Nutshell Series

of

WEST PUBLISHING COMPANY

P.O. Box 64526
St. Paul, Minnesota 55164–0526

Accounting—Law and, 1984, 377 pages, by E. McGruder Faris, Late Professor of Law, Stetson University.

Administrative Law and Process, 2nd Ed., 1981, 445 pages, by Ernest Gellhorn, Former Dean and Professor of Law, Case Western Reserve University and Barry B. Boyer, Professor of Law, SUNY, Buffalo.

Admiralty, 2nd Ed., 1988, about 362 pages, by Frank L. Maraist, Professor of Law, Louisiana State University.

Agency-Partnership, 1977, 364 pages, by Roscoe T. Steffen, Late Professor of Law, University of Chicago.

American Indian Law, 1981, 288 pages, by William C. Canby, Jr., Adjunct Professor of Law, Arizona State University.

Antitrust Law and Economics, 3rd Ed., 1986, 472 pages, by Ernest Gellhorn, Former Dean and Professor of Law, Case Western Reserve University.

Appellate Advocacy, 1984, 325 pages, by Alan D. Hornstein, Professor of Law, University of Maryland.

Art Law, 1984, 335 pages, by Leonard D. DuBoff, Professor of Law, Lewis and Clark College, Northwestern School of Law.

Banking and Financial Institutions, 1984, 409 pages, by William A. Lovett, Professor of Law, Tulane University.

Church-State Relations—Law of, 1981, 305 pages, by Leonard F. Manning, Late Professor of Law, Fordham University.

Civil Procedure, 2nd Ed., 1986, 306 pages, by Mary Kay Kane, Professor of Law, University of California, Hastings College of the Law.

Civil Rights, 1978, 279 pages, by Norman Vieira, Professor of Law, Southern Illinois University.

Commercial Paper, 3rd Ed., 1982, 404 pages, by Charles M. Weber, Professor of Business Law, University of Arizona and Richard E. Speidel, Professor of Law, Northwestern University.

Community Property, 2nd Ed., 1988, about 420 pages, by Robert L. Mennell, Former Professor of Law, Hamline University and Thomas M. Boykoff.

Comparative Legal Traditions, 1982, 402 pages, by Mary Ann Glendon, Professor of Law, Harvard University, Michael Wallace Gordon, Professor of Law, University of Florida and Christopher Osakwe, Professor of Law, Tulane University.

Conflicts, 1982, 470 pages, by David D. Siegel, Professor of Law, St. John's University.

Constitutional Analysis, 1979, 388 pages, by Jerre S. Williams, Professor of Law Emeritus, University of Texas.

Constitutional Federalism, 2nd Ed., 1987, 411 pages, by David E. Engdahl, Professor of Law, University of Puget Sound.

Constitutional Law, 1986, 389 pages, by Jerome A. Barron, Dean and Professor of Law, George Washington University and C. Thomas Dienes, Professor of Law, George Washington University.

Consumer Law, 2nd Ed., 1981, 418 pages, by David G. Epstein, Dean and Professor of Law, Emory University and Steve H. Nickles, Professor of Law, University of Minnesota.

Contract Remedies, 1981, 323 pages, by Jane M. Friedman, Professor of Law, Wayne State University.

Contracts, 2nd Ed., 1984, 425 pages, by Gordon D. Schaber, Dean and Professor of Law, McGeorge School of Law and Claude D. Rohwer, Professor of Law, McGeorge School of Law.

Corporations—Law of, 2nd Ed., 1987, 515 pages, by Robert W. Hamilton, Professor of Law, University of Texas.

Corrections and Prisoners' Rights—Law of, 2nd Ed., 1983, 386 pages, by Sheldon Krantz, Dean and Professor of Law, University of San Diego.

Criminal Law, 2nd Ed., 1987, 321 pages, by Arnold H. Loewy, Professor of Law, University of North Carolina.

Criminal Procedure—Constitutional Limitations, 4th Ed., 1988, about 461 pages, by Jerold H. Israel, Professor of Law, University of Michigan and Wayne R. LaFave, Professor of Law, University of Illinois.

Debtor-Creditor Law, 3rd Ed., 1986, 383 pages, by David G. Epstein, Dean and Professor of Law, Emory University.

Employment Discrimination—Federal Law of, 2nd Ed., 1981, 402 pages, by Mack A. Player, Professor of Law, University of Georgia.

Energy Law, 1981, 338 pages, by Joseph P. Tomain, Professor of Law, University of Cincinnatti.

Environmental Law, 1983, 343 pages by Roger W. Findley, Professor of Law, University of Illinois and Daniel A. Farber, Professor of Law, University of Minnesota.

Estate and Gift Taxation, Federal, 3rd Ed., 1983, 509 pages, by John K. McNulty, Professor of Law, University of California, Berkeley.

Estate Planning—Introduction to, 3rd Ed., 1983, 370 pages, by Robert J. Lynn, Professor of Law, Ohio State University.

Evidence, Federal Rules of, 2nd Ed., 1987, 473 pages, by Michael H. Graham, Professor of Law, University of Miami.

Evidence, State and Federal Rules, 2nd Ed., 1981, 514 pages, by Paul F. Rothstein, Professor of Law, Georgetown University.

Family Law, 2nd Ed., 1986, 444 pages, by Harry D. Krause, Professor of Law, University of Illinois.

Federal Jurisdiction, 2nd Ed., 1981, 258 pages, by David P. Currie, Professor of Law, University of Chicago.

Future Interests, 1981, 361 pages, by Lawrence W. Waggoner, Professor of Law, University of Michigan.

Government Contracts, 1979, 423 pages, by W. Noel Keyes, Professor of Law, Pepperdine University.

Historical Introduction to Anglo-American Law, 2nd Ed., 1973, 280 pages, by Frederick G. Kempin, Jr., Professor of Business Law, Wharton School of Finance and Commerce, University of Pennsylvania.

Immigration Law and Procedure, 1984, 345 pages, by David Weissbrodt, Professor of Law, University of Minnesota.

Injunctions, 1974, 264 pages, by John F. Dobbyn, Professor of Law, Villanova University.

Insurance Law, 1981, 281 pages, by John F. Dobbyn, Professor of Law, Villanova University.

Intellectual Property—Patents, Trademarks and Copyright, 1983, 428 pages, by Arthur R. Miller, Professor of Law, Harvard University, and Michael H. Davis, Professor of Law, Cleveland State University, Cleveland-Marshall College of Law.

International Business Transactions, 2nd Ed., 1984, 476 pages, by Donald T. Wilson, Late Professor of Law, Loyola University, Los Angeles.

International Law (Public), 1985, 262 pages, by Thomas Buergenthal, Professor of Law, Emory University and Harold G. Maier, Professor of Law, Vanderbilt University.

Introduction to the Study and Practice of Law, 1983, 418 pages, by Kenney F. Hegland, Professor of Law, University of Arizona.

Judicial Process, 1980, 292 pages, by William L. Reynolds, Professor of Law, University of Maryland.

Jurisdiction, 4th Ed., 1980, 232 pages, by Albert A. Ehrenzweig, Late Professor of Law, University of California, Berkeley, David W. Louisell, Late Professor of Law, University of California, Berkeley and Geoffrey C. Hazard, Jr., Professor of Law, Yale Law School.

Juvenile Courts, 3rd Ed., 1984, 291 pages, by Sanford J. Fox, Professor of Law, Boston College.

Labor Arbitration Law and Practice, 1979, 358 pages, by Dennis R. Nolan, Professor of Law, University of South Carolina.

Labor Law, 2nd Ed., 1986, 397 pages, by Douglas L. Leslie, Professor of Law, University of Virginia.

Land Use, 2nd Ed., 1985, 356 pages, by Robert R. Wright, Professor of Law, University of Arkansas, Little Rock and Susan Webber Wright, Professor of Law, University of Arkansas, Little Rock.

Landlord and Tenant Law, 2nd Ed., 1986, 311 pages, by David S. Hill, Professor of Law, University of Colorado.

Law Study and Law Examinations—Introduction to, 1971, 389 pages, by Stanley V. Kinyon, Late Professor of Law, University of Minnesota.

Legal Interviewing and Counseling, 2nd Ed., 1987, 487 pages, by Thomas L. Shaffer, Professor of Law, Washington and Lee University and James R. Elkins, Professor of Law, West Virginia University.

Legal Research, 4th Ed., 1985, 452 pages, by Morris L. Cohen, Professor of Law and Law Librarian, Yale University.

Legal Writing, 1982, 294 pages, by Lynn B. Squires and Marjorie Dick Rombauer, Professor of Law, University of Washington.

Legislative Law and Process, 2nd Ed., 1986, 346 pages, by Jack Davies, Professor of Law, William Mitchell College of Law.

Local Government Law, 2nd Ed., 1983, 404 pages, by David J. McCarthy, Jr., Professor of Law, Georgetown University.

Mass Communications Law, 3rd Ed., 1988, 538 pages, by Harvey L. Zuckman, Professor of Law, Catholic University, Martin J. Gaynes, Lecturer in Law, Temple University, T. Barton Carter, Professor of Public Communications, Boston University, and Juliet Lushbough Dee, Professor of Communications, University of Delaware.

Medical Malpractice—The Law of, 2nd Ed., 1986, 342 pages, by Joseph H. King, Professor of Law, University of Tennessee.

Military Law, 1980, 378 pages, by Charles A. Shanor, Professor of Law, Emory University and Timothy P. Terrell, Professor of Law, Emory University.

Oil and Gas Law, 1983, 443 pages, by John S. Lowe, Professor of Law, Southern Methodist University.

Personal Property, 1983, 322 pages, by Barlow Burke, Jr., Professor of Law, American University.

Post-Conviction Remedies, 1978, 360 pages, by Robert Popper, Dean and Professor of Law, University of Missouri, Kansas City.

Presidential Power, 1977, 328 pages, by Arthur Selwyn Miller, Professor of Law Emeritus, George Washington University.

Products Liability, 3rd Ed., 1988, about 350 pages, by Jerry J. Phillips, Professor of Law, University of Tennessee.

Professional Responsibility, 1980, 399 pages, by Robert H. Aronson, Professor of Law, University of Washington, and Donald T. Weckstein, Professor of Law, University of San Diego.

Real Estate Finance, 2nd Ed., 1985, 262 pages, by Jon W. Bruce, Professor of Law, Vanderbilt University.

Real Property, 2nd Ed., 1981, 448 pages, by Roger H. Bernhardt, Professor of Law, Golden Gate University.

Regulated Industries, 2nd Ed., 1987, 389 pages, by Ernest Gellhorn, Former Dean and Professor of Law, Case Western Reserve University, and Richard J. Pierce, Professor of Law, Southern Methodist University.

Remedies, 2nd Ed., 1985, 320 pages, by John F. O'Connell, Dean and Professor of Law, Southern California College of Law.

Res Judicata, 1976, 310 pages, by Robert C. Casad, Professor of Law, University of Kansas.

Sales, 2nd Ed., 1981, 370 pages, by John M. Stockton, Professor of Business Law, Wharton School of Finance and Commerce, University of Pennsylvania.

Schools, Students and Teachers—Law of, 1984, 409 pages, by Kern Alexander, President, Western Kentucky University and M. David Alexander, Professor, Virginia Tech University.

Sea—Law of, 1984, 264 pages, by Louis B. Sohn, Professor of Law, University of Georgia and Kristen Gustafson.

Secured Transactions, 2nd Ed., 1981, 391 pages, by Henry J. Bailey, Professor of Law Emeritus, Willamette University.

Securities Regulation, 3rd Ed., 1988, about 350 pages, by David L. Ratner, Dean and Professor of Law, University of San Francisco.

Sex Discrimination, 1982, 399 pages, by Claire Sherman Thomas, Lecturer, University of Washington, Women's Studies Department.

Taxation and Finance, State and Local, 1986, 309 pages, by M. David Gelfand, Professor of Law, Tulane University and Peter W. Salsich, Professor of Law, St. Louis University.

Taxation of Individuals, Federal Income, 3rd Ed., 1983, 487 pages, by John K. McNulty, Professor of Law, University of California, Berkeley.

Torts—Injuries to Persons and Property, 1977, 434 pages, by Edward J. Kionka, Professor of Law, Southern Illinois University.

Torts—Injuries to Family, Social and Trade Relations, 1979, 358 pages, by Wex S. Malone, Professor of Law Emeritus, Louisiana State University.

Trial Advocacy, 1979, 402 pages, by Paul B. Bergman, Adjunct Professor of Law, University of California, Los Angeles.

Trial and Practice Skills, 1978, 346 pages, by Kenney F. Hegland, Professor of Law, University of Arizona.

Trial, The First—Where Do I Sit? What Do I Say?, 1982, 396 pages, by Steven H. Goldberg, Professor of Law, University of Minnesota.

Unfair Trade Practices, 1982, 445 pages, by Charles R. McManis, Professor of Law, Washington University.

Uniform Commercial Code, 2nd Ed., 1984, 516 pages, by Bradford Stone, Professor of Law, Stetson University.

Uniform Probate Code, 2nd Ed., 1987, 454 pages, by Lawrence H. Averill, Jr., Dean and Professor of Law, University of Arkansas, Little Rock.

Water Law, 1984, 439 pages, by David H. Getches, Professor of Law, University of Colorado.

Welfare Law—Structure and Entitlement, 1979, 455 pages, by Arthur B. LaFrance, Professor of Law, Lewis and Clark College, Northwestern School of Law.

Wills and Trusts, 1979, 392 pages, by Robert L. Mennell, Former Professor of Law, Hamline University.

Workers' Compensation and Employee Protection Laws, 1984, 274 pages, by Jack B. Hood, Former Professor of Law, Cumberland School of Law, Samford University and Benjamin A. Hardy, Former Professor of Law, Cumberland School of Law, Samford University.

Hornbook Series

and

Basic Legal Texts

of

WEST PUBLISHING COMPANY

P.O. Box 64526

St. Paul, Minnesota 55164–0526

Admiralty and Maritime Law, Schoenbaum's Hornbook on, 1987, 692 pages, by Thomas J. Schoenbaum, Professor of Law, University of Georgia.

Agency and Partnership, Reuschlein & Gregory's Hornbook on the Law of, 1979 with 1981 Pocket Part, 625 pages, by Harold Gill Reuschlein, Professor of Law Emeritus, Villanova University and William A. Gregory, Professor of Law, Georgia State University.

Antitrust, Sullivan's Hornbook on the Law of, 1977, 886 pages, by Lawrence A. Sullivan, Professor of Law, University of California, Berkeley.

Civil Procedure, Friedenthal, Kane and Miller's Hornbook on, 1985, 876 pages, by Jack H. Friedental, Professor of Law, Stanford University, Mary Kay Kane, Professor of Law, University of California, Hastings College of the Law and Arthur R. Miller, Professor of Law, Harvard University.

Common Law Pleading, Koffler and Reppy's Hornbook on, 1969, 663 pages, by Joseph H. Koffler, Professor of Law, New York Law School and Alison Reppy, Late Dean and Professor of Law, New York Law School.

Conflict of Laws, Scoles and Hay's Hornbook on, 1982, with 1986 Pocket Part, 1085 pages, by Eugene F. Scoles, Professor of Law, University of Illinois and Peter Hay, Dean and Professor of Law, University of Illinois.

Constitutional Law, Nowak, Rotunda and Young's Hornbook on, 3rd Ed., 1986, 1191 pages, by John E. Nowak, Professor of Law, University of Illinois, Ronald D. Rotunda, Professor of Law, University of Illinois, and J. Nelson Young, Late Professor of Law, University of North Carolina.

Contracts, Calamari and Perillo's Hornbook on, 3rd Ed., 1987, 1049 pages, by John D. Calamari, Professor of Law, Fordham University and Joseph M. Perillo, Professor of Law, Fordham University.

Contracts, Corbin's One Volume Student Ed., 1952, 1224 pages, by Arthur L. Corbin, Late Professor of Law, Yale University.

Corporations, Henn and Alexander's Hornbook on, 3rd Ed., 1983, with 1986 Pocket Part, 1371 pages, by Harry G. Henn, Professor of Law Emeritus, Cornell University and John R. Alexander.

Criminal Law, LaFave and Scott's Hornbook on, 2nd Ed., 1986, 918 pages, by Wayne R. LaFave, Professor of Law, University of Illinois, and Austin Scott, Jr., Late Professor of Law, University of Colorado.

Criminal Procedure, LaFave and Israel's Hornbook on, 1985 with 1986 pocket part, 1142 pages, by Wayne R. LaFave, Professor of Law, University of Illinois and Jerold H. Israel, Professor of Law University of Michigan.

Damages, McCormick's Hornbook on, 1935, 811 pages, by Charles T. McCormick, Late Dean and Professor of Law, University of Texas.

Domestic Relations, Clark's Hornbook on, 2nd Ed., 1988, about 1100 pages, by Homer H. Clark, Jr., Professor of Law, University of Colorado.

Economics and Federal Antitrust Law, Hovenkamp's Hornbook on, 1985, 414 pages, by Herbert Hovenkamp, Professor of Law, University of Iowa.

Employment Discrimination Law, Player's Hornbook on, about 650 pages, 1988, by Mack A. Player, Professor of Law, University of Georgia.

HORNBOOKS & BASIC TEXTS

Environmental Law, Rodgers' Hornbook on, 1977 with 1984 Pocket Part, 956 pages, by William H. Rodgers, Jr., Professor of Law, University of Washington.

Evidence, Lilly's Introduction to, 2nd Ed., 1987, 585 pages, by Graham C. Lilly, Professor of Law, University of Virginia.

Evidence, McCormick's Hornbook on, 3rd Ed., 1984 with 1987 Pocket Part, 1156 pages, General Editor, Edward W. Cleary, Professor of Law Emeritus, Arizona State University.

Federal Courts, Wright's Hornbook on, 4th Ed., 1983, 870 pages, by Charles Alan Wright, Professor of Law, University of Texas.

Federal Income Taxation, Rose and Chommie's Hornbook on, 3rd Ed., 1988, about 875 pages, by Michael D. Rose, Professor of Law, Ohio State University and John C. Chommie, Late Professor of Law, University of Miami.

Federal Income Taxation of Individuals, Posin's Hornbook on, 1983 with 1987 Pocket Part, 491 pages, by Daniel Q. Posin, Jr., Professor of Law, Catholic University.

Future Interest, Simes' Hornbook on, 2nd Ed., 1966, 355 pages, by Lewis M. Simes, Late Professor of Law, University of Michigan.

Insurance, Keeton and Widiss' Basic Text on, 1988, about 1000 pages, by Robert E. Keeton, Professor of Law Emeritus, Harvard University and Alan I. Widiss, Professor of Law, University of Iowa.

Labor Law, Gorman's Basic Text on, 1976, 914 pages, by Robert A. Gorman, Professor of Law, University of Pennsylvania.

Law Problems, Ballentine's, 5th Ed., 1975, 767 pages, General Editor, William E. Burby, Late Professor of Law, University of Southern California.

Legal Ethics, Wolfram's Hornbook on, 1986, 1120 pages, by Charles W. Wolfram, Professor of Law, Cornell University.

Legal Writing Style, Weihofen's, 2nd Ed., 1980, 332 pages, by Henry Weihofen, Professor of Law Emeritus, University of New Mexico.

Local Government Law, Reynolds' Hornbook on, 1982 with 1987 Pocket Part, 860 pages, by Osborne M. Reynolds, Professor of Law, University of Oklahoma.

New York Estate Administration, Turano and Radigan's Hornbook on, 1986, 676 pages, by Margaret V. Turano, Professor of Law, St. John's University and Raymond Radigan.

New York Practice, Siegel's Hornbook on, 1978 with 1987 Pocket Part, 1011 pages, by David D. Siegel, Professor of Law, St. John's University.

Oil and Gas Law, Hemingway's Hornbook on, 2nd Ed., 1983, with 1986 Pocket Part, 543 pages, by Richard W. Hemingway, Professor of Law, University of Oklahoma.

Property, Boyer's Survey of, 3rd Ed., 1981, 766 pages, by Ralph E. Boyer, Professor of Law Emeritus, University of Miami.

Property, Law of, Cunningham, Whitman and Stoebuck's Hornbook on, 1984, with 1987 Pocket Part, 916 pages, by Roger A. Cunningham, Professor of Law, University of Michigan, Dale A. Whitman, Dean and Professor of Law, University of Missouri, Columbia and William B. Stoebuck, Professor of Law, University of Washington.

Real Estate Finance Law, Nelson and Whitman's Hornbook on, 2nd Ed., 1985, 941 pages, by Grant S. Nelson, Professor of Law, University of Missouri, Columbia and Dale A. Whitman, Dean and Professor of Law, University of Missouri, Columbia.

Real Property, Moynihan's Introduction to, 2nd Ed., 1987, 239 pages, by Cornelius J. Moynihan, Late Professor of Law, Suffolk University.

Remedies, Dobbs' Hornbook on, 1973, 1067 pages, by Dan B. Dobbs, Professor of Law, University of Arizona.

Secured Transactions under the U.C.C., Henson's Hornbook on, 2nd Ed., 1979 with 1979 Pocket Part, 504 pages, by Ray D. Henson, Professor of Law, University of California, Hastings College of the Law.

Securities Regulation, Hazen's Hornbook on the Law of, 1985, with 1988 Pocket Part, 739 pages, by Thomas Lee Hazen, Professor of Law, University of North Carolina.

Sports Law, Schubert, Smith and Trentadue's, 1986, 395 pages, by George W. Schubert, Dean of University College, University of North Dakota, Rodney K. Smith, Professor of Law, Delaware Law School, Widener University, and Jesse C. Trentadue, Former Professor of Law, University of North Dakota.

Torts, Prosser and Keeton's Hornbook on, 5th Ed., 1984 with 1988 Pocket Part, 1286 pages, by William L. Prosser, Late Dean and Professor of Law, University of California, Berkeley, Page Keeton, Professor of Law Emeritus, University of Texas, Dan B. Dobbs, Professor of Law, University of Arizona, Robert E. Keeton, Professor of Law Emeritus, Harvard University and David G. Owen, Professor of Law, University of South Carolina.

Trial Advocacy, Jeans' Handbook on, Soft cover, 1975, 473 pages, by James W. Jeans, Professor of Law, University of Missouri, Kansas City.

Trusts, Bogert's Hornbook on, 6th Ed., 1987, 794 pages, by George T. Bogert.

Uniform Commercial Code, White and Summers' Hornbook on, 3rd Ed., 1988, about 1250 pages, by James J. White, Professor of Law, University of Michigan and Robert S. Summers, Professor of Law, Cornell University.

Urban Planning and Land Development Control Law, Hagman and Juergensmeyer's Hornbook on, 2nd Ed., 1986, 680 pages, by Donald G. Hagman, Late Professor of Law, University of California, Los Angeles and Julian C. Juergensmeyer, Professor of Law, University of Florida.

Wills, Atkinson's Hornbook on, 2nd Ed., 1953, 975 pages, by Thomas E. Atkinson, Late Professor of Law, New York University.

Wills, Trusts and Estates, McGovern, Rein and Kurtz' Hornbook on, 1988, by William M. McGovern, Professor of Law, University of California, Los Angeles, Jan Ellen Rein, Professor of Law, Gonzaga University, and Sheldon F. Kurtz, Professor of Law, University of Iowa.

Advisory Board

AGENCY – PARTNERSHIP
IN A NUTSHELL

By

ROSCOE T. STEFFEN

Late Professor of Law, University of
California, Hastings College
of the Law

Formerly

John P. Wilson Professor of Law,
University of Chicago

Professor of Law,
Yale University

ST. PAUL, MINN.
WEST PUBLISHING CO.
1977

Library of Congress Catalog Card Number: 77–78399
ISBN 0–314–33236–7

Steffen-Agency Nutshell
5th Reprint—1988

TO

MY COLLEAGUES AND STUDENTS

*

PREFACE

This Nutshell is the product of long teaching. The outline of subjects follows, to a large extent, those developed in my casebook on Agency-Partnership (3rd Ed. 1969, West Publishing Co.). Over the years, the subjects discussed in the course on Agency-Partnership have grown and evolved so that relationships between different subjects may be explored and all matters of importance treated fully. I have organized the subjects in much the same way one would for classroom discussion (the relation inter se, dealings with the world and finally the form of the enterprise organization).

Thus, in a very real sense this Nutshell is the end product of some fifty years of teaching: the first 25 years at Yale Law School; the next 12 years at the University of Chicago Law School; and the last 14 years at the University of California, Hastings College of the Law.

One important function of teaching is to raise questions for the future and, in this context, to discuss the important considerations which go into the process of reaching answers which stand the test of time. This Nutshell provides many of the answers that I believe to be the working premises which underlie the law of Agency-Partnership (citations to relevant authorities are included where appropriate). Not all the questions in this field are settled, nor should they be, because the quest for answers is and will always remain an ongoing process.

In writing this Nutshell, I owe much to my colleagues and to generations of students with whom I have discussed questions and problems in the law of Agency-Partnership. I also wish to acknowledge the conscientious work of Dorothy Farrar who typed the manuscript.

ROSCOE T. STEFFEN

San Francisco, California
May 14, 1976

OUTLINE

INTRODUCTORY MATTERS

PART I. ENTERPRISE RELATIONS INTER SE

PART II. ENTERPRISE TRANSACTIONS

A. TORTS

B. CONTRACTS

PART III. FORMS OF ENTERPRISE

APPENDICES

TABLE OF CASES

References are to Pages

TABLE OF CASES

TABLE OF CASES

TABLE OF CASES

TABLE OF CASES

TABLE OF CASES

*

AGENCY – PARTNERSHIP
IN A
NUTSHELL

INTRODUCTORY MATTERS

§ 1. Scope

Comment will be useful, preliminarily, to indicate something of scope and plan. Most importantly, as the title indicates, it is proposed to integrate the law of Agency and that of Partnership. The custom, heretofore, has been to treat the two subjects separately. So, for example, Paley, Story and Mechem wrote on Agency, and Lindley, Burdick and Crane, on Partnership, to mention only some of the leading texts.

Many courts, however, have stated, in effect, that partnership is "nothing but a branch of the general law of principal and agent." Per, Willis, J., in Watteau v. Fenwick [1893] 1 Q.B. 346. Accepting this as a valid premise, it is assumed that a combination of the two titles not only will afford a fuller perspective but, hopefully, will give greater insight. Even though the subjects are closely related, or parts of one whole, different solutions to common problems have developed over the years. Strangely, however, when the two subjects are brought together, a subtle change takes place. Attention comes to center on the institution of agency and not so much on separate rules. Much more is involved than the few "peculiarities," which Holmes said alone "makes agency a proper title in the law." Holmes, Agency (1891) 4 Harv.L.Rev. 345, 348.

With the subject so centered it divides easily into three main areas. First, the relation of the various persons inter se; partners to co-partners and the firm, agents to principal, and so on. By way of illustration, questions are discussed concerning tenure, fiduciary duties, negative covenants, indemnity, and the personal injury risks. These last, of course, invite an examination of F.E.L.A. and Workmen's Compensation, a particularly fruitful study as prelude to an examination of respondeat superior.

The second area is concerned with transactions between the enterprise—whether in the form of partnership, individual proprietorship, joint venture, corporation, business trust, or some other —and third persons. This is the area of traditional agency. Perhaps "transactions" is not the right word, for the material includes not only references to contracts and conveyances, but to third party tort claims as well. Herein, also, the traditional agency and partnership problems concerning authority, ratification, notice, undisclosed principal, and so on, are dealt with.

Finally, in the third area, a more careful look is had at the form of the enterprise organization. The problem of when a joint venture or partnership exists comes here, or, for further example, problems concerning unincorporated associations, business trusts and joint stock associations. Lastly, the issues involved in dissolution are examined, particularly those concerned with incoming and outgoing partners, winding up procedures, priorities between creditors, to mention only a few.

In the pages immediately to follow, some of the terms and concepts most frequently met with are defined, for the sake of clarity. Of course, no definition is final, for, like the subject itself, definitions are continually changing, to meet changing notions of social and economic policy.

§ 2. Agency, Defined

Agency is a consensual fiduciary relationship between one person—the agent—who agrees to act *for*, and under the direction or control *of*, another—the principal. See, Restatement, Second, Agency § 1. In other words, Agency—in a broad sense—is that pervasive and infinitely varied institution by and through which most things are done in the free world. One may employ another to do his work, sell his goods, acquire property on his behalf, all to the same effect as if he were present and acting in person. Enterprise, as we know it, could scarcely exist were this not true.

The basic idea, that of making the agent's actions binding on his principal, and, conversely, of giving the principal the benefit of rights or property acquired by his agent, seems to have been settled very early, almost as a matter of course. An instance is Combes' Case (1613) 9 Co.Rep. 75a, where it was held that, since a copyholder in fee (acting in person) might surrender his estate by the common law, he could do so likewise through attorneys, "as a thing incident by the common law."

According to Holmes, it is only common sense that a person should be liable, in tort or contract, for his directed acts; in fact, he tells us that is the true meaning of the maxim: *qui facit per alium facit per se,* and, he adds, "The English law has recognized that maxim as far back as it is worthwhile to follow it." Holmes, Agency (1891) 4 Harv.L.Rev. 345, at 347.

Having said so much, what of the vast number of actions and transactions where the agent— through negligence, fraud, misunderstanding or

[4]

whatever—has departed from instructions? These, too, are very much a part of the institution. As also are the cases where a ship's captain, a factor, a brewmaster, an attorney, a corporation president, or any other, must proceed in some measure on his own initiative. Cases of this sort, too, are legion, and supply much of the raw material with which Agency-Partnership deals.

§ 3. Theories of Liability

Holmes' position was that the courts have used a "fiction of identity," tempered by common sense, to decide cases of the sort last mentioned. Holmes, Agency (1891) 4 Harv.L.Rev. 345 at 350. Moreover, he left no doubt that he considered it a mistake ever to make one person liable for another's torts, unless the act had been directed, or was later ratified. Ibid. 5 Harv.L.Rev. 1 at 14. Compare, Wigmore, Responsibility for Tortious Acts: Its History (1894) 7 Harv.L.Rev. 315.

Nonetheless, Lord Holt had long before declared broadly for the master's liability in tort, Jones v. Hart (1698) Holt, K.B. 642, 90 Eng.Reprint, 1255,—though on unstated grounds—and subsequent courts, mainly by use of the maxim *respondeat superior,* have gone far to establish a doctrine of vicarious liability, that is, liability without fault. See infra, § 30. Indeed, it seems never to have been a defence that the master may have used care in the selection and training of his servants. See, Dansey v. Richardson (1854) 3 El.Bl. 144, 161.

There has been a problem how to reconcile this development with the rule, much debated last century, that tort liability derives only from "fault." See, Brown v. Kendall (1850) 6 Cush. 292, 60 Mass. 292. Recently, the fashion has been simply to assert that the servant's negligence is to be "imputed" to the employer. See, Prosser, Law of Torts (1971) 458. Semantically, that has kept the fault principle alive. The Restatement takes a different tack—equally assertive—that liability in such case is a matter of "inherent agency power." Restatement, Second, Agency § 8A.

The principal's liability in contract, when the agent has gone beyond his express mandate, presents a similar problem. By use of "apparent authority," infra § 47, courts have gone a good way to charge the principal with contract responsibility in such cases. And, beyond that, when apparent authority will not apply, the Restatement has again made use of "inherent agency power," § 195, Comment b, to hold the principal liable. See infra § 60.

A number of writers have suggested that liability in tort, at least, should be treated as a function of enterprise. See: Douglas, Vicarious Liability and Administration of Risk (1929) 38 Yale

L.J. 584; Ehrenzweig, Negligence Without Fault (1966) 54 Cal.L.Rev. 1422. The suggestion obviously borrows from Workmen's Compensation, where the employer's liability to pay compensation to an injured workman, regardless of fault, was promoted on the principle that "the risks of industry should be borne by industry." See, Smith, Frolic and Detour (1923) 23 Col.L.Rev. 444 at 456. Whether "enterprise liability" will apply on the contract side is a question; it would seem, however, that "inherent agency power" has no other plausible means of support. See generally, Mearns, Vicarious Liability for Agency Contracts (1962) 48 Va.L.Rev. 50; Steffen, Enterprise Liability: Some Exploratory Comments (1965) 17 Hastings L.J. 165.

§ 4. Agent, Defined

According to Restatement, Second, Agency § 1, an "agent" is anyone who has manifested "consent" to "act" in a "fiduciary relation" on "behalf" of another, and "subject to his control."

This represents a change. Blackstone used "servant" as the generic term, but added: "There is yet a fourth species of servants, if they may be so called, being rather in a superior, a ministerial, capacity; such as stewards, factors and bailiffs . . ." 1 Bl.Comm. *427. During the last century or more, with the great and increasing development, first of mercantilism and then of industrialization, there has been a proliferation of "agents," or the "fourth species of servants." By 1933, when the Restatement of Agency was published, "agent" had become the generic term, and "servant," infra § 5, a species of agent.

Some things about the present definition require comment. In the first place, although the agency relationship is a consensual one, no contract is necessary. A gratuitous agent is as much an agent as any other. Malloy v. Fong (1951) 37 Cal.2d 356, 378, 232 P.2d 241, 254. Next, anyone, including infants and demented persons, may be an agent, whether or not they have capacity to contract for themselves. Of course, as to the principal—individual, partnership, corporation, or some other—general requirements as to capacity apply. These, not being peculiar to agency, need not be discussed here.

The next identification mark, that an agent is one who acts "on behalf" of his principal—and not for his own profit—is a *sine qua non* of the relationship. The further requirement, that he serve in a "fiduciary" relation, would seem to add little but emphasis; it is really a legal attribute, not part of an objective definition. That is, the courts have long provided special remedies—injunction, constructive trust and so on—to make sure that obligations of trust and confidence, i. e., fiduciary duties, are carried out faithfully. Other situations are: Parent and child; trustee and beneficiary; partner and co-partner or partner and firm. See, U.P.A. § 21.

The second mark is equally important, that is, an agent is one who consents to act "subject to" the principal's "control." Probably no more was needed than to say that an agent consents to act pursuant to his principal's *direction*. But, however phrased, this requirement, too, is a *sine qua non* of the relationship; trustees act for and on behalf of beneficiaries, but they may not act under their control or direction without becoming agents. Brown v. Bedell (1934) 263 N.Y. 177, 188 N.E. 641. See infra, Business Trust, § 77. Strictly applied, even persons who hold a "power coupled with an interest," or a "security power"— though long spoken of as agents—no longer qualify. Restatement, Second, Agency § 12. And see infra, § 17.

§ 5. Servant

Restatement, Second, Agency § 2, defines "servant" as an "agent" employed by a "master" to perform "service" in his affairs, and whose "physical conduct" is "controlled" or is "subject to the right to control" by the "master."

Thus, a "servant" is now a species of "agent," and we have come full circle from Blackstone's time. Even so, the term "servant" is something of an anachronism in today's world.   One does not speak of an accountant, a truck driver, a business manager, as a "servant," or, for that matter, one does not speak of his employer as "master." These terms are still used in court opinions, however, and may once have been useful, since they pointed to early law holding the head of a family responsible to third persons for the acts of his household.   Holmes, Agency (1891) 4 Harv.L.Rev. 345.

The Restatement definition of "servant" takes meaning from Restatement, Second, Agency § 219(1) where it is provided that a master is "subject to liability" for the torts of his "servants" committed while acting "in the scope of their employment."   Putting the two sections together, they say that a master may be liable for torts of assault, negligence, and the like, that is, for those growing out of the "physical conduct" of his servants.   This, of course, is subject to the limitation, as stated, that they must be committed in the "scope" of the servants' "employment."

While it is true that most cases under respondeat superior, infra § 30, have had to do with "physical conduct" torts, it is believed the doctrine is not limited to them.   For example, it was held in Barwick v. English Joint Stock Bank (1867) L.R. 2 Ex. 259, that a bank manager—in common parlance, an "agent," and not a "servant"—could subject his bank employer to tort liability in deceit, for false representation. This, the court said it could do by analogy to the "running down" cases, today's traffic accident cases. In any event, there is a large catalog of torts not involving physical injury, where an "agent"—even a partner or an independent contractor agent—may subject his "principal" to liability. See infra, § 41.

Indeed, under a "multiple hat" doctrine, the manager in *Barwick*, supra, may well have been both an "agent" and a "servant." That is, not only could the manager subject his principal to contract liability, but had he carelessly injured the customer in the course of the transaction—physical conduct—the bank would probably have been liable in tort as well. See infra, § 43.

§ 6. Employee

The term "employee" was not of significance to common law agency. With adoption of the Workmen's Compensation statutes, however, as in the case of much recent social legislation, the term has come into prominence. Speaking generally, it means any agent (other than an independent contractor agent), ranging from director to office boy, who has an appointment or contract "for hire." See, West's Ann.Cal.Labor Code § 3351.

In essence this means that only those agents or servants who work for pay may qualify as "employees." This, of course, squares with the theory underlying the Compensation acts, that provision is to be made to compensate the injured worker for loss of *earning power*—not to give him damages, when pain and mental suffering might be an item. In any case, it is necessary to consult the particular statute to get an accurate reading on the term. For F.E.L.A., see Kelley v. Southern Pacific (1974) 419 U.S. 318, 95 S.Ct. 472.

§ 7. Partnership; Partners

The Uniform Partnership Act, which now has been adopted in all States, defines "partnership" very simply: "A partnership is an association of two or more persons to carry on as co-owners a business for profit." U.P.A. § 6. The Act does not define "partner," as such, but it is evident that a partner is any member of a partnership association. Members are sometimes spoken of as "general" partners but, since all partners—including "dormant" or "silent" partners—have equal rights in the conduct of firm business, U.P.A. § 18(e), the term has little utility.

When, however, a limited partnership is formed, under the Uniform Limited Partnership Act, it is *necessary* to make a distinction. "Limited" or special partners, so-called, have no responsibility for the obligations of the firm, U.L.P.A. § 1, as do the "general" partners, and stand only to lose their contribution. They, however, have no power to act for the business. In fact, if they do take part in management, they may be treated as general partners, and then become liable as such for partnership debts, U.L.P.A. § 7.

For the moment, it is enough to note, as the Uniform Partnership Act states, that "the law of agency shall apply under this act." U.P.A. § 4(3). The general partners in a limited partnership are given similar powers to carry on the business, U.L. P.A. § 9. Neither act provides, in terms, that a partner is a "servant" of the firm; nor is there any mention of "control" as a necessary ingredient either of partnership or of partnership liability. U.P.A. § 6, supra. Yet the statute clearly recognizes, U.P.A. § 13, as did the common law, Champion v. Bostwick (1837) 18 Wend. 175, 31 Am. Dec. 376, that a partnership may be liable for a partner's torts, physical injury torts or any others, when committed in course of the business.

There has been a running debate, for a century or more, whether a partnership is to be regarded as an entity. Under the common law or "aggregate" theory, the firm was held not to be a "legal person"; thus, suit could only be had against the several partners individually,—"trading under the firm name and style" of the company name, as the pleadings put it. In 1912, when the Uniform Act was drafted, a compromise position was taken; the "partnership" might hold title to real property, for example, but business creditors still could sue only the partners. See, Crane & Bromberg, Partnership (1968) § 3(e). Perceptible change toward the entity theory has occurred in recent years; particularly, a number of states now allow the firm to sue or be sued. See, West's Cal.Civ. Code § 388. Infra § 78.

The point is one of considerable importance, and comes up for decision in any number of cases. It may make all the difference, for example, whether an employee is deemed to be hired by the firm, or by the partners individually. See, Mazzuchelli v. Silberberg (1959) 29 N.J. 15, 148 A.2d 8, discussed infra § 78.

§ 8. Independent Contractor

The term "independent contractor," as defined in Restatement, Second, Agency § 2(3), refers to a person who contracts "to do something for" another, and who is "not controlled" by the other with respect to his "physical conduct" in performance of the work. Nor, for good measure, may he be subject to the other's "right to control" such conduct. An older test, still used by many courts, is whether the employer retains control of the "means and methods" by which the work is to be accomplished. Huffcut, Agency (2d ed. 1901) 9. See also, West's Ann.Cal.L.Code § 3353.

Under either wording, the purpose is clear enough, namely, that the employer is to have immunity from liability for torts of "physical conduct" committed by the contractor or his employees in the course of the work. In this respect, "independent contractor" is the opposite of "servant." Examples abound: One is not liable for the taxi driver's negligence; for carelessness of a building contractor; or, for the negligence torts of a bank when handling a collection item. At the same time, the independent contractor may be an "agent" in the broad sense, Restatement, Second, Agency §§ 2(3), 14N, and subject his principal to contract liability, as also to tort liability, that is, for torts not involving physical conduct. See infra, § 44.

There are, of course "exceptions"; so many in fact that a few writers question the rule itself. See, Prosser, Law of Torts (1971) § 71, where the authorities are cited. On examination, however, these so-called "exceptions" turn out only to be rather obvious limitations. That is, as one might expect, an employer remains liable for his own negligence, if any, or upon a contract or statutory obligation, notwithstanding he employed an independent contractor. See, Hole v. Sittingbourne R. Co. (1861) 6 H. & N. 488, 123 Rev.Rep. 636. As owner of land, he continues to be liable for creation of a nuisance. Schwartz v. Merola Bros. Const. Corp. (1943) 290 N.Y. 145, 48 N.E.2d 299. He may not employ an independent contractor to do a quiet murder, or to do work involving "extra hazard" or "inherent danger," without responsibility. See, infra, § 45. For the great range of daily transactions, however, the rule remains intact, and the employer may not be held liable to third persons for the physical conduct of the contractor, or his employees. Steffen, Independent Contractor and the Good Life (1935) 2 U.Chi.L. Rev. 501. See generally, § 43 infra.

§ 9. Lent Servant

There are occasions when one employer *loans* a "servant," i. e., an employee, to another, usually for a short time or to do a particular job. One frequent situation is where a piece of equipment, say, a truck or a crane, is rented with one person or a crew to operate it. The rental, ordinarily, will be for a lump sum, with the initial employer continuing to pay the employee, i. e., "servant," his wages. While the arrangement is thus quite simple, there has been difficulty in determining whether the new employer or the initial one should be responsible for torts of the employee, which may occur in the course of the work. Seavey, Agency (1964) § 86.

The courts are fairly agreed here that the test is whether the employee, with respect *to the very action in question,* was under the direction or "control" of the new employer. The presumption is that he continues as a servant of the initial employer until a change is established. Charles v. Barrett (1922) 233 N.Y. 127, 135 N.E. 199. Moreover, in some states the Workmen's Compensation statute, sensibly, continues the initial arrangement throughout, for purposes of the statute. See, Conn.Gen.Stat.1935, § 1616C. The cases are quite uniform, however, that if the new employer was in control at the time of the injury, he may be held liable to third persons under respondeat superior. See, McCollum v. Smith (C.A.Hi.1964) 339 F.2d 348.

The use of "control" in this situation is not subject to serious criticism. The case assumes that two separate enterprises are involved, so the independent contractor question does not arise. A few cases have held that the employee acted for both employers, but they have involved special facts. Gordon v. S. M. Byers Motor Car Co. (1932) 300 Pa. 453, 164 A. 334.

§ 10. Organization; Management; Sub-Agents

The Uniform Commercial Code, § 1–201(28), uses the term "organization" to include a "corporation," "business trust," "estate," "partnership," "association," or "any other legal or commercial entity." In other words, "organization," in agency terms, will usually refer to the "principal" or "master," that is, the proprietor or employer. Of course, it is also true that an organization, as so defined, may very well be appointed as an "agent." Even a partnership, such as a real estate brokerage firm, though perhaps not a "legal" entity, as heretofore noted, is at least a "commercial" entity and, as such, may serve as an agent. In such case, the salesmen and others employed by the agent to do the particular work, are called "sub agents." Restatement, Second, Agency § 5.

By way of contrast, the word "organization" is often used to refer to personnel, that is, to the officers and directors, the managers, foremen, employees and other agents, who carry on the work of the enterprise. This development, by which large numbers of persons, i. e., agents, are assembled in one business enterprise, though not new, has vastly increased during the past century.

When speaking of the "management" of an organization such as a bank, no certain group can be named. The term refers rather loosely to the persons—directors, principal officers, and so on—who from time to time come to take a leading part in the operation and control of the business. These are all "agents," as above defined, with the possible exception of the directors. See, infra, § 11. While it is useful in business to refer generally to "management," the term has little *legal* significance,—aside from its use in Labor Law, not treated here.

§ 11. Directors; Committees; Employees

There has been question whether "directors" are to be classified as "agents." They have been said not to be subject to "control," and so may not qualify for that reason. Restatement, Second, Agency § 14C; and see, Washington and Bishop, Indemnifying the Corporate Executive (1963) 87 et seq. This, at best, is a doubtful position. Directors, like officers and other representatives, are paid by and owe fiduciary duties to the corporation; they have indemnity today in most states like any other agent, infra, § 23; they do not share, as proprietors, in company gains and profits; and, they are subject to the "control" stated in the by-laws, or as the shares may determine from time to time. For example, when sale or purchase of a principal's property is to be made, special shareholder authority or direction may be required. See, Jeppi v. Brockman Holding Co. (1949) 34 Cal.2d 11, 206 P.2d 847.

Also, with further regard to control, the power to elect is alone sufficient "control" to convert "trustees" into "agents," in the business trust field. Goldwater v. Oltman (1930) 210 Cal. 408, 292 P. 624, 71 A.L.R. 871. No doubt the similar power in the hands of corporation shareholders to elect directors is not the type of "control" that a "master" employs, when directing a "servant" to sweep out the shop. But it should be plain that "control"—insofar as significant—comes in infinite variety. The "control" to which a bank cashier or any executive is subject also differs greatly in extent and kind, but no one doubts that corporation officers, like partners, are to be classified as "agents."

Directors are unique, it seems, mainly in that they happen to be at the top of the personnel hierarchy. They are not the corporation. Their duty, as most corporation statutes provide, is a simple agency task, to "manage." It is true, directors act only as a body, but the same is true of any "committee" of agents in any modern organization; likewise, a single director has no power to act in daily transactions, unless specially authorized, but this also is true of committee members generally.

There once was doubt whether officers of a corporation—and especially directors—were covered by Workmen's Compensation. Infra, § 26. But that question is at rest in most states; directors—like "working partners"—are "employees," within the statute, if they receive pay,—and most do. See, Cal.L.Code § 3351(c). This makes still more dubious the Restatement dictum, that directors are not "agents."

§ 12. Authority

The Restatement definition of "authority" combines two quite different things: One, the principal's instructions or directions to the agent (called "manifestations"); and, two, the agent's "power" to affect the legal relations of the principal with third persons by acts done in accordance with such manifestations. Restatement, Second, Agency § 7. Courts and writers have often used the one word, "authority", to include both senses. But "power" is a broad *legal* concept, and it makes for clarity to use "authority" to describe the *facts* of the principal's authorization, whether in the form of oral instructions, a written power of attorney, or any other. Corbin, The "Authority" of an Agent—Definition (1925) 34 Yale L.J. 788. Whether a duly "authorized" agent has "power" to bind his principal, while the usual case, is still a separate determination.

Authorities are of several kinds. "Implied" authority refers simply to the ambit of things not referred to specifically by the principal, but which may reasonably be inferred from the grant. An agent authorized to borrow money, for example, would have been given authority, by inference, to sign a note in the principal's name. "Apparent" authority or, "ostensible," the term used in some states (West's Ann.Cal.Civ.Code, § 2300), is a very different thing. According to the Restatement it is the "power" to affect the principal's legal relations with others by action "in accordance" with the principal's "manifestations to such third persons." Restatement, Second, Agency §

8. Again it will be convenient to limit the term to its factual connotation, that is, to the principal's "manifestations" to the third person. Matters of interpretation, and the obvious relation to estoppel, are discussed infra, §§ 46 and 47.

The term "authority" is not often used in respondeat superior situations; a master, for example, will seldom instruct an employee to drive negligently. The idea of authority, though concealed, is there just the same. That is, in order to charge a "master" with liability to third persons, it is necessary that the "servant's" conduct was "of the kind" he was employed "to perform," and, further, that such conduct occurred substantially within "authorized" time and space limits. Restatement, Second, Agency § 228.

The Partnership Act employs different words, but would seem to serve the same ends. Thus, it is provided that "the act of every partner . . . for apparently carrying on in the usual way the business of the partnership . . . binds the partnership." U.P.A. § 9(1). This statement conforms most closely to "apparent" authority, but, as paragraph (2) of the section makes plain, any other act will "bind" the partnership when "authorized by the other partners." As for tort liability, the partnership is stated to be bound "by any wrongful act" of any partner "acting in the ordinary course of the business". U.P.A. § 13. Thus, a partner's "authority," in simple agency terms, is found basically in the partnership agreement, as it may have been modified from time to time by course of dealing. A partner in a firm engaged in general merchandise, for example, may have no "authority" to buy race horses or bootleg whiskey for resale. See, Cummings v. S. Funkenstein Co., Ltd. (1919) 17 Ala.App. 7, 81 So. 343, discussed infra § 46.

§ 13. Agency Concept; Sale Distinguished

Preoccupation with definition tends to obscure the significant fact that "agency" is one of the basic legal concepts. Like contract, conveyance, tort, pledge, trust, sale, gift, and such, it is part of the stuff of the law, used by the courts in deciding cases and in writing their opinions. It would be possible to pause at this point, and draw the many distinctions called for—one such, that between "agent" and "trustee" was noted, supra, § 4,—but questions of this sort can best be deferred until later, when they come up in specific situations.

An exception, perhaps, is the need to draw a line between "agency" and "sale." In many businesses goods are shipped to a dealer "on consignment," as the parties say, for purposes of sale at retail. If it has been agreed that the consignor retains title to the goods, has the insurance and tax costs, and the right to fix prices,—probably the arrangement is one of "agency." An early case so held on similar facts for purposes of the antitrust laws.   United States v. General Electric Co. (1926) 272 U.S. 476, 47 S.Ct. 192, 71 L.Ed. 849.

On the other hand, where the dealer's books show an obligation to pay the invoice price, insurance costs are his, and he resells at his own prices —probably the transaction is one of sale and not of agency.   See Dr. Miles Medical Co. v. John D. Park & Sons (1911) 220 U.S. 373, 31 S.Ct. 376, 55 L.Ed. 502, and Simpson v. Union Oil Co. (1964) 377 U.S. 13, 94 S.Ct. 1051.   That the dealer may have been known as an "Agency" of the manufacturer is ordinarily not significant; the dealer's agency, if any, may have been limited to a single factor, such as the extension of the manufacturer's warranty to prospective customers.   If this is thoroughly ambivalent, it nonetheless is an accurate appraisal.

§ 14.   Factor;   Del Credere

An old and well defined type of agent is the "factor."   A factor is said to be an "agent," engaged in "an independent calling," who is employed "to sell property" for another and is "vested by the latter" with the "possession or control" of the property.   West's Ann.Cal.Civ.Code § 2026. Cf. Gazzola v. Lacy Bros. & Kimball (1927) 156 Tenn. 229, 299 S.W. 1039.   In the seventeenth and eighteenth centuries, particularly, the factor flourished in the business of selling raw products, such as cotton, tobacco, sugar, hides, grain. In recent times, he has come also to operate extensively in the textile industry, where his banking function, i. e., the making of advances of money to shippers with a lien on the goods as security, has been significant. See, Steffen and Danziger, The Rebirth of the Commercial Factor (1936) 36 Col.L.Rev. 745.

One variation, the *del credere* agency, must be mentioned. Here the agent—often a "factor"— engages not only to sell, but to be responsible, either for the performance, or at least for the solvency, of the buyer. Chorley, Del Credere (1929) 45 L.Q.Rev. 221. Ordinarily such an apportionment of risks does not represent a change in the basic agency pattern; the buyer, thus, continues in privity with the shipper and, for example, may recover directly from him for defects in the goods. On the other hand, it has been held to be a violation of the Sherman Act to use a group of del credere agents in a scheme to fix prices. United States v. Masonite Corp. (1942) 316 U.S. 265, 62 S.Ct. 1070.

PART I

ENTERPRISE RELATIONS INTER SE

§ 15. Plan

The essentials of "agency" are few, as above noted, supra, § 2. First, the relation is a *consensual* one; an agent *agrees* or as least *consents* to act under the *direction* or *control* of the principal. Second, the relation is a *fiduciary* one, an agent agrees to act *for* and *on behalf* of the principal. He is in no sense a proprietor entitled to the *gains* of enterprise—nor is he expected to carry the *risks*.

Partnership, too, is a *consensual* relation, an *association* of two or more persons to carry on a business as co-owners for profit. U.P.A. § 6. Partners act *for* the firm, or for their co-partners, and in a *fiduciary* capacity. U.P.A. § 21. Since each partner is at the same time both a co-proprietor and an agent, the element of *control* is more complex; a partner is not subject to control in his day to day activities, for partners are co-equals, yet each must abide by policy decisions reached by a majority. U.P.A. § 18(e)(h).

Again, the treatment of enterprise gains is different. In simple agency, gains or profits go in full to the principal; in partnership, they are shared by the partners on some agreed basis. However, since partners as a group share *all* the profits as co-proprietors—not as agents—there would seem to be little real difference. Both in partnership and agency, the law has made it very clear that profits go to the proprietor, that is, to enterprise, which in our system is increasingly being called upon to carry risks and losses.

Returning to the ingredients of agency first mentioned—consent, control, fiduciary, absence of gains or risk—it will be noted that these are of first concern to the parties themselves, that is, to the relation inter se. They present housekeeping questions, so to speak. Although "agency", as a *useful device*, is mainly concerned with dealings between enterprise and third persons, it will be most convenient, first, to explore the inter se relationship, that between the principal and his various servants, agents, officers, co-partners, and others who conduct the enterprise. Thus, Part I takes form as an *elaboration* of "agency" essentials.

In Part II, enterprise dealings with third persons will be discussed. Of course, the two areas may not be kept entirely apart, for the incidence of many risks and losses growing out of third party transactions will have to be allocated between principal and agent—or partner and partners—in the inter se relationship. These will be discussed in context as they arise.

§ 16. A Consensual Relationship

Little need be said on this point, for the concept is not unique to agency. Essentially it is the general contract requirement that the parties voluntarily agree to enter into the relationship. The classical example, where no consent exists, is presented by the rule in some ports that a vessel must take on a compulsory pilot. In such case, it is usually held that the pilot is not an agent, there being no voluntary agreement to his appointment, and therefore, that the vessel owners are not responsible for damage caused by the pilot's negligence. See, Homer Ramsdell Transp. Co. v. La Compagnie Generale Transatlantique (1901) 182 U.S. 406, 21 S.Ct. 831, 45 L.Ed. 1155.

Perhaps a better example, certainly one of more frequent occurrence, concerns the *substitute* agent. A deliveryman—having personal matters to attend—gives over the employer's car to another, who has an accident. Plainly the master is not liable at common law, unless he should ratify the transaction. Dempsey v. Chambers (1891) 154 Mass. 330, 28 N.E. 279, 13 L.R.A. 219, 26 Am. St.Rep. 249. So, a sales agent may not assign his agency. Like the deliveryman, the sales agent would have no power to employ others—even to transfer his agency to a closely held corporation—without the assent of the principal. Barber Agency Co. v. Co-Operative Barrel Co. (1916) 133

Minn. 207, 158 N.W. 38. See Corbin, Contracts § 865.

In partnership, "consensual" means first that the parties must have agreed to become associated together in the particular venture. U.P.A. § 18 (g). It means, further, that one member may not thereafter assign his place in the firm to some other, without the approval of all firm members. Paige v. Faure (1920) 229 N.Y. 114, 127 N.E. 898, 10 A.L.R. 649 (transfer by withdrawing partner). So too, neither the heirs of a deceased partner, nor the administrator of his estate, will automatically become a partner, absent full consent. Blumer Brewing Corp. v. Mayer (1936) 223 Wis. 540, 269 N.W. 693, 111 A.L.R. 1087. Indeed, it would be financially precarious ever to join a partnership, were all this not true.

Probably consent need not be specific in order to become a "partner" or an "agent." See infra §§ 66 and 71. The point is a threshold one when seeking to establish a "joint venture", that is, a form of partnership, usually for short duration, usually set up informally, and often for mutual benefit, rather than profit. Mechem, The Law of Joint Adventures (1931) 15 Minn.L.Rev. 644. Thus, in Judge v. Wallen (1915) 98 Neb. 154, 152 N.W. 318, it was enough to show that two traveling salesmen had agreed to cover their territories in a car owned by one of them, and to share expenses. Whether they expected to form a "joint venture", as such, was beside the point; they had voluntarily associated together in the venture and both, accordingly, were held liable for the negligence of one in carrying it on. See, Carboneau v. Peterson (1939) 1 Wash.2d 347, 95 P.2d 1043 ("community of interest" necessary to joint venture).

The need for consent, of course, is met when the parties enter into a contract. While this is not usual in many employments—or even in the case of some partnerships—a term contract is essential if the parties would preserve a damage sanction. Otherwise the relationship, either partnership or employment, is one at will. Moreover, if not to be performed within one year, there is need of writing to satisfy the statute of frauds. See, Nickerson v. Harvard (1937) 298 Mass. 484, 11 N.E.2d 444, 114 A.L.R. 414. Many agencies, of course, are formed by bare appointment, as by power of attorney given to and received by the agent. See infra, § 50. This arrangement, too, is one at will.

§ 17. Control or Direction

The factor most clearly distinguishing agency from other legal concepts, is control; one person —the agent—agrees to act under the *control* or *direction* of another—the principal. In the long journey from the household servant to the factory employee, the corporation officer, the foreign sales representative, and beyond, *control* has been a *constant*. Indeed, the very word, "agency", has come to connote control by the principal.

True, the quality of control has varied, from the strict duty of obedience expected of servants, to the considerable independence of the sales agency. But, even there, when basic questions arise, say, whether to sell goods and for how much, it is the principal's directions which must prevail. So in the case of an attorney, instructed by his client to garnish or attach a debtor's property, it is no defense to say that the attorney acted reasonably in not doing as directed. W. L. Douglas Shoe Co. v. Rollwage (1933) 187 Ark. 1084, 63 S.W.2d 841. Similarly, a broker's failure to obtain insurance as instructed, leaves the broker liable to his principal for ensuing losses. Elam v. Smithdeal Realty & Ins. Co. (1921) 182 N.C. 599, 109 S.E. 632, 18 A.L.R. 1210.

Neither the attorney nor the insurance broker, in the cases just cited, may have been subject to control as to *how* they would accomplish the principal's mandate, that is, as to the means and methods of doing the job. Hence they would be treated as independent contractors, not servants—and the principal would not be liable to third persons for their torts, if any, involving physical conduct. Restatement, Second, Agency §§ 2(2) & 219(1). Nonetheless, independent contractors may be

"agents" in the broad sense, Restat. 2d Agency §
2(3), and be fully subject to control, or the right
of control, as to *what* should be done. Usually
this is stated at the outset in the specifications
for the job. When the work calls for co-operation
as the work progresses, however, it is sometimes
difficult to draw the line between *what* and *how*.
See, Nepstad v. Lambert (1951) 235 Minn. 1, 50
N.W.2d 614, 17 A.L.R.2d 1388. (Operation of
crane.)

It is tempting, at this point, to draw the conclusion that "control" is the *basis* of a principal's
vicarious liability to third persons. Of course, it
is a factor. Many courts have listed the master's
choice of servant and his right of control as a sufficient basis. Quarman v. Burnett (1840) 6 Mees.
& W. 499, 151 Eng. Reprint, 509. In the last
century, however, it has come to be recognized
that, in most employments, *actual* control is not a
realistic thing, hence it is usual to add, or "right
to control". Restatement, Second, Agency § 2.
While this serves well enough, when it is only
sought to distinguish agency from other concepts,
it is not a complete or satisfactory statement of
the basis for vicarious liability.

An illustration is found in partnership. As
pointed out above, § 15, a partner is not subject
to "control" in his day to day actions; he is a
co-proprietor. Indeed, the statute makes no mention of control when defining "partnership".

U.P.A. § 6. But it is also clear that the law of agency applies, U.P.A. § 4(3), and that any partner may subject the firm to liability either in tort or contract, when acting within the scope of the business. U.P.A. §§ 13 and 15. This suggests that "control" is of lessening significance; liability for losses is being regarded as a function of enterprise conducted for benefit or gain. The point is explored more fully, infra, § 30.

§ 18. A Personal Relationship

Probably the *control* factor, more than any other, has caused the courts to put contracts between principal and agent in a separate category. Or, more specifically, to imply a term in the employment contract that, upon death or incapacity of the agent, there should be no breach giving rise to a damage action; the contract would simply be "dissolved" at that point. Nor does it matter that it is the master, not the servant, who has died; "It is not everyone" to whom the servant will bind himself "knowing that he must be obedient and render the service required." Lacy v. Getman (1890) 119 N.Y. 109, 23 N.E. 452, 6 L.R.A. 728, 16 Am.St.Rep. 806 (farmhand, term contract).

There, of course, have been cases testing boundary lines; at some point supervision may be so remote as to constitute a virtual independent contractor relationship. For example, in Dumont v.

Heighton (1912) 14 Ariz. 25, 123 P. 306, 39 L. R.A., N.S., 1187, the plaintiff was engaged to do assessment work in Arizona on some mining claims owned by his New York employer, who, however, died before the work was completed. It was held that plaintiff might still recover as for a total breach of contract.   And see, In re Mallory's Estate (1929) 99 Cal.App. 96, 278 P. 488; there an attorney recovered his agreed fee, although his client had died some time before the work was finished and judgment obtained.

Perhaps the rule, that equity will not specifically enforce a personal service contract, stems from these same factors.   It is usually put on the ground of impossibility; the court cannot make an artist sing, Lumley v. Wagner (1952) 1 D.M. & G. 604, nor compel an editorial writer to write editorials, Tribune Ass'n v. Simonds (Ch. N.J. 1918) 104 A. 386.   But, it is suggested, the rule rests simply on the fact that it would be intolerable, as a personal matter, either to force the agent to work until the very end of his contract, or to compel the principal to continue the employment so long.   Such being the case, it is easy to apply the usual formula and say that equity will not intervene, since "damages at law would be adequate."   Auerbach v. Northland Rubber Co., Inc. (1916) 161 N.Y.S. 396 (general sales manager).   See, however, comments by Megarry, J., in Giles & Co. v. Morris (1972) 1 All E.R. 960 at 969.

It once was questioned whether this law applied to corporation officers. Since their tenure and many of their duties were stated in the by-laws—or perhaps in some statute—they were sometimes said to have a "franchise" in their office. It is still true that tenure and by-law duties often may not be changed by the directors, but it is current practice, not only to give directors the power to elect, but also the power to dismiss at will. Thus the relationship is simply one at will. When an officer wishes to preserve a damage action in case of dismissal, it is customary to contract separately with the corporation for a stated term. See, In re Paramount Publix Corp. (C.C.A.1937) 90 F.2d 441.

Finally, a distinction is to be drawn between the employment contract, on the one hand, and the concept of authority on the other. While it is true, for example, that death of the principal not only "dissolves" the contract but terminates the agent's authority as well, Charles V. Webster Real Estate v. Rickard (1972) 21 Cal.App.3d 612, 98 Cal.Rptr. 559, the latter result would seem to derive from the principal's right of control, not the personal nature of the relationship. That is, unless the agent's power or authorization is one coupled with an interest, infra § 21, it may be revoked or modified at any time by the principal without breach of contract. However, there are now cases, Courtney v. G. A. Linaker (1927) 173 Ark. 777, 293 S.W. 723, and a few statutes, Calif.

Civil Code § 2356, which continue the agent's power for the protection of third persons without notice. The point is developed more fully infra, § 50.

§ 19.   Delectus Personae

The writers on partnership are all agreed that the relationship between partners, like that between principal and agent generally, is a personal one, and, for most of the same reasons. Thus, Crane writes: "Because of the powers which a partner has in the disposition of partnership property and in the making of obligations binding on the partners, one is naturally particular in his choice of partners. It is a relation in which *delectus personae* is an important element." Crane, Partnership (1952) 34. See also, Warren, Corporate Advantages Without Incorporation (1929) p. 19.

Consistently with the agency rule, death of a partner is held to work a *dissolution* of the partnership. U.P.A. § 31(4). The partnership is not *terminated*, but continues until it can be wound up. U.P.A. § 30. But, as at common law, the authority of a surviving partner is limited to the winding up process, and is ended as to new transactions. See, Bass Dry Goods Co. v. Granite City Mfg. Co. (1902) 116 Ga. 176, 42 S.E. 415. However, it is now provided in the case of former dealers with the dissolved partnership that they must have actual notice, and, in the case of persons merely acquainted with the business, that notice be given by publication. U.P.A. § 35(1). Otherwise, a partner's authority or power will continue as to them. See infra, §§ 50 and 51.

Whether existing personal service contracts with the firm are likewise dissolved, has been a disputed question. In an early Massachusetts case, Holmes, J., said that "it could not be ruled, as a matter of law, that the contract of service was dissolved by the death of a partner. . . ." Hughes v. Gross (1896) 166 Mass. 61, 43 N.E. 1031, 2 L.R.A. 620, 55 Am.St.Rep. 375. However, the court there proceeded on the assumption that the contract was one with the partners individually, not the partnership as such. On the entity theory, it is difficult to say that a service contract would not fall when the partnership is dissolved. And, it has usually been so held. Shumate v. Sohon (1926) 56 App.D.C. 290, 12 F.2d 825, 59 A.L.R. 291.

Upon the broader question, whether equity will enjoin breach of a term partnership agreement— no cause being shown—there was a sharp conflict at common law. The English courts, and many American as well, held that an attempt by one partner to dissolve the partnership in breach of contract could be enjoined. See, Tankersley v. Norton (1920) 142 Ark. 339, 218 S.W. 660. But when the Uniform Act was drafted, the supposed analogy to the personal service contract in agency prevailed, and the law now is that any partner, at any time, may force dissolution of the partnership, subject to a damage claim. U.P.A. § 31(2). While machinery is set up—by posting bond and so on—to require that the withdrawing partner's capital contribution remain in the business, U.P.A. § 38(2), it does not appear to have been much used.

It is possible to avoid some of these consequences by contract. For example, a partnership in the form of a joint stock association, with transferable shares, is not dissolved when one partner sells his shares, or even when he dies. As a safeguard, however, the authority of any single partner to act for the business, is usually so limited in the agreement as to be non-existent. See, Spotswood v. Morris (1906) 12 Idaho 360, 85 P. 1094, 6 L.R.A., N.S., 665. Also, it has been decided that one partner in such an association may not bring about dissolution without cause, as he could in the case of an ordinary partnership. State Street Trust Co. v. Hall (1942) 311 Mass. 299, 41 N.E.2d 30, 156 A.L.R. 13. Even so, the joint stock association is not in general use today.

§ 20. Negative Covenants

Granting the rule to be that personal service contracts may not be specifically enforced, § 18, supra, does the principal have other legal means to assert at least a measure of control? For example, it has long been customary for employment contracts to provide that the agent will not engage in the same line of work with another employer, either during the course of his employment or for a period after its termination for any reason. Plainly, this does not represent the type of "control" used to define an "agent", Restatement, Second, Agency § 1, but, to the extent that clauses of the sort are enforceable, they may indirectly serve much the same purpose. In addition, the employer may hopefully avoid loss of customers and good will, as well as loss of personnel.

An illustration is Tribune Ass'n v. Simonds (Ch.N.J.1918) 104 A. 386. There, *Tribune* sought to enjoin an editorial writer with a reputation as a war correspondent, from joining another paper and writing for it,—all in violation of his negative covenant. Undoubtedly the plaintiff could recover "a judgment at law for a money damage," the court said, but did the law have an "adequate" means of measuring the damage? Here the services were of a "peculiar character"—or, "unique", as most courts would say—and, in order to prevent "irreparable" injury, the court granted an injunction in the language of the covenant. See also, Warner Brothers Pictures, Inc. v. Nelson (1937) 1 K.B. 209 (Bette Davis enjoined from making pictures except for Warner's: "She will not be driven, although she may be tempted, to perform the contract . . . ").

Since such a remedy verges on a "work for the plaintiff or starve" affair, it has been criticized. See: Stevens, Involuntary Servitude by Injunction (1921) 6 Cornell L.Q. 235; Blake, Employee Agreements Not to Compete (1960) 73 Harv.L. Rev. 625. Moreover—perhaps for that reason— the courts have sanctioned it with caution. Most, for example, will not *imply* a negative covenant, even though the agent has agreed to give his whole time. Whitwood Chemical Co. v. Hardman (1891) 2 Ch. 416. Again, the covenant must be reasonable in space and time, otherwise it may be void for restraint of trade. See, Wark v. Ervin Press Corp. (C.C.A.Ill.1931) 48 F.2d 152. Finally, the critical test, that the remedy can apply only in the case of "unique" employments, where damages for breach would not be "adequate", excludes the vast range of agencies. Lynch v. Bailey (1949) 300 N.Y. 615, 90 N.E.2d 484 (accountant—not unique).

The negative covenant, likewise, has been of utility in partnership, where it may serve, first, in holding the firm together and, second, as a safeguard against loss of *good will*. Since the firm may, as a matter of course, have damages in case of breach of the partnership agreement, the question, here too, has been to find grounds to support a remedy in equity. In most partnerships, as indeed in most employments, it is hard to say that the offender is "unique" in any relevant way. Menter Co. v. Brock (1920) 147 Minn. 407, 180 N.W. 553, 20 A.L.R. 857 (manager of retail store).

An illustration is Bauer v. Sawyer (1956) 8 Ill.2d 351, 134 N.E.2d 329. That was a derivative action brought by 5 of 11 erstwhile partners in a Clinic to enjoin a 12th (who had withdrawn) from setting up practice in violation of his negative covenant. The court first disposed of the restraint of trade point by saying that to subtract one doctor, from 70 or more in the area, would not affect the public adversely. Little effort was made, on the positive side, to show that Dr. Sawyer was "unique"; on the contrary, the case was put on the analogy to the sale of business holdings. When a partner withdraws, he disposes of his interest in the firm for a price; as a seller of "good will" he parts with not much of anything except as his hands may be tied by injunction. Hence, judgment was for plaintiff.

A word upon policy! From the standpoint of a partner or an agent, ordered not to carry on his usual work, the remedy seems harsh. Balanced against that is the fact that artists, pugilists, editorial writers and many others could not sell their services, for the price they do, were the employer limited to a damage action in case of breach. See comment by Judge Buffington dissenting in Madison Square Garden Corp. v. Braddock (C.C.A.N.J. 1937) 90 F.2d 924. So also the seller of a business, or a partner upon withdrawing from a firm, is paid more than he otherwise could get, if a suit for damages were to be the only remedy in case of breach. At this point in time the negative covenant, specifically enforced in limited situations, is favored.

§ 21. Irrevocable Agencies

It may be a confusion of terms ever to speak of agencies as being *irrevocable*. Perhaps the holders of irrevocable powers are not "agents" at all, "because they do not have the duty to act primarily for the benefit of the giver of the power, nor are they subject to his right of control." Restatement, Second, Agency § 12 Comment (c). Of course, the mere presence of an irrevocability clause in a power of attorney does not make the holder a non-agent. In fact, prior to confrontation on the irrevocability issue, such an agent acts as any other, for and on behalf of the principal, and as a fiduciary.

Upon confrontation, however, what is the situation? An irrevocability clause in a realty agent's contract, for example, would not alone deprive the principal of control. If supported by consideration, the contract might well be "binding," giving rise to a cause of action for damages in case of breach. Blackstone v. Buttermore (1867) 53 Pa. 266. But "irrevocable" means something more and, on such facts alone, the agent could not enjoin the principal from breaching his contract. Piper v. Wells (1938) 175 Md. 326, 2 A.2d 28; Schilling v. Moore (1912) 34 Okl. 155, 125 P. 487. Damages at law for loss of prospective commissions would be *adequate*.

For a century or more, however, it has been settled that if, in addition, the agent's authority is one "coupled with an interest," the principal may *not* revoke. The leading case, Hunt v. Rousmanier's Adm'rs (1823) 21 U.S. 174, 8 Wheat. 174, 5 L.Ed. 589, had to do with powers of attorney giving a lender authority to sell certain vessels in case the loan was not paid when due. Thus, a typical security power! Chief Justice Marshall was clear that the borrower "could not, during his life, by any act of his own, have revoked this letter of attorney." Whether the holder had at some point become a non-agent, the court did not say.

That Hunt's power could have survived the death of Rousmanier, however, was another matter; the court said that, in order to do so, "the power must be engrafted on an estate in the thing"—whatever that means—and Hunt's letter of attorney was held not to meet the test. No reason was given why a power, which was irrevocable during the life of the parties, should suddenly become revocable when perhaps most needed—except to assert that it would be a "gross absurdity" to permit an attorney to sign in the name of a dead man. In this the court ignored the purpose of the suit, which was to compel the borrower's administrator to join in a sale. Today, procedures exist in most states giving lenders power in such cases to sell the pledged security. Merry v. Lynch (1878) 68 Me. 94.

Later courts have come to see that a "power coupled with an interest" is not an isolated phenomenon, but is governed by usual principles of equity. Thus, a power to manage a building, which had been given to the holder of a 20 year lease as protection against possible forfeiture of the ground lease, was held to be "a power coupled with an interest" and enforceable by injunction. Lane Mortg. Co. v. Crenshaw (1928) 93 Cal.App. 411, 269 P. 672. Plainly the holder's 20 year lease was a unique value, and damages at law would not compensate for its loss. Hence, the agency was irrevocable.

The constructive thing to do, were it not too late, would be to reword the rule, and substitute *equity* for *interest*, thus, "a power coupled with an *equity*" may not be revoked. This would at once preserve the essence of the rule, and end the uncertainty. To illustrate, consider State v. Pacific Waxed Paper Co. (1945) 22 Wash.2d 844, 157 P.2d 707, 159 A.L.R. 297. The court there enforced a mutual proxy agreement, stated to be irrevocable, even after one of the signers had died. The court had trouble in determining the "interest" to which the power was "coupled", but the "equity" in favor of the surviving proxy holder was clear enough, since it gave him voting control, a unique value.

§ 22. Fiduciary

So much for *control*, or the lack thereof, as a distinguishing factor. Of what significance is the point that agency is a "fiduciary" relationship, in which the agent agrees to act "on behalf of" the principal? In fact, it is critical to the concept of enterprise—as an on-going institution, capable of bearing risks—that a line be drawn between what belongs to the agent, and what to the principal. This is not always an easy thing to do factually, even though special procedures have been developed to aid in the task. These, too, need to be examined since, to a degree, they have come to define the obligation.

A case which occurs all too frequently will illustrate the remedy situation. The purchasing agent for a company is given money, i. e. a bribe, to favor the goods of a particular seller. Obviously, the agent will have breached his fiduciary duties in taking the money, for his duty is to work for the best interests of the principal, but what may his employer do about it? Plenty! Of course, the agent may be discharged, and held liable in damages. Also, the transaction with the third person, seller, may be rescinded for fraud, or the seller, too, may be held liable in damages. It will be presumed that his sale price was "loaded by the amount of the bribe." Donemar, Inc. v. Molloy (1930) 252 N.Y. 360, 169 N.E. 610.

And, that is not all. The principal also has the option to recover the bribe money—which may be considerable—from the agent. This may be done either in equity as a constructive trust, Boston Deep Sea Fishing v. Ansell (1886) 39 Ch.Div. 339, or, at law, in an action for money had and received. See, Robert Reis & Co. v. Volck (1912) 151 App.Div. 613, 136 N.Y.S. 367. Nor would it be essential in either case to prove damage of any sort. The test in each is whether the agent may "in good conscience" retain the benefit. See, Beatty v. Guggenheim Exploration Co. (1919) 225 N.Y. 380, 122 N.E. 378.

What are the dictates of "good conscience," however, is sometimes a perplexing question. On a day, back in the 1930's, one Guth, the president and a director of Loft, Inc., (which had a considerable candy and soft drink operation in the New York area) received a telephone call from an acquaintance, Megargel, saying in effect that the formula and trademark for Pepsi-Cola could be acquired in a bankruptcy settlement,—was Guth interested? The upshot was that Guth and Megargel bought the formula and trademark for themselves, at a cost of only $12,000, and formed a new company to carry on the business,—which was quite successful. Did Guth breach his fiduciary duties?

When the question reached the courts, they held in the affirmative, on two grounds. Loft, Inc. v. Guth (1938) 23 Del.Ch. 235, 5 A.2d 503. First, Guth was held to have "diverted and personally appropriated" a business "expectancy," which belonged to Loft. That is, when Megargel's call came in, Guth's fiduciary duty was to place the matter before the Loft directors. Since he had not done so, he was said to hold his stock in the new venture as a constructive trustee, and was required to turn it over to Loft, without recompense. There have been many "business opportunity" cases, so called, reaching similar results. See, Duane Jones Co., Inc. v. Burke (1954) 306 N.Y. 172, 117 N.E.2d 237. (Officers and directors quit and formed new business, taking customers of former employer.)

The second ground afforded an equally solid basis for the decision. That is, Guth had used Loft resources, Loft executives and, above all, Loft stores to promote the new drink. The court said that a business built in that fashion was "in contemplation of equity the property of Loft." As much so, in fact, as if it were "a piece of real estate which Guth had unwarrantably taken Loft assets to purchase . . . '' The cases are many supporting that proposition, even though the taken money has been fully repaid, with interest.

The patent cases, though troubled, are further illustration. When an agent discovers a new and useful invention, on his employer's time, through the use of his employer's facilities and materials, a similar question is presented. Unless the agent was expressly hired to invent, it is clear that the patent belongs to the agent,—it was his personal discovery. See, Standard Parts Co. v. Peck (1924) 264 U.S. 52, 44 S.Ct. 239, 68 L.Ed. 560, 32 A.L.R. 1033. But the courts have recognized that the employer has an equity in the case, and have granted him a so-called "shop right" in the invention, that is, a non-exclusive license to make, use, or vend. See: Gemco Engineering & Mfg. Co. v. Henderson (1947) 82 Ohio App. 324, 77 N.E.2d 742; Morris, American Shop Right Rule (1960) 39 Tex.L.Rev. 41.

How does this law apply to partners, who, as agents, are also fiduciaries? See, U.P.A. § 21. In Meinhard v. Salmon (1928) 249 N.Y. 458, 164 N.E. 545, 62 A.L.R. 1, Cardozo, C. J., put it this way: "Joint adventurers, like copartners, owe to one another, while the enterprise continues, the duty of the finest loyalty." Hence, one of two joint venturers violated his duty when, near the end of the venture, he secretly took a new lease to its property, to hold for himself. "Many forms of conduct permissible in a workaday world for those acting at arm's length, are forbidden to those bound by fiduciary ties. A trustee is held to something stricter than the morals of the market place. Not honesty alone, but the punctilio of an honor the most sensitive, is then the standard of behavior." Per, Cardozo, C. J.

§ 23. Indemnity

The usual definition of Agency, § 2, supra, says nothing about *losses*, attention being directed to *gains*. As to these, Viscount Simonds said in Sterling Eng'r. Co. v. Patchett (1955) A.C. 534, 544, "it is an implied term, though not written at large, in the contract of service of any workman, that what he produces by the strength of his arm, or the skill of his hand, or the exercise of his inventive faculty shall become the property of the employer." No doubt that overstates the matter, but if something of the sort is true, perhaps it also is to be implied that the employer is to bear the *risks* involved?

Looking first to the pecuniary risks—personal injury losses come later, § 25—it has been true for two centuries or more that an agreement to indemnify the agent will, in fact, be implied. Whether this will be done, avowedly, to put the risks of enterprise on enterprise, is a problem. There have been intimations that indemnity is merely a matter of *fairness*.   See, Restatement, Second, Agency § 438(2b).

The early Pennsylvania case of D'Arcy v. Lyle (1813) 5 Binn. 441, which had to do with an unusual set of facts, will illustrate.   In 1804 defendant sent the plaintiff, D'Arcy, to Cape Francois in Haiti, to demand an accounting from Suckley & Co., former agents of the defendant.   Certain goods were turned over to D'Arcy and, although these were attached by Richardson, a creditor of Suckley & Co., the Chamber of Justice awarded possession to D'Arcy.   In 1806 D'Arcy settled all accounts with Lyle and ceased further to represent him.

Then, in 1808, the powers of government having meanwhile been taken over by Christophe, Richardson instituted a new suit against D'Arcy, in the amount of $3,000, for the value of the goods taken in 1804.   Christophe had D'Arcy's lawyer tied and sent to the fort, and ordered a trial by battle between D'Arcy and Richardson.   Ultimately D'Arcy retracted his defense in open court and paid the $3,000 with costs.   Thereafter D'Arcy returned to this country and recovered judgment against Lyle for his losses.

On appeal, Tilghman, C. J., said in part: "In the case before us, the plaintiff has suffered damages without his own fault, *on account of his agency,* and the jury have indemnified him to an amount, very little if at all exceeding the property in his hands, with interest and costs. I am of opinion, that the verdict should not be set aside." (Emphasis added.) Brackenridge, J., dissenting, said: "He was put in fear, fear of his life; a fear that would excuse or justify a constant and resolute man; that is clear. But it is his misfortune, and I can consider Lyle under no obligation to indemnify him for the loss."

Most courts would accept *D'Arcy* as good law; a recurring problem, however, has been whether the agent's loss was one in fact "on account of his agency." In Bibb v. Allen (1893) 149 U.S. 481, 13 S.Ct. 950, 37 L.Ed. 819 (a leading case on the effect of custom), the agent who had sold cotton for future delivery in New York was allowed to recover from his Alabama principals a loss of $19,273.50, which accrued when he had to go into the market to buy cotton to cover. See, Restatement, Second Agency § 438(2a). Recovery was allowed as for "money paid out at the principal's instance and request"—the agent's action being found to be in accord with New York custom. That determined, it was clearly a loss attributable to the agency.

A closer question, often litigated, is whether legal expenses, incurred by an agent in successfully defending suits by third persons, are to be indemnified. The plaintiff, in Admiral Oriental Line v. United States (C.C.A.N.Y.1936) 86 F.2d 201, was a ship's agent in the Philippines who incurred large expenses in defending a suit by cargo owners, the ship having been lost with all hands in a typhoon. The court, by L. Hand, J., said: "Since by hypothesis the agent's outlay is not due to his mismanagement, it should be regarded only as a loss, unexpected it is true, but *inextricably interwoven with the enterprise.*" (Emphasis added.) And, such being the case, the principal was required to pay indemnity: "The doctrine stands upon the fact that the venture is the principal's, and that, as the profits will be his, so should be the expenses." Cf. Restatement, Second, Agency § 439(d).

In New York Dock Co. v. McCollom (1939) 173 Misc. 106, 16 N.Y.S.2d 844, a much cited case, the loss grew out of a minority shareholder's derivative action for alleged mismanagement, in which the directors—making a successful defense—incurred an $86,755.41 expense for attorney fees and costs. Directors, the court said, *are not agents,* "except in a convenient rhetorical sense," and hence, *D'Arcy* law would not apply. The court's ruling would seem to have been in error. Supra, § 11. In fact, there have since been a great many by-law provisions expressly providing indemnity for directors, as well as for officers and other agents. Thus, a pragmatic reversal. See, Ballantine, California's 1943 Statute, etc. (1943) 31 Cal.L.Rev. 515.

The *McCollom* court also refused an alternative ground, that the director's successful defense had conferred a "benefit" on the corporation. Many cases may be cited in which officers or other agents pay debts of the principal, or spend money to protect its property. In these, the agent can be indemnified for his outlay and incidental expenses on equitable principles. See, Restatement, Second, Agency § 439(e). But the court was unable to find any "benefit"; the company had its own counsel present, as is usual in these cases. See: Solimine v. Hollander (1941) 129 N.J.Eq. 264, 19 A.2d 344 (contra); and, Washington and Bishop, Indemnifying the Corporate Executive (1963).

The court in *McCollom* was right, of course, in pointing out that generally a defendant, even when successful, must pay his own lawyer's fees. Thus, there should be no question of indemnity when the agent is sued *directly* by his employer for breach of the employment contract. But a shareholder's derivative action is something else again, more nearly akin to a third party action. Such being the case, the agent's expense might easily be found to be "inextricably interwoven with the enterprise", as Judge Hand put it, and hence entitled to indemnity.

§ 24. Contribution for Losses

Since partners are agents, § 7 supra, the indemnity rules just discussed, § 23, would seem also to apply to them. In fact, this is true; U.P.A. § 18 (b) expressly provides: "The partnership must indemnify every partner in respect of payments made and personal liabilities reasonably incurred by him *in the ordinary and proper conduct* of its business, or for the preservation of its business or property." (Emphasis added.) Not merely as a matter of fairness, these are enterprise losses.

How "contribution" fits into the scheme requires explanation. Contribution connotes a *sharing* of losses, not full indemnity; it is a concept found in many areas of the law. Asylum v. McGuire (1925) 239 N.Y. 375, 146 N.E. 632, 38 A.L.R. 1214 (contribution between co-sureties). At common law, a partner could not sue either the firm (since it was not regarded as a legal entity) or his co-partners, but was required to bring a bill in equity for an accounting, usually upon dissolution. While this procedure has been relaxed, U.P.A. § 22(d), the partner still meets with procedural difficulties not encountered generally by an agent seeking indemnity from an employer.

A few states now allow partnerships or other associations to be sued directly at law. See: Cal.Civ.Code § 388; Smith v. Hensley (Ky.1962) 354 S.W.2d 744, 98 A.L.R.2d 340 (claim by part-

ner for damage to his personally owned truck).
The important thing for present purposes, however, is that when a partner does obtain judgment
against his firm for *full indemnity,* as provided in
U.P.A. § 18(b), supra, he also must share the loss,
as do the other partners. This is provided in
U.P.A. § 18(a): "Each partner . . . must
contribute towards the losses . . . sustained
by the partnership according to his share in the
profits." Thus, the upshot is that an aggrieved
partner—unlike an agent—ultimately obtains
"contribution," not full indemnity.

Consistently, when suit is allowed against a co-
partner, rather than the firm, the claim is merely
for contribution. For example, in United Brokers' Co. v. Dose (1933) 143 Ore. 283, 22 P.2d 204,
plaintiff objected to his co-partner's accounting in
a winding up proceeding. Defendant had asked
for contribution based upon a claim for salary,
and also for losses he had sustained in a traffic
accident, when on firm business. Both claims
were disallowed: The first, because partners are
not entitled to compensation (except by agreement), U.P.A. § 18(f); and, the second, because
plaintiff was found to have been at fault in the
accident. See, U.P.A. § 18(b) supra. So too, an
agent may not have indemnity when the loss in
question was caused by his own fault.

Of course, contribution comes into question
whenever a partnership is being wound up and

there are not assets sufficient to pay losses. That is, losses of whatever kind, including indemnity losses. See: U.P.A. § 18(a); Whitcomb v. Converse (1875) 119 Mass. 38, 20 Am.Rep. 311. In a very real sense, therefore, a partner's initial contributions to capital, infra § 79, are an advance contribution to future indemnity losses. It is but natural, therefore, that the ratios by which losses are to be shared, established at that time, should apply in subsequent cases. Vaughan v. Caldwell (1927) 200 Cal. 572, 253 P. 929.

§ 25. Personal Injury Losses; F.E.L.A.

There is no question that at common law an agent's personal injuries—even though suffered in the course of his work—were his own misfortune. Both majority and dissent in D'Arcy v. Lyle, supra § 23, said as much. Tilghman, C. J., put it this way: "The cases cited by the defendant show, that if the agent on a journey on business of his principal, is robbed of *his own money,* the principal is not answerable. . . . So if he receives a wound, the principal is not bound to pay the expenses of his cure, because it is a personal risk which the agent takes upon himself." The admiralty rule has always been different.

That was in 1808. For the rest of the century, as industrial units became larger and employment less able to guard against injury, there was increasing litigation. In a landmark case, Farwell

v. Boston W. R. Corp. (1842) 45 Mass. (4 Metc.) 49, 38 Am.Dec. 339 (engineer injured by negligence of a switchman), Chief Justice Shaw refused to apply the respondeat superior doctrine, which would give relief to a third person so injured, infra § 30, and denied recovery. It was a matter of *contract,* Shaw said, though why he did not imply an indemnity clause, supra § 23, was not stated.

Thus was established the "fellow servant rule," Restatement, Second, Agency § 474, which compares with the "common employment" rule, previously stated in England. Priestly v. Fowler (1837) 3 Mees. & Welsb. 1. To be charitable, the result may have been in keeping with prevailing notions of social policy at the time. At any rate, the doctrine—also recognized by Shaw, C. J.— that an employer owes a non-delegable duty to maintain reasonably safe working conditions (including *competent* fellow workers), became the agent's main protection at law. See: Flike v. Boston & A. R. Co. (1873) 53 N.Y. 549, 13 Am. Rep. 545; Restatement, Second, Agency § 492. That in turn, however, was pretty well nullified by the twin defences, contributory negligence and, especially, assumption of risk. See: Restatement, Second, Agency § 521; Yaconi v. Brady & Gioe, Inc. (1927) 246 N.Y. 300, 158 N.E. 876 (stevedore held by Cardozo, J., to have assumed risk of injury caused by grease on floor).

Finally, in 1908, at the start of this century, Congress passed the Federal Employers' Liability Act. See, (1954) 45 U.S.C.A. §§ 51–59. F.E.L.A. was a proud achievement of the Theodore Roosevelt administration. Though it applied only to employees of carriers in interstate commerce, it abolished the fellow servant rule as to them with a flourish. Also, it reduced the employer's contributory negligence defense to one of comparative negligence. See, Prosser, Comparative Negligence (1953) 41 Cal.L.Rev. 1. This was all to the good, but unfortunately it left "assumption of risk" untouched. See, (1954) 45 U.S.C.A. § 54.

Of perhaps more significance, the scheme of the act enshrined negligence as the basis of liability. That is to say, the Act provided that every carrier is to be liable for injury or death to any employee "resulting in whole or *in part* from the *negligence* of any of the officers, agents or employees of such carrier . . .." (1954) 45 U.S.C.A. § 51 (Emphasis added). Subsequent cases finally held that this was not the measure of "negligence" required generally in tort law; it was enough, as Mr. Justice Brennan stated in Rogers v. Missouri Pacific R. Co. (1957) 352 U.S. 500, 506, 77 S.Ct. 443, 448, 1 L.Ed.2d 493, if the "employer played any part, *even the slightest,* in producing the injury . . .." (Emphasis added).

Even so, the result was very different from the rule of the indemnity cases, where claims are charged to enterprise, as business losses. Supra, § 23. Or, as in Workmen's Compensation, where personal injury claims also are treated as enterprise losses. Infra, § 26. And, even though the doctrine of assumption of risk was later *obliterated from the law,* by the 1939 amendments, as Mr. Justice Black stated in Tiller v. Atlantic Coast Line R. Co. (1943) 318 U.S. 54, 63 S.Ct. 444, 87 L.Ed. 610, 143 A.L.R. 967, the Act still is criticized for that reason. Mr. Justice Frankfurter, dissenting in *Tiller,* made the point this way: "the common law concept of liability for negligence is archaic and unjust as a means of compensation for injuries sustained by employees under modern industrial conditions   . . . ."

It would be premature to decide now which view is the better. When it was finally realized that "negligence," as used in the Act, is a federal question—Urie v. Thompson (1949) 337 U.S. 163, 174, 69 S.Ct. 1018, 1026, 93 L.Ed. 1282, 11 A.L.R. 2d 252—not governed by local rules applied in traffic cases, for example, much of the litigation ended. See, Arnold, Professor Hart's Theology (1960) 73 Harv.L.Rev. 1298. Moreover, there is little doubt that recoveries are larger in F.E.L.A. cases, than are the awards under Workmens' Compensation. See, Richter and Forer, F.E.L.A.

—A Real Compensatory Law (1951) 36 Corn L.Q. 203.

§ 26. Workmen's Compensation—Scope

State legislatures took a different course than Congress, when it adopted F.E.L.A., and enacted Workmen's Compensation statutes to cover the personal injury losses of employees. The various acts differ in particulars, and are continually being amended, but most were patterned after the early British Workmen's Compensation Act of 1897 (60 & 61 Vict. c. 37), as changed by the act of 1906 (6 Edw. 7, c. 58), and follow more or less closely the formulae adopted by the British Act to fix its boundaries.

The New York provision, McKinney's, N.Y. Workmen's Compensation Law, § 10, is typical: "Every employer . . . shall . . . secure compensation to his employees and pay or provide compensation for their disability or death from injury *arising out of and in the course of* the employment, without regard to fault as a cause of the injury . . ." (Emphasis added). Under the various statutes it is usual to provide a schedule, setting out the compensation—based on loss of earning power—which may be awarded for different injuries. One reason is to facilitate sure and prompt payment to the injured workman; the common law remedy, even when successful, often took years to litigate.

Thus the theory of liability is very different from that of F.E.L.A. Employer fault, as a basis, is gone. Indeed, Workmen's Compensation was promoted on the slogan that "the risks of industry are to be borne by industry." Early employers said the law was revolutionary, a taking of property without due process, and challenged its constitutionality. In due time, however, the law was fully sustained. See, New York Central R. Co. v. White (1917) 243 U.S. 188, 37 S.Ct. 247. (New York statute).

As a matter of perspective, the concept of *liability without fault* is by no means new to agency. As just considered, supra § 23, it is in fact the basis of indemnity liability. Moreover, liability without fault underlies the Respondeat Superior doctrine, governing the principal's liability to third persons, a matter of some consequence. See, infra, § 30; Steffen, Enterprise Liability: Some Exploratory Comments (1965) 17 Hastings L.Rev. 165. Whether we are yet ready to proclaim a new legal principle—enterprise liability—is a question. See, Ehrenzweig, Negligence Without Fault (1966) 54 Cal.L.Rev. 1422.

Nonetheless, the statutory test—"arising out of and in the course of"—has given trouble. Some early courts, when applying the "arising out of" part, looked to find causation or fault, but today, aided by the admonition in all statutes that they "shall be liberally construed," Cal.Labor Code §

3202, that has not been a problem. Fault is not a part of the Workmen's Compensation equation, nor is foreseeability or assumption of risk. See, Chambers v. Union Oil Co. (1930) 199 N.C. 28, 153 S.E. 594; Young v. Liberty Mut. Ins. Co. (1943) 68 Ga.App. 843, 24 S.E.2d 594 (contra). The courts have done a liberal, even an imaginative job, in administering the statute.

In most cases, of course, there is little doubt—as when a workman, while at his bench during regular hours, is injured by a defective machine. But suppose: he is struck by lightning, Madura v. City of New York (1924) 238 N.Y. 214, 144 N.E. 505; is injured by falling bricks during a hurricane, Morris Caswell's Case (1940) 305 Mass. 500, 26 N.E.2d 328; is drowned when trying to rescue some third person, O'Leary v. Brown-Pacific-Maxon (1951) 340 U.S. 504, 71 S.Ct. 470, 95 L.Ed. 483, falls off a bridge, when answering a "call of nature," Haskins Case (1927) 261 Mass. 436, 158 N.E. 845; or, being a salesman, chokes to death on a piece of meat when entertaining a customer at a New York restaurant, Snyder v. General Paper Corp. (1967) 277 Minn. 376, 152 N.W. 2d 743.

In each of the cases just listed, the accident was held to have been one "arising out of" the employment. Also, to have met the second part of the test, that the accident happened "in the course of" the employment. The test being stated in the conjunctive, both phrases are given equal weight. In *O'Leary*, supra, for example, it was strongly argued that the workman, who was on a company sponsored outing at the time, had completely departed from "the course of" his employment when he voluntarily went to the aid of a stranger. But the court held in the negative; both branches of the test were met.

However, even in routine cases, there has been difficulty in fixing a point of beginning. It was early decided that, when the employee had a regular place of work, accidents occurring while coming or going were not "in the course of," thus excluding bus and trolley accidents. But if the workman had boarded his employer's truck to go to work, that would meet the test. Flanagan v. Webster & Webster (1928) 107 Conn. 502, 142 A. 201. And see, Holt L. Co. v. Industrial Comm. (1919) 168 Wis. 381, 170 N.W. 366. Recently, California has extended "in the course of" to include an employee injured while going to work *in his own car,* since the car was used routinely in his work. Smith v. W. C. App. Bd. (1968) 69 Cal.2d 814, 73 Cal.Rptr. 253, 447 P.2d 365.

The question: Who is an "employee?" has also caused litigation. Some of the early cases held that a corporation officer or director could not be an "employee" or "workman." See, Gassaway v. Gassaway & Owen, Inc. (1942) 220 N.C. 694, 18 S.E.2d 120. But that position, too, has been changed, either by decision or statute. See, Cal. Labor Code § 3351(c). Since they, too, contribute to production, "compensation for them is within the scheme .   .   . " Per, Judge Learned Hand, quoted in Gottlieb v. Arrow Door Co. (1961) 364 Mich. 450, 110 N.W.2d 767 (President and sole shareholder awarded compensation for injury).

§ 27. Workmen's Compensation—Immunity

Workmen's Compensation legislation was promoted as something in the nature of a bargain between employer and employee. In case of injury by accident, the employer was to assume a definite obligation to the employee, as for the replacement of broken machinery, and in return the employee was to give up his rights at common law against the employer. The bargaining process was the same, a quarter century later, when the statutes were being amended to bring industrial "disease" within the scheme. See, Smith v. Lau (1939) 135 Ohio St. 191, 20 N.E.2d 232, 121 A.L.R. 1131; Cal.L.Code § 3208. Many courts had held "disease" not to be an "accident" or "injury." See, Cole, Occupational Disease Coverage (1944) 6 La.L.Rev. 85.

The statutes thus represented a gain of great importance to the employee; at common law his recovery sometimes was large, if he could hold out long enough, but often he had no recovery at all.

See, supra, § 25; Thomas v. Parker Rust Proof Co. (1938) 284 Mich. 260, 279 N.W. 504 (silicosis). But the *immunity* given to the employer, Cal.L.Code § 3601, likewise was very important to him; its purpose, "to substitute finite liability for the fortuities of the common law remedy." Per, Weintraub, C. J., in Mazzuchelli v. Silberberg (1959) 29 N.J. 15, 148 A.2d 8. A few states extended immunity to other related employers. See, Smith v. Ostrov (1940) 208 Minn. 77, 292 N.W. 745. The Illinois law, which covered all employers, was held unconstitutional, Grasse v. Dealer's Transport Co. (1952) 412 Ill. 179, 106 N.E.2d 124.

The question most agitated recently has been whether the employer's mantle should also cover management, and negligent fellow servants, as well. Each of the time tested torts arguments —to teach the "wrongdoer" a lesson and so on— points in the opposite direction. See, Lees v. Dunkerley Brothers (1910) 103 L.T.R. (N.S.) 467, 55 Sol.J. 44. Indeed, a few courts have held the negligent fellow servant liable. Zimmer v. Casey (1929) 296 Pa. 529, 146 A. 130. In some states, however, the "vice principal" doctrine was conscripted to exonerate management, Landrum v. Middaugh (1927) 117 Ohio St. 608, 160 N.E. 691 (foreman), and later, in a growing number of states, both management and fellow servants—if not *grossly* negligent—have been exempted from common law suit. See: Caulfield v. Elmhurst

Contracting Co. (1945) 268 App.Div. 661, 53 N.Y.S.2d 25; Cal.L.Code § 3601.

The risks of industry are, thus, finally put on industry, not on co-employees or management. Warner v. Leder (1952) 234 N.C. 727, 69 S.E.2d 6 (president not liable): "[T]o hold otherwise," the court said, "would, in large measure, defeat the very purposes for which our Workmen's Compensation Act was enacted." Nor is that unfair; it is the employer, not the employee, who can best guard against accident, by providing safe equipment, competent fellow employees, and proper working rules.

Thus, the related problem, what to do with the employee's common law action against third persons (not in the same employ), when they have been the cause of injury, has taken on increased importance. At the threshold is the question of election. If the employee takes compensation, must he assign his third party action to the employer? Most courts would answer in the negative; there is no election. See Rosenbaum v. Hartford News Co. (1918) 92 Conn. 398, 103 A. 120, L.R.A.1918F, 521. In fact, the statutes usually provide in detail for suit by either, employer or employee. See, Cal.L.Code §§ 3854, 3855.

What are the priorities? Plainly the action— which often may greatly exceed the compensation recovery—belongs to the injured workman. It is generally provided, however, that the employer is to have a "lien" on any judgment, in order that he may recover his outlay for compensation. Cal.L. Code § 3856. Moreover, this result, too, is probably fair enough. The third person—at fault— has no standing to urge that the loss was a risk of industry; the injured employee has little warrant to claim a double recovery.

When the employer's negligence was a contributory cause of the accident, however, there has been dispute. Under early statutes this was held not to be a defense available to third persons, when sued by the injured employee. Caulfield v. Elmhurst Contracting Co., supra. But, in a series of cases since, the defense has been allowed, measured by the amount of the compensation award. See, Witt v. Jackson (1961) 57 Cal.2d 57, 17 Cal. Rptr. 369, 366 P.2d 641. The employee, it will be noted, neither profits nor loses. In those states which have abandoned the defense of contributory negligence, there will be a problem. See, Nga Li v. Yellow Cab Co. (1975) 13 Cal.3d 804, 119 Cal.Rptr. 858, 532 P.2d 1226.

§ 28. Partial Summary

One point of special interest emerges from the foregoing examination of the salient features of "agency," §§ 15 to 27. The principal, or proprietor, has been called upon increasingly to assume agency, or inter se, losses—both pecuniary and

personal injury—as routine business risks.   On
this evidence, the critical element in the "agency"
definition is not so much "control," as usually
stated, supra § 18, but the fact that the gains or
benefits from—as well as the risks incident to—
the agent's actions, belong to the principal.   The
Restatement makes it clear that the agent works
"for," or "on behalf of" the principal, but leaves
to inference, the many questions of risk.

Out of step, is the remedy provided by F.E.L.A.,
supra § 25, which is based on "fault."   Far from
disappearing—unless the carriers disappear—the
1937 amendments to the Act broadened its scope;
any employee whose duties are in "furtherance
of," or would in any way "affect," interstate commerce, is now covered.   See, 45 U.S.C.A. § 51.
Under the original text, the decisions were approaching a point where it seemed an employee
must in fact be crossing a state line when injured
before the Act would apply.

The amended Act, however, goes very far in the
other direction.   A filing clerk at her desk in an
office building, for example, who was injured
when a cracked window pane gave in, has been
permitted to recover F.E.L.A. damages.   Reed v.
Pennsylvania R. Co. (1956) 351 U.S. 502, 76 S.Ct.
958, 100 L.Ed. 1366.   Not a bad result, perhaps,
since negligence could be established, but the cor-
ollary, that all such employees are in Interstate
Commerce, and thus excluded from Workmen's

Compensation coverage (See, Cal.L.Code § 3203), means that many industrial injuries will go without redress of any kind. See, Miller, F.E.L.A. Revisited (1957) 6 Cath.U.L.Rev. 158.

With F.E.L.A. put to one side, however, it seems fair to say, as suggested above, that "agency" is evolving into a risk bearing institution, thus giving support for the theory of "enterprise liability." It remains, in Part II, to examine whether—or the extent to which—responsibility for third party losses, either in tort or contract, may likewise fit into the pattern.

PART II

ENTERPRISE TRANSACTIONS

A. TORTS

§ 29. More on Scope

It is proposed in Part II to explore the many questions which arise in the course of enterprise dealings with third persons. This is the area of traditional agency. For the moment the form of the organization conducting the enterprise is not of consequence; it may be either an individual principal or master, or a corporation, partnership or some other form, as will be discussed in Part III. The term enterprise, however, is taking on a broader significance than that of principal, master, or employer; it also connotes the relationships discussed in Part I, that is, the on-going business, or, to travel in circles, the enterprise.

First, it is proposed to deal with *tort* liability, the defense side of enterprise. Of course, as Holmes wrote in 1891, "it is plain good sense to hold people answerable for wrongs which they have intentionally brought to pass. . . ." Holmes, Agency (1891) 4 Harv.L.Rev. 345, at 347. And, he continued, "This is the true scope and meaning of 'qui facit per alium facit per se,' and the English law has recognized that maxim as far back as it is worthwhile to follow it." See, also, Wigmore, Responsibility for Tortious Acts (1894) 7 Harv.L.Rev. 42.

The extent to which, and the basis upon which, enterprise should be liable for *non-directed* acts is the question. Holmes would have solved that problem by the "fiction" that, "within the scope of the agency, principal and agent are one." Holmes, Collected Legal Papers (1921) 49. But the law has taken a different course. The problem, moreover, is not simply one of fixing liability as between third person and employer; it is necessary also to examine how such risks or losses are to be allocated as between employer and employee, i. e., between master and servant, thus, presenting further data pertinent to Part I.

In the final sections, §§ 46 to 64, rights and liabilities growing out of *contract* transactions with third persons will be examined. Again, when the agent acts as directed, or, that is, within his authority, there is little difficulty. However, there is a very large area, here too, where losses are to be adjusted, when, because of misunderstanding, carelessness, lack of instructions, fraud or something else, the agent has taken action contrary to the principal's expectation. To an extent, the factors making for liability on the tort side have a bearing.

§ 30. Respondeat Superior

In 1698 Lord Holt declared, positively and without reference to prior authority, that a master must respond to third persons for losses negligently caused by the master's servants. Or, as he put it: "If the servants of A. with his cart run against another cart, wherein is a pipe of wine, and overturn the cart and spoil the wine, an action lieth against A." Jones v. Hart (1698) Holt, K.B. 642, 90 Eng.Reprint 1255 (trover for goods lost by negligence of defendant's servants). See also, Brucker v. Fromont (1796) 6 T.R. 695, 101 Eng.Reprint 758.

Thus, the doctrine of vicarious liability was established well before the great industrial expansion of the 19th century. No name had yet been given the remedy; nor had any reason been assigned for it. In due time, many reasons were given. Holmes said it is a "survival from ancient times of doctrines" which "embodied certain rights and liabilities of heads of families." Holmes, Agency (1891) 4 Harv.L.Rev. 345. Early in the 19th century, however, most courts adopted the maxim, *respondeat superior*—or the law for which it stands—to sanction the action. See generally, Ellis v. Turner (1800) 8 T.R. 531; Wigmore, Responsibility for Tortious Acts: Its History (1894) 7 Harv.L.Rev. 315 (directed act theory); Baty, Vicarious Liability (1916) 154 (The "deep pocket" theory, discussed infra, § 33).

The prevailing rationale in this country, last century, was well stated by Shaw, C. J., in *Farwell* (1842), cited supra, § 25. The "principle indicated by the maxim *respondeat superior,"* he said, is "obviously founded on the great principle of social duty, that every man, in the management of his own affairs, whether by himself or by his agents or servants, shall so conduct them as not to injure another . . ." See also, Wolf v. Sulik (1919) 93 Conn. 431, 106 A. 443.

That was a clear statement of enterprise liability, or liability without fault, but many courts could not go so far. In one of the most influential, Quarman v. Burnett (1840) 6 Mees. & Welsb. 499, 151 Eng.Reprint 509, Park B., said: "Upon the principle that *qui facit per alium facit per se,* the master is responsible for the acts of his servant;" for it was the master "who *had selected him* as his servant" and "whose *orders* he was *bound to receive and obey."* (Emphasis added).

Thus, there have been two main currents of thought, one based on control, that is, fault, and the other on the notion that since the master takes the benefits or profits, if any, he should also be responsible for losses. The Restatement, with its emphasis on "control" in the definition of "servant," supra § 5, would seem to lean to the fault side. But, perhaps in recognition of the fact that "control," or the ephémeral "right to control," is an unrealistic ground of liability, it now

[*73*]

also declares boldly that a master's liability derives from "inherent agency power." Restatement, Second, Agency § 8A.

What, then, is "inherent agency power," and on what is it based? The same questions may be asked about the "imputed negligence" rationale of the Torts writers. See, § 3, supra. In the case of Agency, the answer is found in Comment (a) to § 8A of the Restatement: "It would be *unfair* for an enterprise to have the benefit of the work of its agents without making it responsible to some extent for their excesses and failures to act carefully." (Emphasis added). Thus, a guarded espousal of the enterprise theory. Probably "imputed negligence," likewise, is to be based on some such theory. The point has given difficulty. See, Note (1965) 19 Rutgers L.Rev. 532.

However this all may be, the significant thing is that for two centuries and more, vicarious liability has been the settled rule. And, for nearly two centuries, "respondeat superior" has been accepted doctrine. Speaking of "respondeat superior", Mr. Justice Stone, in Gleason v. Seaboard Air Line R. Co. (1929) 278 U.S. 349, 49 S.Ct. 161, 73 L.Ed. 415, said that "few doctrines of the law are more firmly established or more in harmony with accepted notions of social policy than that of the liability of the principal without fault of his own." Therefore, the defendant railroad was held responsible for pecuniary losses caused when a clerk gave false freight arrival notices.

§ 31. Whether Derivative

A few states have said that vicarious liability is a "secondary" or "derivative" remedy. As stated in Bradley v. Rosenthal (1908) 154 Cal. 420, 97 P. 875: "The employer's responsibility is secondary, in the sense that he has committed no moral wrong, but under the law is held accountable for his agent's conduct." Subsequent California decisions have generalized the point to say: "The responsibility of an employer for the acts of his employees under the doctrine of *respondeat superior* is dependent upon the injured person's right to recover against the employee." Popejoy v. Hannon (1951) 37 Cal.2d 159, 231 P.2d 484.

In the light of the historical background discussed above, this view would seem to turn things upside down. Without entering upon the point whether either employer or employee is a *moral* wrongdoer, there is much evidence that the employer, or enterprise, has more than a residual responsibility. After all, the employer started and controlled the enterprise and, if it prospers, will receive the gains. While it is true the employer's liability in many cases will be determined by the kind of tort committed by the agent, it by no means follows that it is *only* when the agent is liable to third persons that the employer may be held responsible under the respondeat superior doctrine.

A good illustration is Schubert v. August Schubert Wagon Co. (1928) 249 N.Y. 253, 164 N.E. 42, 64 A.L.R. 293. Plaintiff wife had been injured by the negligence of her husband, when driving a company car for defendant. It was urged that, since plaintiff could not recover from her husband at common law, the defendant employer could not be held responsible either. But Cardozo, C. J., ruled to the contrary: "An *employer* commits a trespass by the hand of his servant upon the person of another." (Emphasis added). "The statement sometimes made" that the employer's liability "is derivative and secondary   .   .   . means this, and nothing more: That at times the fault of the actor will fix the quality of the act. Illegality established, liability ensues."

The same result has been reached in a partnership setting. Eule v. Eule Motor Sales (1961) 34 N.J. 537, 170 A.2d 241. In holding for plaintiff wife, who had been injured by partner husband, Weintraub, C. J., said: "In the last analysis .   .   . *respondeat superior* rests upon a public policy that the employer bear the burden as an expense of the operation he expands through the employment of others." And, under U.P.A. § 13, that principle applies to a partnership; thus, it too may not escape liability because, at common law, the plaintiff could not sue the partner at fault. And see, Kangas v. Winquist (1940) 207 Minn. 315, 291 N.W. 292 (negligent partner killed in accident, no effect on firm's liability).

Interspousal immunity, of course, is on the way out, Self v. Self (1962) 58 Cal.2d 683, 26 Cal.Rptr. 97, 376 P.2d 65, so that issue may not come up again. An even broader category, however, is that of an agent's *non-feasance*. See, infra, § 38. While the agent may not be held liable to third persons, since he committed no tort, nothing is clearer than that the employer—in a proper case —may be held responsible for the agent's *failure to act*. See, United States v. Hull (C.A.Mass. 1952) 195 F.2d 64. (Employees of land owner failed to repair defective window).

Indeed, and this may be significant, the owner's duty to so manage his *property* as not to injure another, as in *Hull,* supra, compares closely with that of the policy underlying respondeat superior, as stated by Weintraub, C. J., in *Eule,* supra. That is, to paraphrase and combine, public policy has required that an owner, either of property or of an enterprise, who chooses to expand operations through the employment of others, must manage the *property,* in the one case, or the *enterprise,* in the other, so as not to injure third persons. This burden, the *Eule* court stated, is to be carried "as an expense of the operation."

§ 32. Intermediate Agent

One of the clearest readings on respondeat superior, or, if you will, on enterprise liability, is afforded by the cases in which it has been sought to charge a manager or other intermediate agent with responsibility for the wrongs of subordinates, especially when they have been selected by him and are subject to his control. Stone v. Cartwright (1795) 6 Term.Rep. 411, 101 Eng.Reprint 622, was such a case. Without mention of "enterprise liability," or "respondeat superior" for that matter, Lord Kenyon, C. J., decided for the defendant: "I have ever understood that the action must either be brought against the hand committing the injury, or against the owner for whom the act was done; but it was never heard of that a servant who hires laborers for his master was answerable for all their acts. The present defendant has no interest in the colliery, nor was it worked for his benefit." Accord, Brown & Sons Lumber Co. v. Sessler (1914) 128 Tenn. 665, 163 S.W. 812, Ann.Cas.1915C, 103.

A quarter century after *Cartwright*, in Hall v. Smith (1824) 2 Bing. 156, 130 Eng.Reprint 265, the same question was presented, this time in a public works setting. Certain "artificers" hired by defendants and under their supervision had left a ditch uncovered into which plaintiff had fallen to his injury. In denying that defendant commissioners could be held liable, Best, C. J., said this: "The maxim of respondeat superior is *bottomed* on this principle, that he who expects to derive advantage from an act which is done by another for him, must answer for any injury which a third person may sustain from it." (Emphasis added).

In fact, if respondeat superior should apply, Best, C. J. asked, "who would be hardy enough to undertake" the work? Then he went on to point out that, historically, "respondeat superior" is derived from an Act of Parliament, (1285) Westminster 2, C. 11, applicable to jailers (later extended to sheriffs), which made them responsible for their deputies: "Although the office of sheriffs be now a burthensome one, yet they are entitled to poundage, and other fees, for acts done by their officers, which in old time might be a just equivalent for their responsibility." The road has been a long one, from the sheriffs and jailers of 1285 to the employers of today, but surely it is clear that, not "control," but "benefit" or "profit" taking, has been a consistent basis of liability.

The following excerpt from the opinion of Justice Traynor, in Malloy v. Fong (1951) 37 Cal.2d 356, 378, 232 P.2d 241, 254, makes the point today: "The doctrine of *respondeat superior* is not applicable to the relationship between a supervisor and his subordinate employees. The supervisor occupies an economic and legal position quite different from that of the employer. It is not the supervisor's work that is being performed, nor does he share in the profits which the employees' conduct is designed to produce." Justice Traynor went on to say that: "For these reasons, the law has shifted financial responsibility from the supervisor, who exercises immediate control, to the employer, who exercises ultimate control and for whose benefit the work is done."

This reference to "ultimate control" requires comment. The court had a mixed bag of questions before it to decide. It held, first, that the claim of charitable immunity urged by the Presbytery of San Francisco, the alleged employer, must be denied. Next, it decided that Fong, the negligent driver, was an "agent," even though he acted gratuitously. See, § 4, supra. And, thirdly, it held that Fong was an agent of the Presbytery, not of the supervisor. Plainly, in that context "ultimate control" was not stated as a new ingredient of the respondeat superior equation, but simply as further clarification of the disputed employment relationship. See, § 3, supra.

On the merits, it is of course an important point that an intermediate agent—manager, officer, director—may not be held liable for the acts of subordinates. These are risks of the business. Although there has been some wavering on the point, Murray v. Cowherd (1912) 148 Ky. 591, 147 S.W. 6, 40 L.R.A.,N.S., 617 the great majority of courts have so held, unless the intermediate agent himself was personally guilty of a positive tort. See, Towt v. Pope (1959) 168 Cal.App.2d 520, 336 P.2d 276.

§ 33. Co-Partners

A partnership, of course, is liable to third persons for torts of its *servants* or *agents,* under the respondeat superior doctrine, as any employer would be. There is a question, though, whether similar considerations apply when it is a *co-partner,* who causes tort or contract losses. The easy answer, that co-partners are liable because they agreed—actually or implicitly—that they would share losses, is of little help. It is very clear that, as between partners, a member *at fault* is not entitled to contribution. Supra, § 24. They have not *agreed* to share such losses.

At common law it seems to have been taken more or less for granted that, since partners are in some sense agents, respondeat superior would apply. For example, in Champion v. Bostwick (1837) 18 Wend. 175, 31 Am.Dec. 376, although the tort was done by an employee of one of three partners, who were operating a connecting stage line, the court said: "That one partner is liable in tort for the acts of his co-partner in the prosecution of the co-partnership business, as well as upon contracts for the joint concern, appears to be well settled." Hence, each partner, or the firm, was held liable for the servants' torts. See § 7 supra. See also, Ashworth v. Stanwix (1861) 3 El. & El. 701, 122 Eng.Rep. 906. (Partner liable for co-partner's negligent injury to workman).

Indeed, § 13 of the Uniform Partnership Act, now expressly provides that "the partnership is liable" where "loss or injury is caused to any person" by reason of "any wrongful act or omission of any partner acting *in the ordinary course of the business* of the partnership." (Emphasis added). And U.P.A. § 15(a) provides that all partners are liable, "jointly and severally for everything chargeable to the partnership" under U.P.A. § 13. That surely buttons up the liability question; matters of procedure are examined, infra § 78. It will be noticed, however, that no mention is made of "imputed negligence," "inherent agency power," or any other rationale, but that is of the nature of legislation.

Nonetheless, it will be useful to examine the basis for U.P.A. § 13. In the first place, a partnership is stated to be an association of two or more persons to carry on a business for profit, U.P.A. § 6. Nothing more. There is no mention of "control" as being an essential ingredient. See infra §§ 66 and 67. Thus, the liability of a partner for acts of his co-partner, also, might well be said to be "bottomed," as Best, C. J., would put it, on the fact that each partner receives—or at least shares in—the benefits, gains and profits of the enterprise. Thus, U.P.A. § 13 is not only consistent with Chief Justice Best's analysis, supra § 32, but also would seem greatly to reinforce that analysis. Partnership is pre-eminently an association for "profit."

There has been very little dissent. In 1916, however, Baty examined the whole matter of vicarious liability, and came up with several adverse conclusions. In his view, there is little support, even for respondeat superior, except that "in hard fact . . . the damages are taken from *a deep pocket.*" (Emphasis added). Baty, Vicarious Liability (1916) 154. And, as for a partner's liability for his co-partner's wrong, Baty was sure there should be none; in fact, he said the legislature was in grievous error in stating a remedy, for, as everyone knows, one partner has no "control" of his co-partner's actions. See, U.P.A. § 18 (e). But perhaps Baty proved too much; he may have established, unintentionally, that "control" is not really a significant factor leading to vicarious liability, either in partnership or in respondeat superior.

§ 34. Scope of Employment

Courts have been more occupied, during the last two centuries, in stating limitations upon vicarious liability, than in finding a basis for it.

Limitations have been mainly of two kinds. The first was to define "servant"—as one whose "physical conduct" is subject to "control"—thus carving out the whole area of physical injury torts, and emphasizing control, or fault, as the basis of liability. Supra, § 5.

The second limitation is also essentially sound, that is, to set boundaries. Not every wrong of a servant may be attributed to his employer; respondeat superior is not general public insurance. As a result there has evolved a formula: An employer or master is responsible for only such wrongful conduct of a "servant" that occurs in "the scope of the employment." Restatement, Second, Agency § 219. Compare the formula for co-partners. Supra, § 33.

The Restatement, moreover, has done a good job in sorting out the several components of "scope of employment," Restatement of Agency § 228. After all, it would scarcely do to ask a jury, simply, to find "scope of employment." At all events, the Restatement points out, first, that the questioned act must be of a "kind" which the servant was employed to do; second, that it must have occurred within "authorized time and space limits"; and, third, that it must have been "actuated, at least in part, by a purpose to serve the master."

Though not without difficulty, this is a fairly precise tool with which to work. An illustration is White v. Pacific Telephone & Telegraph Co. (D.C.Or.1938) 24 F.Supp. 871. The action there was for an alleged assault committed by defendant's "special agent" when examining plaintiff concerning his part—if any—in a hold-up of the defendant's offices. Since the agent was clearly doing the "kind" of thing he was employed to do, within authorized "time" and "space" limits, these matters were not submitted to the jury. But there could be a question whether the agent was actuated, at least in part, by a "purpose" to serve his employer. It was held proper, on appeal, to have submitted only this last for the jury's determination. For discussion of the present test, Restatement, Second, Agency § 228(1)(d), see infra, § 36.

Other illustrations of the "scope" problem will be given in later sections, but again it must be stressed that the Restatement rule, as stated in § 228, does not apply to a whole range of torts—deceit, defamation, false representation and so on—which, if committed by agents generally (including servants), may be charged to the employer. These, of course, must be related to the employment, but other factors enter into the equation which make "scope," as defined in § 228, not fully applicable. See infra, § 42.

§ 35. The W/C Test Compared

There has been question whether the test applied in Workmen's Compensation, to fix its boundaries, supra, § 26, is the same as the "scope" test in respondeat superior. And, if not, why should there be a difference; one limits enterprise liability to third persons, the other to employees? Of course the two tests are worded differently, "scope of employment" in one case, and "arising out of and in the course of," in the other. See, § 26, supra. Is the difference significant?

In any case, most courts have declared that W/C provides wider coverage for injured workmen, than respondeat superior does for injured third persons. See, for example, Park Transfer Co. v. Lumbermens Mut. Casualty Co. (1944) 79 U.S.App.D.C. 48, 142 F.2d 100, where the court said: "Workmen's compensation is available in many circumstances where damages are not." Cf. Kohlman v. Hyland (1926) 54 N.D. 710, 210 N.W. 643, 50 A.L.R. 1437.

The issue was squarely raised in Saala v. McFarland (1965) 63 Cal.2d 124, 45 Cal.Rptr. 144, 403 P.2d 400, which had to do with a company parking lot accident caused by defendant employee when leaving after work. Plaintiff was a co-employee, and the special question was whether defendant should be granted the immunity from common law suit generally accorded a fellow employee. Supra, § 27. The court held not, pointing out that the statute gives immunity only to a co-employee who was "acting within the scope of his employment" at the time. Cal.Lab. Code, § 3601. Plainly, defendant could not meet the "scope" test. For one thing, there was no showing that when the accident happened she was "actuated," even in part, by a purpose to serve the employer.

The point does not die easily, however. In a third party setting, the employee being on his way home from work in his own car when the accident happened, the W/C test was held to be persuasive to show that the employee was in fact acting within the "scope of his employment." Huntsinger v. Glass Containers Corp. (1972) 22 Cal. App. 3rd 803, 99 Cal.Rptr. 666. Perhaps we will reach that position one day. Meanwhile, however, it should be noted that W/C was designed for a different purpose. In order to afford sure and prompt protection for employees the W/C test was broadly stated, but, at the same time, recovery was carefully limited according to a schedule based on loss of earning power. The *Huntsinger* court chose to broaden the "scope" test, but ignored the W/C limitation.

§ 36. Use of Force

The Restatement has singled out for special treatment the many cases where an agent—delivery man, collector, bus driver, salesman, conductor, or some other—has made use of force in dealing with third persons. Thus it is said in the Comment to Restatement of Agency § 245 that: "To create liability for a battery by a servant upon a third person, the employment must be one which is *likely* to bring the servant into conflict with others." (Emphasis added). This statement has been quoted with seeming approval in a few cases. See, Plotkin v. Northland Transp. Co. (1939) 204 Minn. 422, 283 N.W. 758.

Probably this was error. No doubt torts of violence are more *likely* to occur in such employments than in others, but there is no apparent reason to limit a master's liability only to torts so occurring. Nonetheless, the error has now been reinforced by adding a *fourth* requirement to the traditional definition of scope of employment, that is: "Conduct of a servant is within the scope of employment if, but only if: . . . (d) if force is intentionally used by the servant against another, the use of force is *not unexpectable by the master*." (Emphasis added). Restatement, Second, Agency § 228(1)(d).

The writers of § 228(1)(d), aside from being too iffy, would appear to have been confused. The respondeat superior doctrine provides for liability *without fault*. Supra, § 30. From very early times, for example, it has been held immaterial whether or not the master used care in the selection of his servants, or in the conduct of his business. See, Holmes, Agency (1891) 4 Harv.L.Rev. 345 at 348. He might be liable for his own action, if he caused injury to others, but not vicariously. Thus, it would seem to be wholly immaterial whether a given action by an agent is foreseeable, or "not unexpectable," to the principal. At most, it might help him determine whether insurance should be taken to cover the risk, but it would seem to have little bearing otherwise.

Most courts have seen this quite clearly. An example is Son v. Hartford Ice Cream Co. (1925) 102 Conn. 696, 129 A. 778. There, defendant had sent its truck driver to plaintiff's shop to deliver ice cream, with instructions to collect, but to use no force. Nonetheless, an altercation arose, the driver undertook to take the money from the cash register; then attempted to carry away the cash register bodily; and, in course of the "transaction," plaintiff was kicked and severely beaten. The trial court gave judgment for plaintiff.

Affirming, Judge Beach, in an able opinion, spent no time in determining whether the episode was "not unexpectable." "It may be more difficult," he said, "for a plaintiff to sustain the burden of proving that a wilful, as distinguished from a negligent, injury was inflicted while the servant was upon the master's business, and acting within the scope of his employment; but when these conditions are shown to exist there is no satisfactory reason for holding a master, who is himself free from fault, liable for his servant's lapses of judgment and attention, which does not apply to the servant's lapses of temper and self control." Cf. Moskins Stores, Inc. v. De Hart (1940) 217 Ind. 622, 29 N.E.2d 948. Nor do the writers of the Restatement offer a "satisfactory reason."

For another illustration, consider Porter v. Grennan Bakeries (1945) 219 Minn. 14, 16 N.W. 2d 906. Two cake salesmen there had gotten into a dispute over display space, and went back of the store to settle the question. Before plaintiff could take off his glasses, defendant's salesman struck him in the face. It was easy to hold that both men had left the scope of their employment, but, on appeal, it was urged that the trial court had erred in excluding evidence that defendant knew its man was "a surly, troublesome fellow," or, that is, that the trouble was "not unexpectable." The court quite properly held that the "personal fault of the master," if any, was not in issue: "In no possible view of the case was it error to exclude the evidence . . ."

Although the assault cases have also given trouble in partnership, there has been no attempt to insinuate "unexpectability" into the statutory test. If the assault occurred "in the ordinary course of the business," to quote the statute, that is enough; the firm would be liable. See, § 33, supra.   In Malanga v. Manufacturers Cas. Ins. Co. (1958) 28 N.J. 220, 146 A.2d 105, for example, one partner, while doing some grading work for the firm, used a bulldozer bodily to remove plaintiff from his way.   The firm was held liable for the resulting injuries.   The main question, whether the *firm* could also be charged with a "wilful" tort—and hence an uninsurable one— was decided in the negative.   Cf. Schloss v. Silverman (1937) 172 Md. 632, 192 A. 343.

§ 37.   Use of Property

The fact that property has been entrusted to a servant, for use and management, would seem to add nothing new to the agency equation.   In fact, negligent use of a master's "cart" was a typical illustration of vicarious liability in Lord Holt's day.   Supra, § 30.   A few courts have even held that, if the agent used merely his own two legs to travel a public way, respondeat superior would *not* apply.   But they are in a distinct minority. See, Annis v. Postal Telegraph Co. (1944) 114 Ind.App. 543, 52 N.E.2d 373.   (Messenger boy collided with lady pedestrian).

Of course, if the entrusted property is inherently dangerous, a master may be responsible on other grounds, apart from respondeat superior. Michael v. Alestree (K.B., 1676) 2 Levinz 172. (Two ungovernable horses).   Again, as landowner, or landlord, or carrier, the employer may be found liable for injuries caused by his employees, even though acting *outside* the scope of their employment. See, Restatement, Second, Torts § 317. The bailment cases also fall in this category, as the bailee's responsibility would seem to turn simply on his contract with the bailor. A few courts, however, have introduced scope of employment ideas to give the bailee a defense. See: Firemen's Fund Ins. Co. v. Schreiber (1912) 150 Wis. 42, 135 N.W. 507, 45 L.R.A.,N.S., 314, Ann. Cas.1913E, 823; Castorina v. Rosen (1943) 290 N.Y. 445, 49 N.E.2d 521.

The greater mobility attained by an agent—first with horse and cart and in this century with the motor vehicle—caused the courts to state limits. In the celebrated case of Joel v. Morison (1834) 6 Car. & P. 501, 172 Eng.Rep. 1338, the defendant's servant had driven the master's horse and cart into the city, taking a different route than usual, and negligently run down the plaintiff. Baron Parke, in a classic statement, said liability would turn on whether the servant was merely making a "detour," while on his master's business, or was going "on a frolic of his own." Verdict for the plaintiff—damages, 30£.

The "frolic" or "detour" test obviously lacks precision. Even as reworded, Restatement, Second, Agency § 228(1)(a)(b) and (c), there has been difficulty. See, § 36, supra. But maybe this is as it should be; at most, the law here can only provide a *process* to settle disputes. By use of a flexible test, the triers of fact may best bring their views of a changing social policy to bear on the problem. See, Smith, Frolic and Detour (1923) 23 Col.L.Rev. 444. Many states have gone part way in aid of the plaintiff (or to save court time) by giving a presumption of regularity, when the name of the supposed employer appears on the truck. See: Fiocco v. Carver (1922) 234 N.Y. 219, 137 N.E. 309; Frick v. Bickel (1944) 115 Ind.App. 114, 54 N.E.2d 436.

The employee who generously invites a "rider" on his vehicle, contrary to orders, has caused litigation. A few courts have denied recovery to the rider, when injured, saying the invitation, as "an unauthorized act," was "beyond the scope of the servant's employment." Thomas v. Magnolia Petroleum Co. (1928) 177 Ark. 963, 9 S.W. 2d 1. The courts which use "scope," in this fashion, to distinguish between differently situated plaintiffs—guests, trespassers, wives, and so on—tend to confuse the issue. But Restatement, Second, Agency § 242, while granting the "scope" point, would still deny recovery to the unauthorized rider. In a well reasoned opinion, however, the California court refused to go along with the Restatement view and granted recovery. Meyer v. Blackman (1963) 59 Cal.2d 668, 31 Cal.Rptr. 36, 381 P.2d 916.

Use of property, this time by members of the owner's family, has contributed another chapter to the law. Faced with the circumstance that an injured person would often have no recovery if he could look only to the infant driver, a number of courts contrived the "family purpose" doctrine. See, Lattin, Vicarious Liability and the Family Automobile (1928) 26 Mich.L.Rev. 846. By analogy to respondeat superior, the owner was regarded as the master, and the members of his family, as servants. See, Durso v. A. D. Cozzolino Co. (1941) 128 Conn. 24, 20 A.2d 392. As might be expected, many courts were unable to go so far. See: Van Blaricom v. Dodgson (1917) 220 N.Y. 111, 115 N.E. 443; Perry v. Simeone (1925) 197 Cal. 132, 239 P. 1056.

In due time the legislatures in most states adopted so-called "permissive use" statutes, which went beyond the family purpose doctrine of the courts. See, Calif.Vehicle Code § 17150. Any owner of a motor vehicle, who permits another—family member or not—to "use" it, is made liable to third persons for injuries caused by the operator's fault. See, Grant v. Knepper (1927) 245 N.Y. 158, 156 N.E. 650, 54 A.L.R. 845, interpreting the New York statute. Moreover, the notion of scope of employment or use would seem to have been abandoned. See, Baker v. Rhode Island Ice Co. (1946) 72 R.I. 262, 50 A.2d 618. But, as in W/C, the statutory recovery has been limited to stated, and quite modest, amounts.

§ 38. Nonfeasance and Such

The question here, broadly speaking, is to see how (or whether) *nonaction* on the part of servants or other agents, officers or partners may be fitted into the respondeat superior doctrine. Many losses are caused by simple failure to act, or to take what hindsight shows would have been reasonable precautions. Moreover, it is often difficult, after a loss has occurred, to point the finger at any individual in the employer's organization who was sufficiently at fault to justify calling him a tort-feasor.

The matter got off to a nice start in the case of Lane v. Cotton (1701) 12 Mod. 472, 88 Eng.Rep. 1458, in which it was held that a postmaster was not to be responsible for the loss of certain Exchequer bills in the mails. Lord Holt dissented, and in the course of a long opinion said: "It was objected at the Bar, that they have this remedy against Breese [the mail clerk]. I agree, if they could prove that he took out the bills, they might sue him for it; so they might anybody else on whom they could fix that fact; but for a *neglect* in him they can have no remedy against him; for they must consider him only as a servant; and then his neglect is only chargeable on his master, or principal; . . . but for a *misfeasance* an action will lie against a servant or deputy, but not *quatenus* a deputy or servant, but as a wrongdoer." (Emphasis added). Cited with approval, Story, Agency (9th ed., 1882) § 319.

There is no question today, of course, that an agent may be held liable to third persons for his positive torts—trespass, deceit, conversion, assault, and so on; these, in Lord Holt's terminology, would be called *misfeasance*. Nor is it ever a defense that the agent acted on behalf of his principal, perhaps under his orders. But there has been a considerable split of authority when the agent has merely failed to act, so-called *nonfeasance*. See: Osborne v. Morgan (1881) 130 Mass. 102, 39 Am.Rep. 437; Murray v. Usher (1889) 117 N.Y. 542, 23 N.E. 564. Some torts writers, seeing mainly the "privity" issue, have urged liability of the agent, in disregard of basic principles of risk allocation in the modern enterprise. See, Prosser, The Assault Upon the Citadel (1960) 69 Yale L.J. 1099.

The agency point is seen well enough, however, by most courts. For example, in Knight v. Atlantic Coast Line R. Co. (5th Cir. 1934) 73 F.2d 76, 99 A.L.R. 405, a section foreman, one Poppell, was held *not* liable, although he had failed one day to have some dry grass and weeds removed from defendant's tracks, and a resulting fire had destroyed plaintiff's property. Nor can the decision well be criticized; after all, Poppell, as a section foreman and wage earner, should not be expected to answer to third persons for the railroad's daily risks of operation. See also, Franklin v. May Dept. Stores Co. (D.C.Mo.1938) 25 F.Supp. 735.

The railroad, of course, would be subject to liability for Poppell's failure to act. Since memory runs not to the contrary, a landowner has been held to a duty to so manage his property as not to injure another negligently. See, Rowland v. Christian (1968) 69 Cal.2d 108, 443 P.2d 561, 70 Cal.Rptr. 97. In that context, it would make no difference whether Poppell's conduct was a mere failure to act, nonfeasance, or a positive tort, misfeasance. For, in either case, it could be found that the railroad had been negligent in the management of its property. See, United States v. Hull (1st Cir. 1952) 195 F.2d 64 (U.S. liable under F.T.C.A. for unidentified employee's failure to repair window). A rule that some agent must have *failed* to act *in the scope of his employment* is really too metaphysical for much use. See, Restatement, Second, Agency § 232.

Typical of the cases which say an agent's failure to act may, itself, be a "misfeasance," making him a tort-feasor, is Tippecanoe Loan and Trust Co. v. Jester (1913) 180 Ind. 357, 101 N.E. 915, L.R.A.1915E, 721. There, the defendant Trust Co., which had been given *full management and control* of a rental property, failed one day to have the catch on an elevator door repaired, and plaintiff had fallen down the elevator shaft, probably to his sorrow.   The agent Trust Co. was held liable.   See also, Lough v. Davis & Co. (1902) 30 Wash. 204, 70 P. 491, 59 L.R.A. 802, 94 Am. St.Rep. 848.   In the *Tippecanoe* court's view, the failure to repair the catch may have been "nonfeasance," but whether so or not, it was "misfeasance" for the Trust Co. to operate the elevator in that condition.   Such a holding is plainly distinguishable from *Knight,* supra;   Poppell never had anything approaching that kind of control and management of the Atlantic Coast Line tracks and roadbed.   Nor, in all probability, did he receive pay commensurate with the risk.

A closer case, perhaps, is Ultramares Corp. v. Touche (1931) 255 N.Y. 170, 174 N.E. 441, 74 A.L.R. 1139.   There, Cardozo, C. J., held the defendant, a firm of accountants *not* liable for mere *negligence* in the preparation of a financial statement, which was later shown by the client to plaintiff lender.   Fraud, the court said, was a different case, for which the agent-accountant *would* be liable.   In drawing this line, Cardozo, C. J., was mindful of the many prior decisions exonerating wage earners, even officers and directors, from liability to third persons for mere negligence in carrying out their duties.   See, Reno v. Bull (1919) 226 N.Y. 546, 124 N.E. 144. They might well be liable to their employer in some measure, § 39 infra, but not to third persons.   Thus, a tribute to the sturdy good sense of

Lord Holt. Cf. Hedley Byrne & Co., Ltd. v. Heller & Partners (H.L.1963) 2 All E.R. 575, 3 W.L. R. 101.

The *Ultramares* case has been criticized; not so much, one suspects, for its basic holding, as for its failure to make new law for an emerging class of independent risk bearers—accountants, managers of property, weighers, surveyors, perhaps even law firms. See, Solomon, Ultramares Revisited (1958) 18 De Paul L.Rev. 56. When the social need is great, as in the products liability cases, the courts have shown a ready willingness to ignore ancient privity boundaries. See: Hanna v. Fletcher (1956) 97 U.S.App.D.C. 310, 231 F.2d 469, 58 A.L.R.2d 847; Steffen, Enterprise Liability (1965) 17 Hastings L.Rev. 165. Whether *lenders,* as in *Ultramares,* are to be given similar protection is at least dubious. Similarly, should the victim of a newspaper libel be given recourse to the editor, most courts have decided in the negative. See, Folwell v. Miller (1906) 75 C.C.A. 489, 145 F. 495, 10 L.R.A.,N.S., 332, 7 Ann.Cas. 455.

The plight of the security buyer, however, was such—as disclosed by the 1929 Stock Market debacle—that Congress felt impelled to pass § 77K of the Securities Act of 1933. By this section almost anyone who may have had something to do with the registration statement for a new issue—director, accountant, officer—is made strictly liable for the correctness of the statement to any person who may have acquired the securities. See, New Civil Liabilities (1947) 14 U.Chi.L.Rev. 471. This plainly is a drastic provision, but one tailored to meet an urgent need.

§ 39. Employer's Indemnity

We have explored two sides of the respondeat superior equation: The principal's liability to third persons, §§ 30 to 38; and, the extent of the agent's direct liability to third persons. The latter, being mainly a question of torts law, except for the nonfeasance problem, § 38 supra, has needed little discussion here. It remains to explore the third side of the triangle, the extent to which the employer may shift his respondeat superior losses back upon the agent at fault.

It perhaps comes as something of a surprise, even to pose the question, for the W/C rule is clearly to the contrary. Enterprise must bear personal injury risks to employees, whether or not caused by their negligence, and, accordingly, it has no recourse to any worker, unless grossly or intentionally at fault. See, § 27, supra. But the notion of "enterprise liability" has not been carried so far in the case of respondeat superior losses. It may well be something of an "anachronism," as Weintraub, C. J., said in *Eule*, supra § 31, but most courts have clung stubbornly to the individualistic view, that enterprise may, indeed, shift its respondeat superior losses.

A few courts hold rather automatically that, whenever an employer has been forced to pay a third party judgment under respondeat superior, he "has the right of recoupment against the negligent employee." Popejoy v. Hannon (1951) 37 Cal.2d 159, 231 P.2d 484. Perhaps most courts would say that the employer, or his insurance carrier, is "subrogated" to the third person's action against the negligent employee. See: Restatement, Second, Agency § 401, Comment (d); Cal.C.Code § 17153. But, either way, the ultimate loss—at least in theory—is put on the negligent employee, who is said to be the real *wrongdoer*.

In a highly controversial case, Lister v. Romford Ice and Cold Storage Co. Ltd. (1957) A.C. 555, the House of Lords reached the same result by implying a term in the driver's contract, that he would—without fail—use care and skill when driving plaintiff's lorry. Having failed one morning to keep an adequate lookout when backing the lorry—thus injuring a fellow employee—it followed that Lister, the driver, was liable to reimburse his employer, the plaintiff, as for a breach of contract.

The *Lister* case, of course, was widely criticized. See, Williams, Vicarious Liability and the

Master's Indemnity (1957) 20 Modern L.Rev. 220, 437. Indeed, it is hard not to agree with Denning, L. J., that no lorry driver "if asked, would give a warranty to his employer that he would at all times, without exception, come up to the standard of the reasonable man of the law, who, so far as I know, when he is driving, never makes a slip or a mistake." (Dissent, in Romford Ice and Cold Storage Co. Ltd. v. Lister (1956) 2 Q.B. 180, 187.) In other words, Viscount Simonds, for the House of Lords, was quite right in treating the question as one of contract, but grievously wrong in implying the contract which he did; no agent engages to be *infallible.*

The same question came up in United States v. Gilman (1954) 347 U.S. 507, 74 S.Ct. 695, 98 L.Ed. 898. The action was by the United States, which had been held liable to a third person under the Federal Tort Claims Act, 60 Stat. 842, 28 U.S.C.A. §§ 1346, 2671, et seq., to recover indemnity from Gilman (a postal employee), the negligent driver. The court, by Douglas, J., refused to imply a term in defendant's contract, to indemnify the United States; that was a matter of policy for the "writers" of law to deal with, not the Court: "We have no way of knowing what the impact of the rule of indemnity we are asked to create might be."

Congress has not yet written a contract of indemnity to apply to government employees in this area. But it has made it very clear that the U. S. is not to be subrogated to the injured third person's cause of action against the employee. This it has done by denying the third person any action at all against the driver, when he has an action against the U. S. See, F.T.C.A. § 2679. In other words, there is no action left to which the U. S. could be subrogated. The upshot would seem to be that the "writers" regard indemnity in this area, at best, to be purely an administrative matter.

Such glimpses of administrative policy as we have in the cases, indicates that a line is being drawn between gross or reckless misconduct, on the one hand, and ordinary negligence, on the other. See, Burks v. United States (S.D.Texas, 1953) 116 F.Supp. 337. The same line is drawn in some labor contracts. The Teamster's Union provided in Art. 10 of their National Master Freight agreement for February 1, 1964 to March 31, 1967 that: "Employees shall not be charged for loss or damage unless clear proof of gross negligence is shown." CCH Lab.L.Rep. 59, 944 (1965). The evident purpose here is to put routine losses on enterprise, where they may be covered by insurance and settled with a minimum of wasteful labor-management controversy.

What appears to be evolving, therefore, is a form of contract which (1) preserves the employee's ancient duty to bring reasonable care and skill to the job, and (2) at the same time, denies that he agrees to be infallible.   Liability for negligence *as to third persons* answers to an urgent social need;   the measure of duty *to an employer* responds to a very different one.   To draw a line between gross and ordinary negligence, although perhaps a crude procedure, at least serves the point.   A similar line is drawn in W/C, when an employee's *immunity* from common law suit at the hands of an injured co-employee is established.   Cal.L.Code § 3601.

§ 40.   The Business Judgment Rule

The indemnity responsibility of officers, directors, managers and other agents, mainly for pecuniary losses to enterprise, has had its own history.   The problem, however, is much the same as that encountered when it is sought to hold a servant responsible for losses incurred in a personal injury action.   Supra, § 39.   The English cases, last century, with no intimation that the two situations were in any way related, said that a director, at least, need only be free of *"crassa negligentia,"* i. e., gross negligence.   See: Overend & Gurney Co. v. Gibb (1872) L.R., 5 E. & I. App. 480;   Steffen, The Employer's "Indemnity" Action (1958) 25 U.Chi.L.Rev. 465.

Whether or not there is any change in substance, the rule has been put in a less provocative form in this century.   That is, a director's duty is now said to be one of "reasonable care," which in turn is "to be measured by the care an ordinary man might be expected to take in the same circumstances on his own behalf." Per, Neville, J., In re Brazilian Rubber Plantations and Estates, Ltd. (1911) 1 Ch. 425, 437. But, Neville, J., was careful to add also: "He is clearly . . not responsible for damages occasioned by errors of judgment."

The point is phrased in much the same way in this country. See, Otis & Co. v. Pennsylvania R. Co. (P.C.Pa.1945) 61 F.Supp. 905, aff'd 155 F.2d 522 (1946). In *Otis,* a shareholder's derivative action, it was sought to hold the Pennsylvania directors responsible for having failed to sell an issue of securities at competitive bidding, thus to obtain the best price available. But the court held for the defendants: "It is . . . clearly established that *mistakes* or *errors* in the exercise of *honest business judgment* do not subject the officers and directors to liability for negligence in the discharge of their appointed duties." (Emphasis added). See generally: Dwight, Liability of Corporate Directors (1907) 17 Yale L.J. 33; Douglas, Directors Who Do Not Direct (1934) 47 Harv.L.Rev. 1305.

One thing seems clear, however the rule is worded, the duty of care, as stated for officers and directors, is less onerous than that for "lorry" drivers. So, why not a "business judgment" rule also for today's truck drivers?   Driving long distances, with valuable cargos, while trying to maintain a schedule, such drivers make more "business judgments" per mile, than many directors do per year.   Actually, however, it may well be that the "gross negligence" rule—discussed supra, § 39—accomplishes exactly the same thing. Interestingly enough, that was the early statement for directors. See, *Overend*, supra.

There appear to be few cases dealing with partners.   But in United Brokers' Co. v. Dose (1933) 143 Or. 283, 22 P.2d 204, the court said partners were to be regarded as agents, and refused to give an erring partner indemnity for losses suffered in a traffic accident while on firm business.   Rather he should be held liable, even as in *Lister*, supra § 39.   However, when the case is one of pecuniary loss, most courts have taken a different course. See, Hurter v. Larrabee (1916) 224 Mass. 218, 112 N.E. 613, where, Rugg, C. J., said: "So far as losses result to a firm from errors of judgment of one partner not amounting to fraud, bad faith, or reckless disregard of his obligations, they must be borne by the partnership."   It may be that the personal injury lawyer lacks perspective.

A word as to policy.   It once was fashionable to criticize the "business judgment" rule as being too lenient to directors and partners.   No doubt there is criticism, likewise, of the "gross negligence" test evolving in the case of truck drivers. It must be noted, however, that it is plainly to the interest of enterprise that personnel be able, unafraid, and innovative; the gains to result therefrom should greatly outweigh the possibility of occasional losses. These, it would seem, should be taken by enterprise as part of the cost of doing business, as are W/C losses.

§ 41. Assorted Frauds

The new ground to be explored, as the heading suggests, is the principal's responsibility—if any —for non-physical conduct torts. These comprise a large family: deceit, bribery, fraud, slander, false representation and so on, which result only in pecuniary loss, not injury to person or damage to property. Again, while physical injury torts are committed by "servants," as above discussed §§ 30–38, it appears that any "agent," including any "servant," may subject his principal to responsibility for non-physical injury torts. See, Restatement, Second, Agency § 257. The logic of all this is not obvious, but such has been the historical development.

One thing, it should be noted, is unchanged; the principal's responsibility for an agent's *frauds,* like that for a servant's *negligence,* is held to come within the broad sweep of the respondeat superior doctrine. A good example is Barwick v.

English Joint Stock Bank (1867) L.R. 2 Ex. 259. There, the manager of defendant bank gave plaintiff a written "guarantee" to cover sales of oats to one of the bank's customers, which the customer in turn expected to re-sell to the Government. It was agreed that checks to plaintiff were to have "priority" over any other payments, "except to this bank." But, as the manager well knew, its customer was largely indebted to the bank at the time, and when the customer's check to plaintiff came through, it was refused payment: No funds! The bank had meanwhile charged the customer's account to cover his prior indebtedness.

On the likely supposition that a jury might find the manager to have committed a "fraud," Willes, J., had no difficulty in holding that the bank would be responsible. "The general rule," he said, "is, that the master is answerable for every such wrong of the *servant* or *agent* as is committed in the course of the service *and for the master's benefit* . . . ." (Emphasis added). Indeed: "That principle is acted upon every day in running down cases," i. e., in traffic cases. In further support, the court pointed to the early case of Hern v. Nichols (1708) 1 Salk. 289, 91 Eng.Reprint 256, as having pretty well settled the point. Accord, Rutherford v. Rideout Bank (1938) 11 Cal.2d 479, 80 P.2d 978, 117 A.L.R. 383.

The phrase, "and for the master's benefit," unfortunately, prompted a half century of wasteful litigation. Given the advantage of hindsight, Willes, J., was merely tailoring the rule to the case before him, not stating the irreducible elements of an action for an agent's fraud. In a series of false bill of lading cases, however, the courts in this country held for the railroad, citing *Barwick;* since the freight agent had no actual authority to issue bills of lading, except on receipt of goods, a purchaser of a false bill could have no action against the road, either in contract on the bill for breach, or in tort for false representation. See, Friedlander v. Texas & Pacific Ry. Co. (1889) 130 U.S. 416, 9 S.Ct. 570, 32 L.Ed. 991.

Not until Gleason v. Seaboard Air Line R. Co. (1929) 278 U.S. 349, 49 S.Ct. 161, 73 L.Ed. 415, was the point made clear. In that case, a clerk (whose duty it was to give arrival notices to consignees of freight) forged some bills, gave false notices of arrival, and defrauded the named consignee of several thousand dollars. It was urged that, since the railroad had not *benefited,* it could not be held liable. But Stone, J., for the court, held bluntly that actual receipt of "benefit" is not a proper "limitation upon the doctrine of respondeat superior." See also, Lloyd v. Grace (1912) A.C. 716.

The court in *Gleason* made a wide departure from the "scope of employment" test used in the "servant" cases. Supra, § 34. The railroad clerk's conduct could be said to have been "of the kind" he was employed to do, and it occurred "substantially within the authorized time and space limits," but he plainly had no "purpose" whatever "to serve the master" in what he did. See, Restatement, Second, Agency § 228. With the change in kind of tort, however, the "purpose" test is dropped; emphasis is put on third party expectations. See, Restatement, Second, Agency § 261. The *Gleason* case would also come within § 261, since the road had put the clerk in a "position" to facilitate the fraud. McCord v. Western Union (1888) 39 Minn. 181, 39 N.W. 315, 1 L.R.A. 143, 12 Am.St.Rep. 636.

In partnership, the basic question—whether the partnership should be liable for a co-partner's fraud—was answered easily enough. For example, in Hamlyn v. John Houston & Co. (1903) 1 K.B. 81, a "sleeping" or dormant partner was held answerable for the fraud of the active partner in bribing one of plaintiff's clerks to obtain trade information. As in respondeat superior cases generally, Collins, M. R., said that this was not unjust since defendant would have the "benefit" of the partners wrong, "if successful." See § 30, supra.

The same result has been reached under the Uniform Partnership Act. See, First Nat. Bank v. Turchetta (1962) 407 Pa. 511, 181 A.2d 285 (partner in used car business sold fictitious customer's notes and mortgages to plaintiff bank), where the court said: "Conversion, embezzlement, fraud and deceit, misapplication of money or other wrongful conduct of a partner or other agent is alone insufficient to remove it from the area imposing firm liability, if otherwise it be committed in actual or apparent furtherance of the business."

The test stated in *Turchetta,* minus the word "furtherance," is a synthesis of the tests stated in U.P.A. §§ 9 and 13. The test in § 9, dealing with contracts, is that the partner's act must be one "for apparently carrying on in the usual way the business of the partnership." For tort liability, § 13, the partner must have been "acting in the ordinary course of the business of the partnership." Neither *Hamlyn* nor *Turchetta,* supra, quite reach the point decided in *Gleason*—where the agent pocketed the fruits of the fraud himself—but U.P.A. § 14, which holds the firm liable for frauds, makes no point of that difference. Accord, as to agents generally, Restatement, Second, Agency § 262.

Referring back to the problems discussed, supra §§ 39 and 40, it goes almost without saying that a principal may hold his agent accountable for losses caused by the agent's *fraud.* This, either on contract or tort principles. Likewise, the defrauded third person has an action in tort against the agent for damages. See, Light v.

Chandler, infra § 42.   Or, it would seem, the third person may hold the agent accountable for breach of his implied warranty of authority.   See infra, § 57.

§ 42.   False Representation

The basic point, that a principal may be answerable for his agent's false representations— as for frauds generally, § 41, supra—is well settled.   Again, it would seem, the usual "scope of employment" test does not apply.   Since representations—false or otherwise—are most commonly made in connection with contract negotiations, the Restatement has adopted the contract test.   That is, a principal is subject to liability for the "tortious representations" of his servant or other agent, when they are "(a) authorized" or "(b) apparently authorized."   Restatement, Second, Agency § 257.   Compare, § 140, for contract liability.

It will be noted that there is no requirement that the representation be for the "benefit" of the principal, or that the agent must have a "purpose" to serve the principal.   The further point, stated in the Comment to § 257, that the "principal's liabilities do not depend upon the theory of respondeat superior," but on contract principles, is at least dubious.   True, the tort is different than one for negligence, and requires other proof, but that aside, the agent's wrong would seem to come easily within the doctrine. See, §§ 30 and 41, supra. In any case, nothing much seems to turn on the point.

Whether an agent's *false* representations are within his "apparent" authority and have been reasonably relied upon by the third person, presents a mixed question of law and fact. The real estate cases will illustrate. In Light v. Chandler Improvement Co. (1928) 33 Ariz. 101, 261 P. 969, 59 A.L.R. 107, the action was to foreclose a mortgage, to which the defendant mortgagor and buyer interposed a defense of fraud and deceit on the part of plaintiff's real estate agent. The evidence indicated that the property had been "listed" with the broker and that he had falsely "represented" that the land was all "fertile" and would "produce good crops."

The "vital" point, the court said, was whether "a real estate broker in the selling of land is impliedly [apparently?] authorized by his principal to make representation in regard to the quality and value of the land." Treating the matter as one of first impression, the court held for plaintiff; that is, a real estate broker was said to have no authority to make such representations. Among the many cases in accord, see Friedman v. N. Y. Telephone Co. (1931) 256 N.Y. 392, 176 N.E. 543.

The Restatement, however, holds the door part way open. It suggests that if an owner authorizes an agent "to enter into negotiations" to which representations are usual, then there may be liability.   Restat. 2d Agency (1958) § 258.   In a sense, this merely illustrates the problem; when are representations usual?   At least, in a case where the broker, by mistake, showed the wrong land to the buyer, the principal was held answerable.   Eamoe v. Big Bear Land & Water Co. (1950) 98 Cal.App.2d 370, 220 P.2d 408.   The agent's authority, it seems, extends at least that far.

The cautious thing to do, of course, is to make use of an exculpatory clause.   In Speck v. Wylie (1934) 1 Cal.2d 625, 36 P.2d 618, the court held such clauses fully effective "to protect an innocent principal" from direct suit for false representation, but said the buyer might rescind. Accord, Restatement, Second, Agency (1958) § 260.   Although the point has been much litigated, there seems to be general agreement that, in rescission cases, as stated by Weist, J., in Plate v. Detroit Fidelity & Surety Co. (1924) 229 Mich. 482, 201 N.W. 457: "The seal of silence as to actual fraud is not imposed by any such provisions."   Accord: Bates v. Southgate (1941) 308 Mass. 170, 31 N.E.2d 551, 133 A.L.R. 1349.

The defrauded buyer has still other remedies, as was pointed out in Light v. Chandler, supra. That is, he may acquaint the seller with the broker's fraud, demand rescission, and, if the seller demurs overly long, claim ratification. Perhaps not ratification of the tort, as such, which would raise problems, infra § 55, but of the contract, burdened with the broker's false representations. At any rate, the buyer then has a free field —either to rescind and get his money back or to keep the land and recover damages for the false representation. Or, as the court said, the purchaser may ratify the transaction, reserving his rights, and then "sue the agent in damages for fraud and deception." This, on ordinary tort principles.

§ 43. Independent Contractor

When an independent contractor is employed, many of the problems just discussed tend to disappear. Of course, they may re-appear in different guise, when the contractor is an agent. Infra, § 44. But, for the moment, we are done with torts involving physical conduct; only a "servant," it seems, may subject a master to liability for them. Supra, § 5. And, we are told, "independent contractor" is the *opposite* of "servant." Supra, § 8.

It would be a mistake, however, to conclude that "all agents who are not servants are independent contractors." Sell, Agency (1975) p. 15. It appears there is a large intermediate group of *agents,* who well may be neither. The question has been a vexed one, as least since N.L.R.B. v.

Hearst Publications (1944) 322 U.S. 111, 64 S.Ct. 851. There it was decided, for purposes of the National Labor Relations Act, 29 U.S.C.A. § 152, that newsboys are "employees" and not "independent contractors." Hence the respondents, publishers of four Los Angeles daily papers, could be required to bargain collectively with their union.

In reaching this result, Mr. Justice Rutledge pointed out that the common law test, supra § 8, had evolved in answer to a very different problem, that is, where to set limits on *vicarious liability,* which really had little to do with the issue before the court. Hence, Justice Rutledge suggested what has come to be called the "economic reality" test: "In short, when .   .   .   the economic facts of the relation make it more nearly one of employment than of independent business enterprise," the statute should apply. Newsboys, however as a matter of *economic reality,* were not independent enterprises. See, Brown v. N.L. R.B. (C.A. 9th Cir. 1972) 462 F.2d 699. (News "dealers" held to be independent contractors).

Congress and various of the state legislatures have taken a hand in the question and declared for the common law test. For example, in Illinois Tri-Seal Products, Inc. v. United States (1965) 173 Ct.Cl. 499, 353 F.2d 216, the question was whether aluminum siding "installers" were employees for purposes of the Federal Insurance

Contributions Act and also The Federal Unemployment Tax Act. In both cases Congress had stipulated the "common law test for ascertaining the existence of the employer-employee relationship." The court noted, therefore, that it could not use the "economic reality" test, but said, nevertheless, that it must apply "the common-law rules *realistically*." (Emphasis added.)

After a very careful examination it was concluded that "installers" were essentially small businessmen, i. e., independent contractors, owning their own equipment, working when and how and for whom they saw fit, carrying their own insurance and so on. Hence, Tri Seal Products need not pay taxes as if they were "employees." The result highlights the point, stated above, that there is a very large group of agents who are not "servants," but who, most assuredly, are not "independent contractors." It would be unfortunate if this were not true, since it would mean, for example, that most managers, clerks, salesmen, directors, and other non-servants, would not be protected under the Workers' Compensation statutes, which uniformly exclude "independent contractors." See, West's Ann.Calif.L.Code § 3353.

The result would seem to be that the common law test, i. e., "control of means and methods," is scarcely adequate by itself. The point, in fact, is recognized by the Restatement for it lists 8 or 10 factors, *including* "control," which are to be considered in determining "whether one acting for another is a servant or an independent contractor." Restatement, Second, Agency § 220. A few courts have considered these to be merely an aid in the process of finding control, but it is submitted that to do this misses the point.

After all, the basic question is whether the "contractor" is one who may be expected to carry on as a separate and independent enterprise, entitled to enjoy the gains, and capable of carrying the risks involved. See, Douglas, Vicarious Liability and Administration of Risk (1929) 38 Yale L.J. 584. There is little justification for the category otherwise. The control of "means" test is an aid in the inquiry, for no truly independent contractor can brook control as to *how* the work is to be done, and expect to stay in business very long. However, the amplified Restatement test, § 220, is a far more efficient tool. See generally, Steffen, Independent Contractor and the Good Life (1935) 2 U.Chi.L.R. 501.

Even so, there are many close questions. The courts have been divided, for example, on where to place a realty or appliance salesman. See: Stockwell v. Morris (1933) 46 Wyo. 1, 22 P.2d 189 (Maytag salesman, owned own car, independent contractor); Sinclair v. Perma-Maid Co. (1942) 345 Pa. 280, 26 A.2d 924 (contra, on similar facts). Perhaps, again a multiple hat doctrine should be used supra, § 5. The salesman in *Stockwell* was an "agent" in making contracts for Maytag, Restatement, Second, Agency § 12; he was held to be an "independent contractor" in the use of his car; he well could be a "servant" if he injured a customer, Restatement, Second, Agency § 220, comment (1) (e); and, an "employee" for purposes of Workers' Compensation. Why not?

§ 44. Independent Contractor as Agent

It may seem a contradiction in terms to speak of an independent contractor as an "agent." See, however, Restatement, Second, Agency § 2. In fact, a sizeable part of the world's business is done by independent contractors when acting as agent. A commercial bank, for instance, acts as agent for its customer when handling collection items. U.C.C. § 4–201. A brokerage house acts as an agent in executing an order to buy or sell securities. And, of course, both bank and broker would be independent contractors, in that they conduct separate enterprises, with no control over the "means and methods" by which they carry on their businesses. Supra, § 43.

For another example, consider the early case of Hern v. Nichols (1708) 1 Salk. 289, 91 Eng.Reprint 256, cited supra § 41, which had to do with a deceit on the part of a "factor beyond sea," when selling defendant's goods. No doubt the factor was an independent contractor, since it is not customary for shippers to exert any control whatever over the way the factor conducts his business. This would insulate the shipper-employer from torts involving the *physical conduct* of the factor or his employees. But, as an *agent,* the factor *is* authorized to contract on behalf of his employer for the sale of the goods, subject, for example, to the employer's control as to price and terms of sale.

On these facts, Lord Holt held the shipper liable in deceit for the factor's false representations: "For seeing somebody must be a loser by this deceit, it is more reason that he that employs and puts a trust and confidence in the deceiver should be a loser, than a stranger." Thus was started that hardy *substitute for thought,* which has it that "when one of two innocent persons must suffer, etc., etc." See, Cal.Civ.Code § 3543. No one questions that the case was well decided, but today, it would be put on different grounds, that is, the question would be whether the plaintiff reasonably relied on the "apparent authority" of the factor. Restatement, Second, Agency § 265.

Probably the most typical independent contractor today, certainly the most prevalent, is the building contractor. He sells immunity from loss due to physical injury torts, almost as part of his stock in trade. Yet, he too, may at times have authority, as an agent, to purchase materials for the job. See, for example, North Carolina Lumber

Co. v. Spear Motor Co. (1926) 192 N.C. 377, 135 S.E. 115, where it was held that a *cost-plus* contractor had authority to purchase a carload of flooring, for which defendant owner-employer was held responsible. Thus the question is not whether an independent contractor may be an agent, but whether the particular facts make out an agency relationship. Most courts would say that a "cost-plus" term is not enough to give a building contractor agency powers. See, Kruse v. Revelson (1927) 115 Ohio St. 594, 155 N.E. 137, 55 A.L.R. 289.

In the case of a "management company," which would usually be an independent contractor, the authority question often would not be difficult. In Costan v. Manila Electric Co. (C.A.N.Y.1928) 24 F.2d 383, 385, for example, the J. G. White Management Corp. had been put in the position of manager for Manila Electric. Thus it had authority to hire and control employees for the company. In denying that it also should be answerable for their torts, Judge Swan said: "While its powers as manager were very broad, still it was acting as an agent, not as an owner *pro hac vice*, in operating the railway. It was subject to supervision and control by the board of directors of its employer, the holding company. Therefore its principal, and not it, should be responsible for the negligence of subordinate employees." See, supra, § 32.

A closer case, perhaps, concerns parent and subsidiary corporations. It is not usual to classify a subsidiary corporation as an independent contractor—and it may not be useful to do so—but they would seem to qualify under any of the usual tests. See, § 43, supra. In any case, since a corporation, like an independent contractor, may be an agent, there is no reason why a subsidiary may not be an agent in the service or employ of its parent shareholder. And it has been so held. Steele v. Meaker Co., Inc. (1928) 131 Misc. 675, 227 N.Y.S. 644. Again, the problem is one of fact, whether an agency situation was in fact established. See, Gledhill v. Fisher & Co. (1935) 272 Mich. 353, 262 N.W. 371, 102 A.L.R. 1042 (parent held not liable as undisclosed principal).

§ 45. Strict Liability

When the business at hand is lawful, it has long been true that an employer is under no duty, at his peril, to hire only a competent, careful, financially capable, independent contractor. Of course, he may need to do so to meet a safe place to work duty to his own employees, or he may want to do so to insure that the job will go smoothly, but, generally speaking, one is free to take the low bidder, whoever he may be. Nor, is it significant that possible injury to third persons or their property is a "foreseeable" risk. Indeed, one purpose in forming a corporation is to attain limited liability in just such circumstances; it is equally respectable to engage an independent contractor for the purpose. Steffen, Independent Contractor and the Good Life (1935) 2 U.Chi.L.Rev. 501.

The case, of course, is not that simple. So long ago as Rylands v. Fletcher (1868) L.R. 3 H.L. (E. & I.App.) 330, it was held that a landowner who had built a reservoir on his property should be liable for damage done when water broke out and flooded his neighbor's mine. It was not material that defendant had employed a competent engineer and contractor to do the work. As Blackburn, J., said, the person who "brings on his lands and collects and keeps there anything likely to do mischief, if it escapes, must keep it in at his peril . . ." (1866, L.R. 1 Exch. 265, 279). This was the old notion of absolute liability for fire and wild animals. And while the early American courts (See, Brown v. Collins (1873) 53 N.H. 442, 16 Am.Rep. 372) refused to follow suit on similar facts, the notion is a stubborn one and later courts have held the employer liable. See, Green, Hazardous Oil and Gas Operations (1955) 33 Tex. L.Rev. 574.

The same point was made again in Bower v. Peate (1876) 1 Q.B.Div. 321, 326, a routine construction case, in which the independent contractor, doing excavation work, had failed to provide adequate shoring to protect plaintiff's building.

Again the employer was held liable. The court said that handing work over to a contractor "from which mischievous consequences will arise unless preventive measures are adopted," can only be done at the peril of the employer.

In this country, at the turn of the century, there was little disposition to follow a similar course. Thus, in Berg v. Parsons (1898) 156 N.Y. 109, 50 N.E. 957, 41 L.R.A. 391, 66 Am.St.Rep. 542, a blasting case, the court held quite confidently that the employer could not be held responsible for damage to plaintiff's property. This, in spite of a strong dissent—based largely on Norwalk Gaslight Co. v. Norwalk (1893) 63 Conn. 495, 28 A. 32—that it must be shown that the employer had used due care to select "a competent and careful contractor." On the facts, this probably could not have been done.

However plausible, care in hiring has not become a condition of employer immunity. The idea that he must hire a financially capable contractor has had even less acceptance. Both have been swept aside by the notion that there is to be "strict liability" for "inherently dangerous" work, or, shall we say, work which may entail "mischievous consequences." Most states, would now put "blasting," and "demolition" work, in that category. Prosser, Law of Torts (1971) § 78. Or, in Agency terms, the employer owes a "nondelegable duty" as to such work. See, § 8 supra.

The "inherent danger" category has been a growing one. Like its counterpart, "products liability," it responds to a social policy designed to shift certain unexpected and unavoidable personal injury and property damage losses directly to enterprise. We could say, as the products courts once did, that the employer "represents" that his job will be safe. See, Greenman v. Yuba Power Products, Inc. (1963) 59 Cal.2d 57, 27 Cal.Rptr. 697, 377 P.2d 897. That, of course, was and is a needless step; it is enough to conclude, simply, that the doctrine of "strict liability" applies to work which is "inherently dangerous," as it does in the "products liability" cases. See, McPherson v. Buick Comes of Age (1937) 4 U.Chi.L.Rev. 461.

B. CONTRACTS

§ 46. Whether Authorized

As a matter of perspective, the business employer is usually more concerned with *enforcing* his agent's contracts with third persons, than in denying liability upon them. Property and profits are so acquired; and, agency is a "useful device" to that end. Supra, § 15. Of course, recognition by the principal of the agent's action, will usually operate as a "ratification" (See, infra, § 55), and thus cure, or render moot, any question concerning the agent's "authority" or "apparent authority." Supra, § 12. There are, however, a great many times when the employer, i. e., principal, will wish to contest whether his agent-officer, co-partner, servant—acted within his powers.

First it should be noted that, as in vicarious liability, supra § 30, the third person has the burden of proof. Or, as it is often put, the third person must ascertain at his peril the existence and extent of the agent's authority. Even when authority is in writing, as when the agent has a letter or power of attorney, (See infra § 50) there are problems of interpretation. Since interpretation is not a matter peculiar to agency, however, perhaps an example will suffice.

In Le Roy v. Beard (1850) 8 How. 451, 12 L.Ed. 1151, a leading case, the question was whether an authority given in New York "to sell" and execute "deeds of conveyance" for lands in Wisconsin, gave the agent power to give a "warranty" deed. After examining the situation of the parties, the custom in Wisconsin, and so on, the decision was in the affirmative; defendant principal was liable on his warranty.

Written authority, however, is probably the exception; unless the equal dignity rule applies, infra, § 52 a writing ordinarily is not necessary. Thus most agents are instructed orally and, as might be expected, change is the usual order of things. A third person, therefore, must make out his case by showing what the "course of dealing" was at the time. If he calls the agent to the stand, he asks him what his duties are, that is, what does he do? Strictly, it should also be necessary to show that the employer knew about and approved the agent's actions, before a course of dealing can ripen into an authority; but, practically, that issue often gets lost at the trial. It is more or less assumed the principal knows how his business is run.

The partnership case is no different. If the firm was established by a written agreement, that is the best evidence of what the partnership does, and, hence, of each partner's authority. But, as Holmes has said, "a partnership, although constituted by a contract, is not the contract but is a result of it." See, United States v. Kissel (1910) 218 U.S. 601, 31 S.Ct. 124, 54 L.Ed. 1168. Hence, as in agency generally, the person dealing with a partner is not limited to the contract, but, ordinarily, may also show what the "course of dealing" has been to establish the partner's actual authority.

An example, in which the third person failed to make out his case, is Cummings v. S. Funkenstein Co., Ltd. (1919) 17 Ala.App. 7, 81 So. 343. The question there was whether a partner in a general merchandise firm, doing business in a prohibition district, had authority to buy a stock of whiskey for the firm. The court held for the defendant. Probably the result would be the same under U.P.A. § 9, where the test is whether the partner's action was one "for apparently carrying on in the usual way the business of the partnership." The § 9 test, quite plainly, is not limited to the terms of the partnership agreement.

§ 47. Apparent Authority

The problem of proving an apparent authority case is very different. The third person still has the burden, but the theory of his case has changed. In the case of actual authority, the contract requirements of offer and acceptance, for example, are met by showing that the agent acted within the principal's express or implied mandate. With apparent or ostensible authority, however, the principal's manifestation runs to the third person, not the agent, and may even be contrary to instructions given directly to the agent. See, supra, § 12. Thus, the third person must show (1) a holding out by the principal, and (2) reasonable reliance on the agent's apparent authority.

The evident relation to estoppel calls for comment. Obviously, there is an element of holding out in each, but in theory they then take different ways. Estoppel requires "change of position" and, strictly, the third person's recovery is limited to his losses so caused. Moreover, the other party to the transaction—in this case the principal— would have no action at all. Estoppel is a one-way street. The apparent authority equation, on the other hand, leads to contract, enforceable by either the principal or the third person, even though there may be only a promissory consideration. See, Restatement, Second, Agency § 140. For a case involving estoppel only, see Metropolitan Club, Inc. v. Hopper (1927) 153 Md. 666, 139 A. 554.

A typical illustration of the apparent authority problem is presented by North Alabama Grocery Co. v. J. C. Lysle Milling Co. (1921) 205 Ala. 484, 88 So. 590. The question there was whether one Fitzhugh, sales manager for defendant Milling Co., had authority to sell flour to Grocery Co., without "confirmation" from the home office. Rather plainly he had no express authority to do so, but, if we may assume (1) that he told Grocer he did have authority and, (2) that he said it was customary in the flour business for "sales managers" to sell without confirmation, we have the problem stated.

To begin with, Fitzhugh's statement, that he had authority, would be inadmissible in evidence to prove the fact, and this for two reasons. In the first place, it would be hearsay, an unsworn statement not subject to cross examination, and therefore procedurally untrustworthy. Du Bois-Matlack Lumber Co. v. Henry D. Davis Lumber Co. (1935) 149 Ore. 571, 42 P.2d 152. Second, it would be inadmissible for the solid substantive reason that the statement did not proceed from the principal. An agent may not lift himself by his own bootstraps, so to speak, into a position of authority.

The second statement, however, that it was customary in the industry for sales managers to sell without confirmation, *would* be admissible. Not to prove authority, or even that there was such a custom, but to lay a basis for apparent authority. Grocer, no doubt, could be required to stipulate that he would produce other evidence later to show that the statement was in fact true. See, Butler v. Maples (1870) 76 U.S. (9 Wall.) 766, 19 L.Ed. 822. Then, to complete the equation, he must show that he relied reasonably on the fact that there was such a custom. An earlier law was built around the concept of "general agent" to reach the same result. See: *Butler,* supra; Restatement, Second, Agency § 3.

The reliance factor surely is *subjective,* and it should not be material what a reasonably prudent man might have done. Such is the negotiable paper rule; good faith means "honesty in fact," a personal quality. U.C.C. § 1–201(19). And see, Murray v. Lardner (1864) 69 U.S. (2 Wall.) 110. Thus, Grocer would have made out a case, to go to the triers of fact, on the theory of apparent authority; Milling Co. gave its man the title "sales manager" and put him in a territory where the custom was for sales managers to sell without confirmation. It can make no real difference that Grocer first learned of the custom from the manager himself, if, in fact, it was true and he relied on it.

The *North Alabama* case, itself, went off on a question as to the correctness of the trial court's instructions. Instruction A was to the effect that, unless Grocer relied "on Fitzhugh's authority to make contracts without confirmation," it would "make no difference . . . what Fitzhugh's authority was in the premises." This was properly held to be error; the trial court had confused authority and apparent authority.

There is little doubt that a third person need not rely on, or even know about, an agent's actual or real authority. See, Kansas Educational Ass'n v. McMahan (C.C.A. 10, 1935) 76 F.2d 957, 100 A.L.R. 384. Evidence of the fact may therefore come in at the trial. Thus, in *North Alabama,* if the facts had shown that Fitzhugh followed a course of dealing to sell without confirmation, he may well have acquired actual authority to do so, and it would then be quite immaterial whether or not Grocer knew and relied on that fact. The court's instruction pretermitted consideration of that possibility and hence was in error.

§ 48. Corporate Officers

The scene changes: Corporations are principals in this section, and officers are the representatives; authority is often differently described as "inherent," "ex-officio," "prima facie" and so on; transactions are of a larger order, often involving impressive sums. However, in the background, is the same basic conflict, namely, whether the principal should be given wide protection, or, on the other hand, whether full security is to be given those third persons who in good faith have dealt with the officers supposing them to be the corporation, or the proper agents thereof, with *actual* or *apparent authority*.

Most courts agree that the president has no significant inherent authority. See, Myers, The Inherent Powers of Corporation Presidents (1937) 23 Wash.U.L.Q. 117. Thus, directors' action may be needed, but, here too, a pitfall awaits the unwary third person. The possibility always exists that purported board action authorizing a transaction may have been irregular: A quorum may not have been present; due notice may not have been given to each director; or, indeed, no meeting of the board may ever have been held. Incidentally, the officer conducting the transaction may not have been regularly elected. These involve important shareholder safeguards, but, from the standpoint of third persons—at least as to those dealing at arm's length—doing business with corporations must not be made unduly precarious.

The problem may be illustrated by Citizens' Bank v. Public Drug Co. (1921) 190 Iowa 983, 181 N.W. 274. That was a suit by Bank, as indorsee and holder of an $800 note payable to the Partin Mfg. Co., which had been signed in the name of defendant, Drug Co., as maker, by Bronson, its president. Drug Co. pleaded that Bronson had no authority to sign the note and the trial court refused to admit it in evidence. On appeal, the court granted that a president has no authority by virtue of his office to sign notes, but pointed to the additional evidence that Bronson was also "one of its three directors and the manager of its business," and held that a sufficient basis had been laid for admission of the note.

The fact that Bronson was one of three directors should do little to show authority. Directors act only as a board, unless authority has been specially delegated to one of their number to act. See, Jones v. Williams (1897) 139 Mo. 1, 39 S.W. 486. But, at least, it would be difficult to say that the board was not fully aware of, and had not consented to, the fact that Bronson's duties included the actual, day by day, management of the Drug Co. business. This would surely include authority to contract for advertising, the consideration for which the note had been given to Partin, the payee.

Incidentally, the case presents a close question, not discussed by the court. Should Bronson's authority—at least as a prima facie matter—be classified as *actual authority,* derived from the course of dealing, or should it be put in the *apparent authority* category? It would make a difference, since there was no evidence that Bank, a remote holder, had ever heard of Bronson, much less relied on his course of dealing. The payee, Partin Mfg., must have known of Bronson's activities, and hence its position would be sound enough; perhaps Partin Mfg. could transfer rights so acquired. The point is not clear. On the assumption, however, that Bronson's apparent authority had ripened into actual authority, no Bank reliance would be needed, and the court's position is clearly supported. See, § 47, supra.

Today, the *Public Drug* case, supra, would be governed by the notion that Bronson, at least, had *prima facie* authority. That is, a president or other officer, may be *deemed* to have any authority the board of directors might have delegated to him in usual course of the business. See, Italo-Petroleum Corp. v. Hannigan (1940) 40 Del. 534, 14 A.2d 401. This means that when a plaintiff has proven the agent's signature to a note or other writing, it may be admitted in evidence, and, if no contrary evidence is offered, plaintiff may take judgment. But, if other evidence *is* introduced, the plaintiff must carry the ultimate burden of showing that the signing was in fact within the agent's authority or apparent authority.

Such is the position now taken by the Code, with reference to negotiable instruments. U.C.C. § 3–307. Indeed, the Code provision applies to *any* "signature," whether made by a corporation officer or any other. And while strictly the section deals only with negotiable paper, the provision is a reasonable one, saving court room time, and so it may be expected that it will be adopted as to writings generally. The provision gives the plaintiff, third person, a tactical advantage; when the defendant puts on a witness to dispute the agent's prima facie authority, the plaintiff has an opportunity to make out his case during cross examination.

Returning to *Public Drug,* supra, if Bronson had sought to borrow from Bank the $800 needed to pay Partin, a typical situation would be presented. Bank, most surely would not care to rely on the chance that, at a later date, it could prove the course of dealing by which Bronson had managed the business. It might do so, but the custom is to demand a certificate, signed and sealed by the company Secretary, which recites any by-law or resolution authority which Bronson might have. Such authority would be examined carefully; it was held in *Italo-Petroleum*, supra, that a by-law saying merely that certain officers were authorized "to sign" notes and so on, was not an authority to *borrow*.

The bank would be most happy if it were furnished with a certificate saying that at a meeting of the board of directors, duly called with a quorum present, a majority voted to authorize Bronson to borrow $800 from Bank, on such terms as he might think proper, and to sign and deliver a Drug Company note for its repayment. Then, even if the call was not regular or if, in fact, no directors' meeting had been held at all, Bank would have a solid position. That is, the Secretary's certificate would clearly have given Bronson *apparent authority* to borrow; Bank, of course, could easily establish the necessary reliance.

This supposes an arm's length transaction; obviously, if Bank knew that there had been no proper directors' action, it could not recover. See, Aetna Casualty Co. v. American Brewing Co. (1922) 63 Mont. 474, 208 P. 921. When the transaction *is* at arm's length, however, the law is fairly clear that a third person may not be required to go behind the Secretary's recitals, and inquire into what has been termed the "indoor management" of the corporation. See: Royal British Bank v. Turquand (1856) 6 El. & Bl. 327; Louisville, N. A. & C. R. Co. v. Louisville Trust Co. (1899) 174 U.S. 522, 19 S.Ct. 817, 43 L.Ed. 1081.

§ 49. Goods or Documents

The situation here is varied from that of the preceding sections by one additional fact, namely, goods, documents or securities have been placed in the hands of the agent. Another difference, of uncertain import, should also be noted, the greater degree of disassociation between principal and agent. Often the agent, as factor, commission merchant, dealer or broker, conducts a separate business, and at a distance from the principal. With the use of the *del credere* agency contract, moreover, the agent is often financially as important as his principal. See, supra, §§ 14 and 44.

The cases illustrate a long-standing conflict between notions of static security in property and the mercantile idea of what is essential to trade, viz., security of transactions. In the early case of Paterson v. Tash (1743) 2 Strange 1178, 93 Eng.Reprint 1110, traditional views as to the sanctity of property won, it being held "that though a factor has power to sell, and thereby bind his principal, yet he cannot bind or affect the property of the goods by pledging them as security for his own debt   .   .   . " Since then, by application of the "apparent authority" concept, by talk of "quasi-negotiability," and by recourse to legislation, there has been a steady advance toward the security of transaction viewpoint, though by no means on an unbroken front. See: Steffen and Danziger, The Rebirth of the Commercial Factor (1936) 36 Col.L.Rev. 745.

The case which, more than any other, foreshadowed the modern development, was Pickering

v. Busk (1812) 15 East 38, 104 Eng.Reprint 758. There the owner of certain hemp had it warehoused and transferred into the name of Swallow, his agent. Lord Ellenborough held that this gave Swallow "an implied authority to sell." Probably we would say Swallow had an "apparent authority," but, in any event, a purchaser from Swallow was given title to the hemp—and the door was open to take further steps in aid of transactions in the regular course of trade.

The *Paterson* case, which had been pressed upon the court, was said to have "considerably distressed our decision." Then, in 1824, following the decision in *Pickering,* supra, the first of the so-called Factor's Acts was adopted in England, to be followed by similar statutes in this country. See, 1 Williston, Sales (2 ed. 1924) § 318. Under the English pattern the factor or agent entrusted with goods *for sale,* was deemed to be "the true owner" thereof, so far at least as to give sanction to a sale in ordinary course of trade, or to protect a good faith pledgee. Even though the pledgee knew that the pledgor was not the real owner! Associates Discount Corp. v. C. E. Fay Co. (1941) 307 Mass. 577, 30 N.E.2d 876, 132 A.L.R. 519.

A problem in the Factor's Acts, however, was the requirement that the goods be put in the factor's hands "for the purpose of sale." How was a subsequent good faith taker from the factor to know that fact? See, Gazzola v. Lacy Bros. &

Kimball (1927) 156 Tenn. 229, 299 S.W. 1039, where the pledgee was defeated, even as in *Paterson,* supra.

At all events, when the Commercial Code was drafted a different course was taken: "Any entrusting of possession of goods to a merchant" who deals in goods of the kind "gives him power to transfer all rights of the entruster" to a buyer "in ordinary course of business." U.C.C. § 2–403 (2). Thus the crucial test now is simply whether the owner *entrusted* his goods to a "merchant," who deals in such goods, and no inquiry is needed as to purpose, whether or not for sale. In agency terms, this means that the merchant has been given an "apparent authority," long a disputed point in the automobile car lot cases. See: Carter v. Rowley (1922) 59 Cal.App. 486, 211 P. 267; Mori v. Chicago Nat. Bank (1954) 3 Ill.App.2d 49, 120 N.E.2d 567.

The phrase, in ordinary course of trade or business, as the Code puts it, requires comment. Even in the early cases, when an agent had an "authority" to sell, it was limited to a sale in usual course. Thus, it did not include sale at auction. See, Towle v. Leavitt (1851) 23 N.H. 360, 55 Am.Dec. 195. Late last century an irregular situation developed in which a dealer would procure a stock of goods on consignment, and then sell out everything, store and goods, in one transaction. A few courts held the sale unauthorized, that the dealer's authority was limited to sale in usual course at retail.   See, Romeo v. Martucci (1900) 72 Conn. 504, 45 A. 1, 99, 47 L.R.A. 601, 77 Am.St. Rep. 327.   Even so, most states passed "bulk sales" laws to require prior notice to creditors as a condition.   These statutes have now, in turn, been displaced by U.C.C. Art. 6.   See generally, Billig, Bulk Sales Laws (1928) 77 U. of Pa.L.Rev. 72.

The decisions with respect to entrusted documents and securities took a different course. They avoided the sound common law rule, that a bare entrusting of goods to another gives him no authority to dispose of them, by saying that a blank indorsed share certificate is different than ordinary goods.   Being indorsed by the owner, it is in order for sale or transfer.   Hence, in McNeil v. Tenth Nat. Bank (1871) 46 N.Y. 325, the court sanctioned the position of a bona fide pledgee as against the real owner.   The case represented a highwater mark, but of course it gave no aid at all, if the security, though properly indorsed, had been lost by, or stolen from the owner.

The next step, therefore, was to declare the share certificate "negotiable."   This was done by the Uniform Stock Transfer Act, drafted by Williston at the start of the century.   See, Turnbull v. Longacre Bank (1928) 249 N.Y. 159, 163 N.E. 135.   In fact, the Stock Transfer Act has now been superseded by Art. 8 of the Code, which not only covers share certificates but bonds, coupons and other securities as well. Likewise, and for the same basic reasons, bills of lading and other documents are similarly treated. See, U.C.C. Art. 7.

In sum, if one should ask what the law is, the answer must be: That depends on a number of things, includes a close reading of U.C.C. § 2–403 (2). "The times, they be a changing." By one device or another, however, we can say now that law will usually be found to support the good faith transaction in usual course of trade.

§ 50. Limitations and Revocation

The two areas, limitations and revocation, have much in common. Certainly as between principal and agent this is true, for a principal is equally free, at any time, either to limit or wholly revoke an agent's authority or apparent authority, except of course as the agent may have some form of irrevocable power. See, § 21, supra. And, being a consensual relation, mere notice to the agent will alone suffice to end his authority. Thus, the area to be explored is whether—as to third persons—there may nevertheless be a lingering authority or apparent authority of some sort.

Looking first to limitations, a more or less typical situation is that before the court in the well used case of Mussey v. Beecher (1849) 57 Mass. (3 Cush.) 511. Defendant there had given his agent a power of attorney to buy books for his store to an amount not to exceed $2000. After more than this amount had been purchased, plaintiff, relying on the agent's statement that he had not yet purchased up to the limit, sold the order of books in suit. The court gave judgment for defendant, Shaw, C. J., saying, "no one is bound to deal with the agent" and "whoever does so is admonished" of the limits put on the agent's authority; therefore, he must, at his "own peril," ascertain whether such limits have been exceeded. There is support for that position. See, First Nat. Bank v. St. John's Church (1929) 296 Pa. 467, 146 A. 102.

In contrast, secret limitations on the agent's authority are usually disregarded. An agent with authority to buy a horse or a car, for example, but with a private limitation on the amount he may pay, has full authority. So too, attempts to limit the *use* to which an authority may be put are ineffective. Thus, a clause in a by-law or corporate resolution, that certain officers have authority to sign notes and borrow money, "for purposes of the business," would appear to add nothing. With or without such a clause, if the third person has notice that the agent signs in breach of trust, he could not enforce the contract at common law.

[*142*]

The problem, thus, is not at all one of apparent authority, but of notice of misuse of authority. So, in Morgan v. Hall & Lyon Co. (1912) 34 R.I. 273, 83 A. 113, a company treasurer, who had authority to apply for letters of credit *in usual course of business*, and to sign a guaranty of repayment, was held to have obligated the company, when he applied for a letter of credit *to accommodate* a friend. There was nothing in the transaction, the court said, to put Morgan on notice of a misuse of authority. The cases have been at odds on whether a corporate officer—with authority to indorse receivables for company purposes—may indorse in the company name and deposit the paper in his personal account. He may take cash; he may *not* pay his personal debt to the indorsee. See, McIntosh v. Detroit Sav. Bank (1929) 247 Mich. 10, 225 N.W. 628.

In the leading English case, Hambro v. Burnand (1904) 2 K.B. 10, the agent had been given written authorities to underwrite policies of insurance, at Lloyds, in defendants' names. The policies in suit were signed to help keep a company afloat, in which the agents were personally interested. In reversing a judgment for defendants, Collins, M. P. said: "It would be impossible, as it seems to me, for the business of a mercantile community to be carried on, if a person dealing with an agent was bound to go behind the authority of the agent in each case, and inquire whether his motives did or did not involve the application of the authority for his own private purposes."

It appears that the "ultra vires" problem is similarly controlled. That is, a corporation with no charter power—or a partnership with no agreement power—to issue notes for the accommodation of others, may nevertheless be held liable to purchasers, who have no notice of the accommodation, as upon "business paper." See, Mechanics Banking Ass'n v. New York & S. White Lead Co. (1866) 35 N.Y. 505. Or, if you prefer, the corporation or partnership has acquired charter power in such cases.

Turning now to revocation, the case of Courtney v. G. A. Linaker Co. (1927) 173 Ark. 777, 293 S.W. 723, will illustrate the problem. The defendant, Mrs. Courtney, sold a store which she owned to her two sons, who had been operating it for her as her agents. Later, without notice of the sale or that the sons' authority had been revoked, plaintiff—a former dealer—sold the bill of merchandise in suit. The court held that Mrs. Courtney must answer for the purchase: "after a principal has appointed an agent in a particular business, parties dealing with him in that business have a right to rely upon the continuance of his authority until in some way informed of its revocation."

[144]

The court buttressed its opinion by reference to partnership law. There, it is true, when a firm is dissolved, the erstwhile partners who may continue the business have power to obligate the firm on contracts with *former dealers,* unless and until such dealers have notice of the dissolution. U.P.A. § 35. To put the thing in agency terms, continuing partners, like Mrs. Courtney's sons, are thus given something in the nature of an apparent authority.

It should be noted that this law is valid only as to *former dealers*, a term which is ordinarily limited to dealers on credit. As to the considerable number of persons who may have known generally of the firm, but not previously dealt with it, partnership law requires *publication* of the facts, to give constructive notice. U.P.A. § 35. Whether agency will ultimately adopt this refinement is not clear.

§ 51. Termination

The common law dealt harshly with third persons who contracted with an agent after his authority had been terminated *by operation of law.* This upon the principle, stated in Smout v. Ilbery (1842) 10 Mees. & W. 1, 152 Eng.Reprint 357, noted 126 A.L.R. 120, that "the continuance of the life of the principal was, under the circumstances, a fact equally within the knowledge of both contracting parties." While it is easy to dispute this assumption today, not much change in court-made law has taken place. Such a case as Farmers' Loan & Trust Co. v. Wilson (1893) 139 N.Y. 284, 34 N.E. 784, 36 Am. St.Rep. 696, which also put the risk of post termination dealings on the third person, has survived at least two Law Revision studies. See, Law Rev.Comm. (N.Y.1957) 293.

The consideration, more than any other, which has sustained the rule that death terminates an agent's authority, has been the need to protect the principal's estate from fraud. There has, however, been some legislative nibbling at the rule. For example, a proxy in many states may be voted even after death of the shareholder, unless "written notice of such death is received by the corporation" before the vote. See: Mc-Kinney's 1957 Session Laws, 356. So, too, the banks have been given authority to pay checks, in spite of the death or incompetence of the drawer, "until the bank knows of the fact . . . and has reasonable opportunity to act on it." See: U.C.C. § 4–405(1)(2).

A few states have gone farther. For example, California provides that "any bona fide transaction" with an agent after his authority has been terminated *for any reason*, if entered into by "a person acting without actual knowledge" of the termination, "shall be binding" on the principal or his estate, as the case may be. Cal.

Civ.Code § 2356. This would seem to go all the way, but, although the proviso has been on the books since 1943, it does not appear to have been litigated. Is a transaction "bona fide" when the agent intends to defraud his erstwhile principal or the estate? Probably so, if at least the third person acted in good faith.

The partnership scheme is not only more discriminating, but probably fairer, all things considered. See, supra § 50. While the court in the *Courtney* case was able to adopt the partnership rule as to former dealers, in the case of a voluntary revocation, it is doubtful that it could have done so if the case had been one of termination by operation of law. That is, it has been so well established, and for so long, that death terminates an agency, that it probably needs explicit legislative action now to fasten liability on the estate for post-death acts of a former agent. Indeed, when a partnership is dissolved by death of a partner, U.P.A. § 31(4), it is not too clear that the estate itself may be made liable by action under U.P.A. § 35, although, of course, its interest in partnership assets may be charged. The section says "the partnership" may be liable, but neither the estate nor its representative is a partner.

The cautious thing for a third person to do, therefore, is to ask for the customary clause in the agent's power of attorney, where that is possible. That is, the principal may properly be asked to agree to hold harmless any third person who *without notice* either of revocation or termination deals with the agent on the supposition that his power of attorney is still in effect. An agreement of the sort will survive and be binding on the estate. It goes without saying, almost, that the agent's continued possession of the power of attorney gives him no apparent authority.

§ 52. Formalities

An agent may have been fully authorized, in the senses discussed above, and yet he would need more, if he were to contract for the sale or purchase of land, or were to give a conveyance in the name of the principal. At common law, since both contract and conveyance must have been under seal, the agent's authority to execute them, likewise, was required to be in writing and under seal. This was the "equal dignity" rule. See, Heath v. Nutter (1862) 50 Me. 378. The courts early made an exception, when, as in Gardner v. Gardner (1850) 5 Cush. (59 Mass.) 483, 52 Am.Dec. 741, the instrument was signed by the agent in the principal's presence: "The name being written by another hand, in the presence of the grantor, and at her request, is her act."

Today, of course, the seal has lost its significance in most states. In California: "All distinctions between sealed and unsealed instruments are abolished." See, (1872) Cal.Civ.Code, § 1629. In New York: "Except as otherwise expressly provided by statute, the presence or absence of a seal upon a written instrument . . . shall be without legal effect." See, Report, N.Y.Law Rev.Comm. (1936) pp. 291–382. With this breakup in the use of seals, however, greater stress has been put upon the importance of *written* authority. In many states it is provided either in the statute of frauds, in the statutes concerning conveyances, in the broker or agency contract statutes, or in all three, that the agent's authority must be in writing.

California has a general provision: "An oral authorization is sufficient for any purpose, except that an authority to enter into a contract required by law to be in writing can only be given by an instrument in writing." Cal.Civ.Code, § 2309. This provision has wide application. Thus, an agent must have *written* authority to sign a simple contract to buy or sell goods when the amount is $500 or more, since the statute of frauds requires such contracts to be in writing to be effective. U.C.C. § 2–201(1). One exception, "no particular form of appointment is necessary" to authorize an agent to sign a negotiable instrument. U.C.C. § 3–104(1).

There has been litigation when land is listed with a real estate broker "for sale." May the broker sign a binding sales contract, in his principal's name, according to the terms of the listing? The courts have been divided on how to construe "for sale" in such context. Probably the majority hold that the broker's only authority would be to find a purchaser. He may take a contract as evidence that he has found a purchaser, ready and willing, but it would not be binding on the principal. See, Landskroener v. Henning (1923) 221 Mich. 558, 191 N.W. 943 (granted "the exclusive right to sell"). The contract would not be binding for two reasons: (1) the agent had no authority *to sell*, and (2) he had—for the same reason—no authority *in writing.*

At common law there was litigation involving conveyances, when one or more blanks may have been filled in by a person not having authority under seal. See, Bretta v. Meltzer (1932) 280 Mass. 537, 182 N.E. 827. The problem has persisted when only a written authority is required. Probably most courts would say that if the third person knew the blank was filled in by an agent who did not have written authority, a conveyance so executed would be ineffective. See, Harris v. Barlow (1919) 180 Cal. 142, 179 P. 682. However, there is good authority to the contrary, that such a conveyance *would be effective*, if the third person acted in good faith without notice of the improper filling. See, White v. Duggan (1885)

140 Mass. 18, 2 N.E. 110, 54 Am.St.Rep. 437, where Holmes, J., remarked that a specialty based on an estoppel is "somewhat like Nebuchadnazzar's image with a head of gold supported by feet of clay."

Whether, or the extent to which, this law applies to partners and corporate officers is a separate matter. Partners, of course, are agents, and it would be easy to make out a showing of written authority, in most cases, by introducing the partnership agreement. But this was probably not necessary, even at common law. See, Fincher & Womble v. Hanson (1913) 12 Ga.App. 608, 77 S.E. 1068, where the equal dignity rule was held not to apply: "it is entirely immaterial whether the partnership articles be under seal or not." Today the point is reasonably well settled, since U.P.A. § 9(1) provides that every partner has authority to act for the firm, "including the execution in the partnership name of any instrument." See, Lawer v. Kline (1928) 39 Wyo. 285, 279 P. 1077 (no written authority needed by partner to sign term lease).

It is not clear that the "equal dignity" rule applied to corporate officers at common law. See: Savings Bank of New Haven v. Davis (1830) 8 Conn. 191. Modern provisions, such as California § 2309, discussed supra, would literally require that a corporate officer, like any agent, have written authority to sign either a contract or conveyance within the statute of frauds. But there is case law to the contrary. For example, in Potter v. Fon du Lac Park Dist. (1929) 337 Ill. 111, 168 N.E. 908, the court said "The rule as to agency does not apply to an executive officer of a corporation, who is *more than an agent*." (Emphasis added). To the same effect, Jeppi v. Brockman Holding Co. (1949) 34 Cal.2d 11, 206 P.2d 847.

Plainly this is a lame rationalization; it might fit partners, who are both agents and co-proprietors, but not corporate officers. Which suggests that there may be dissatisfaction with the equal dignity rule itself. But that calls in question the policy underlying the statute of frauds, to which the rule is a mere adjunct. It is clearly beyond the scope of this writing to evaluate the statute of frauds, except to remark that it has become a fixture of our jurisprudence. While there is dissent, there is also strong support. For example, in Byrd v. Piha (1927) 165 Ga. 397, 141 S.E. 48, the court sustained the ouster of a tenant, whose agent had acted without written authority, by saying "the same formality" rule, Civ.Code § 3574, is "a stroke of genius," and should be strictly enforced: "Otherwise the purpose of the statute of frauds, which is to prevent frauds and perjuries, would be virtually done away with."

In any case, the rule has produced some interesting by-products. Most important, it brings to a virtual halt the development of an expansible apparent authority. That is, except possibly in the case of partners and corporation officers, the third person is on notice that he must, at his peril, examine the agent's credentials. See, Harrigan v. Dodge (1914) 216 Mass. 461, 103 N.E. 919. So also, the "two innocent persons" rule, § 44, supra, may not apply. Thus, in Ernst v. Searle (1933) 218 Cal. 233, 22 P.2d 715, the court said that Civil Code § 3543 (the two innocent persons rule) would not help the third person, since "the injury never would have occurred had appellant properly performed the duty imposed upon it by law to investigate the authority of the agent with whom it was dealing."

§ 53. Notice

There is a question of terminology at the outset; the two terms, *notice* and *notification,* are often used interchangeably. Thus, it may be said either that *notice* has been given to a third person or that he has been *notified.* Both are correct, but for present purposes *notice* will be treated as the knowledge or information which one has, or is deemed to have, and *notification* as one of the means by which notice may be conveyed. It will be convenient to discuss notice first, and, in § 54, notification.

That a principal, who carries on business through others—agents or servants—will be charged or credited to some extent at least with their knowledge does not require citation. But the theoretical basis on which this is put, and hence its scope, is another matter. It has been said that the reason, at least to begin with, was the fiction of identity, that principal and agent are one. See, Holmes, The Common Law (1890) 232. The "better view," however, has long been to improvise a duty on the part of the agent to communicate pertinent information to his principal. Whether he does so or not, the principal, in cases to be discussed, is deemed to have "notice" of the fact.

The problem takes on complexity in the case of the corporation, which of course can know nothing except as it is charged with knowledge possessed by its various agents. But it would seem strange if all their bits of information might be added up and charged to the fictitious entity known as the corporation. See, Neal v. Cincinnati Union Stockyard Co. (1903) 15 Ohio Cir.Ct.R. 299, 1 O.C.C.,N.S., 13. However, we are told in this very connection, "that great business houses" are not to be "held to less responsibility than small ones." Holmes, J., in United States v. National Exchange Bank (1926) 270 U.S. 527, 46 S.Ct. 388, 70 L.Ed. 717.

There has long been a dispute whether a principal may be charged with information obtained by his agent *prior to appointment.* Or, subsequent to employment, but while not on duty. For example, a lawyer, when handling work for a prior client, may have learned of an unrecorded mortgage on property which his present client wishes to buy. If the purchase is made, is the buyer to be charged with notice of the prior mortgage? Most courts today would answer in the affirmative, that is, if the lawyer had the fact in mind at the time he acted for the buyer. See also, Restatement, Second, Agency, § 276.

Pennsylvania is usually cited as following the old English rule to the contrary. In Houseman v. Girard Mut. Building & Loan Assn (1876) 81 Pa. 256, the court, quite logically, said its position was supported by the point "that it is only during the agency that the agent represents, and stands in the shoes of his principal." Which, of course, is true, but the question is not whether the agent represented the principal when he *obtained* the information. That is surely irrelevant. The question is whether it was in his mind when he *acted* for the principal.

Another significant point is implied. The agent with the knowledge must have acted in the scope of his employment. For illustration, an attorney is engaged to make a title search. If, by chance, he knows of an unrecorded lien, but reports only that the record title is clear, which is true, should the client nevertheless be charged with his attorney's knowledge? There is strong authority in the negative, since the attorney's job was limited to a record search. In Trentor v. Pothen (1891) 46 Minn. 298, 49 N.W. 129, which involved this situation, Mitchell, J., said that were the law otherwise, "it would be very dangerous to employ an attorney at all for any such purpose."

For other illustration, if the agent acts *adversely,* as where he sells his own securities to his principal, though knowing of a defence, his information will not be charged to the principal. There are two rationalizations. First, since the agent acted adversely, as a citizen and at arm's length, he was not in the scope of his employment at the time. Innerarity v. Merchants' Nat. Bank (1885) 139 Mass. 332, 1 N.E. 282, 52 Am.Rep. 710. Second, since he sought to defraud his principal, it cannot be presumed that he communicated the fact to his principal. To this last, however, there is an exception the "sole actor" doctrine. Thus, if an assistant cashier acts on both sides of the transaction, say, as seller of stolen bonds and as agent for his principal, a bank, to buy them, the bank, at least, may not retain the stolen securities as against the real owner. Munroe v. Harriman (D.C.N.Y.1936) 85 F.2d 493.

The rules in the case of partnership are essentially the same. Thus it is provided that "the

[*156*]

knowledge of the partner acting in the particular matter, acquired while a partner or *then present to his mind* . . . operate as notice to or knowledge of the partnership, *except in the case of a fraud* on the partnership . . ." U.P.A. § 12 (emphasis added). It will be noted that the partnership is regarded as an entity for the purpose.

The above results, for the most part, square with the "communication" rationalization. However, there has been doubt, for, as Judge Swan said in *Munroe*, supra, "The presumption of communication is a pure fiction, contrary to the fact, for it is only when the agent has failed to communicate" that it comes into use. Judge Swan disposed of the case quite simply, "common justice requires that one who puts forward an agent to do his business should not escape the consequences of notice to, or knowledge of, his agent."

In so holding, Judge Swan appears to have aligned the case with the early formulations concerning respondeat superior. See, § 30, supra. Moreover, it is fair to say that the "notice" question is, in fact, but another aspect of that doctrine. If an employer is to answer for an agent's propensity to accident—wherever acquired—so also is he charged with his knowledge and information, as above discussed.

§ 54. Notification

It is not easy to generalize concerning what is essential to a "notification." Much depends on the transaction, and the measure of diligence expected of the sender. In a carefully drawn guaranty agreement, for example, the guarantor will stipulate for demand and written notice of any default, the same actually to be received by the guarantor. Cf. St. Louis & St. Charles Bridge Co. v. Union Electric Light & Power Co. (1925) 216 Mo.App. 385, 268 S.W. 404. On the other hand, it is not unusual for corporate by-laws to provide that a timely letter addressed and mailed to a director or shareholder, at the last known address, will be sufficient notice or notification of a forthcoming meeting—whether or not the letter ever arrives. See, Stockton, etc. v. Houser (1895) 109 Cal. 1, 41 P. 809.

The "notice" required to charge an indorser upon a negotiable instrument affords a different comparison. The indorser engages that, if upon due presentment to the maker the instrument is not paid, he will pay it, providing he is "given" due notice of dishonor. N.I.L. §§ 66, 89. But by N.I.L. § 105, it is further provided that "notice" is sufficient, if it is properly mailed, "notwithstanding any miscarriage in the mails." The Code provisions are to the same effect. U.C.C. §§ 3–414(1), 3–508(4). And, to make doubly sure, the Code has a general provision—perforce applicable only to Commercial Code situations— which states that a person "notifies" or gives "notice" to another "by taking such steps as may be reasonably required to inform the other . . . whether or not such other actually comes to know of it." U.C.C. § 1–201(21).

Again, upon dissolution of a partnership— whether by death of a partner or for any other reason—there is the problem of giving "notice" to those who may have extended credit to the partnership prior to dissolution. Otherwise, the withdrawing partner or the estate of a deceased partner may become obligated on future transactions. U.P.A. § 35; § 51, supra. The wording of the statute, "and had no knowledge or notice," is ambiguous at best, but may fairly be construed to say that the prior dealer must actually *receive* "knowledge or notice." Moreover, that seems to have been the court-made law. See, Torvend v. Patterson (1933) 136 Cal.App. 120, 28 P.2d 413.

A more controversial situation involves the *lost* or *stolen* bearer bond, or blank indorsed share certificate. If subsequently sold to a purchaser *without notice,* or pledged as collateral, the real owner stands to lose the total value. Accordingly, there is a practice to send out "loss notices" to banks, security houses and others who might be expected to take in the securities in regular course. The question is not so much whether the notice must be actually received, that is assumed. The question is as to the effect. May the bank or other recipient simply throw the notice in the waste basket? Probably not!

Central to the problem is the concept of notice to a principal—in this case a corporation, partnership or other "organization," U.C.C. § 1–201 (28)—when its agents are quite without notice. It was well decided at common law, however, that when notice has once been brought home to a bank, for example, it would be immaterial whether or not the discount committee, which later purchased the paper in suit, had knowledge of the fact that defendant had previously withdrawn from the drawer firm. Bank of Pittsburg v. Whitehead (1840) 10 Watts 397, 36 Am.Dec. 186. The fact of withdrawal had been discussed at a director's meeting of plaintiff bank and Gibson, C. J., said: "notice to the government, or head, is necessarily notice to the body . . ." Hence, defendant could not be held liable.

The Code softens any notion that notice to an *organization,* defined, § 10 supra, operates instantaneously. It provides that such notice does not become "effective" until brought to the attention of the individual conducting the transaction, or "in any event from the time when it would have been brought to his attention if the organization had exercised due diligence . . . " U.C.C. § 1–201(27). This is reasonable enough. Compare, U.C.C. § 4–403(1), with respect to "stop payment" notices. In the process, however, a significant point is confirmed, that the "organization" may have "notice," quite apart from what its agents may know, and in any event from the time when it could have been brought to their attention, if "due diligence" were used.

This means there may be some future case law changes. In perhaps the leading case today, Graham v. White-Phillips Co. (1935) 296 U.S. 27, 56 S.Ct. 21, 80 L.Ed. 20, 102 A.L.R. 24, the court sided with the purchaser as against the real owner, basing its decision in part on a Michigan holding, in which the court had said that it must give weight to "the well-established rule that though one has received actual notice, if by forgetfulness or negligence he does not have it in mind when he acquires the bonds, he may still be a good-faith purchaser." Actually, the Michigan court appears to have failed to grasp the significance of notice to an "organization." See, *Bank of Pittsburg,* supra. For all that appeared the purchaser still held plaintiff's loss-notice in its files, and hence *it* had not forgotten. That its agents may have, was not material, they were not the purchaser. See, Merrill, *Unforgettable Knowledge* (1936) 34 Mich.L.Rev. 474.

So, at long last, we have workable machinery to help the innocent loser of negotiable securities recoup his losses. Nor would it seem to impose an onerous burden on the financial community, particularly if the services of a computer are available.

§ 55. Ratification

The transactions here in question are those beyond the power of the agent to do, that is, they fall outside his authority or apparent authority, or any power he might have in excess of those limits. See § 57, infra. That some of these may be *ratified* is familiar ground, the theory on which this proceeds and its consequences are another matter. Most courts and writers are agreed, however, that it does not rest on estoppel, but is a consensual matter. See, Forsyth v. Day (1858) 46 Me. 176. The essence of the thing is that upon ratification—of a contract, let us say—the one ratifying, i. e., the purported principal, is put into the contract as if present when it was negotiated by the pretended agent, with all the rights and liabilities of a party.

Of course, this involves some departures from orthodox contract law, and Holmes was prompted to describe these as "absurdities introduced by ratification." Agency, (1891) 4 Harv.L.Rev. 14. It is suggested, however, that if one views the third person's signature to the contract as an offer, most requirements fall into place. The principal's "ratification," so called, thus becomes an acceptance. Consistently with the rule concerning counter offers, the ratification must be of all or none. The acceptance, moreover, need not be communicated to the third person; indeed, it would serve no purpose, as he already has what purports to be a binding contract. See, Restatement, Second, Agency, § 95. Also, in the nature of the case, no new consideration is needed, as that supporting the contract as negotiated will suffice.

However, the "relation back" factor—as it is usually described—needs further examination. May acceptance, i. e., ratification, be effective even after the third person has attempted to withdraw? The leading English case on the point, Bolton Partners v. Lambert (1889) 41 Ch.Div. 295, held in the affirmative, "the ratification is thrown back to the date of the act done . . . " Evidently such is still the English law, with the qualification that the principal must act within a "reasonable time." Portuguese Cons. Copper Mines, Ltd. (1890) 45 Ch.D. 16. Even so, the result is to give the principal a period, when he may await developments, before deciding whether or not to ratify.

The American courts took an opposite course. See: Clews v. Jamieson (1901) 182 U.S. 461, 21

S.Ct. 845, 45 L.Ed. 1183; Restatement, Second, Agency, § 88. Indeed, a minority of one or more has gone farther and insisted that ratification cannot be effective until later, when the third person in turn has agreed to it. This to one side, ratification may take place at any time; there is no reasonable time requirement. Whether a contract for insurance may be ratified *after loss,* however, has caused some litigation. See, Robinson, Ratification after Loss, etc. (1933) 18 Corn. L.J. 161. The insurance case, however, differs only in degree; a principal will seldom ratify any contract unless he expects to gain something by so doing.

Other conditions are that the principal must have full knowledge of the transaction he proposes to ratify. Needless to say, he will not be charged with the purported agent's knowledge. See, § 53, supra. This requirement squares, rather plainly, with the notion that ratification is but acceptance of the third person's offer, as above discussed. The requirement of full knowledge, however, has at times been overstressed; it surely should mean no more than that the principal has knowledge of the terms of the disputed contract, and of such additional facts as he might want to know about, were he to have made the contract himself. See, Blen v. Bear River, etc. (1862) 20 Cal. 602. Of course, the principal may determine to ratify even without facts, but this

[*164*]

may be difficult to establish. See, Currie v. Land Title Bank & Trust Co. (1939) 333 Pa. 310, 5 A.2d 168.

The "all or none" requirement has caused litigation. In Cram v. Tippery (1945) 175 Ore. 575, 155 P.2d 558, the owner's ranch agent sold 70 tons of hay, when the owner claimed he had authority to sell only 30 tons,—the buyer, however, had already taken $3\frac{3}{4}$ tons in excess of that amount. Ultimately, the buyer brought suit for breach of the 70 ton contract, and the ranch owner counterclaimed for the price of the $3\frac{3}{4}$ tons. The court was on sound ground when it held that the counterclaim was an effective ratification, citing Mechem to the point that bringing suit to enforce a contract is "one of the most unequivocal methods of showing a ratification." Mechem, Agency, 2d Ed. 329, § 446. The court also has strong support for the point that suit for the price of $3\frac{3}{4}$ tons was necessarily ratification of the full contract. Restat.2d Agency § 97(b).

The obvious course for the ranch owner—since it may be assumed he did not wish to donate $3\frac{3}{4}$ tons of hay to the buyer—would have been to sue in replevin, or, better, in restitution for the fair value of the $3\frac{3}{4}$ tons. By so doing he would not have affirmed the contract. In a few cases it has been possible to split the transaction into two contracts, and thus avoid the rule. For example, in

Murray v. Standard Pecan Co. (1923) 309 Ill. 226, 140 N.E. 834, 31 A.L.R. 604, defendant's agent to sell stock had found it an aid in his work to give the buyer a re-purchase agreement as well. On these facts the court held that defendant might keep the purchase price for the stock and repudiate the re-purchase contract, when later advised of it. No doubt, the buyer might still rescind for mutual mistake.

The possibility of ratifying a tort encounters another condition, that the agent's act must have been done in the name of the pretended principal. In the leading case, Dempsey v. Chambers (1891) 154 Mass. 330, 28 N.E. 279, 13 L.R.A. 219, 26 Am. St.Rep. 249, a substitute driver had broken plaintiff's window when delivering coal. The court held that, by collecting for the coal, defendant had ratified the *employment*, and this carried with it responsibility for the negligence. Holmes, J., had doubt that a person could ratify an assault, merely because the assaulter "called himself my servant," but there have been cases going so far. See, Kansas City, etc. v. Shain (1939) 345 Mo. 543, 134 S.W.2d 58. It was not necessary to reach the point in *Dempsey*. As to undisclosed principals, see § 60, infra.

Courts at one time decided that a forgery could not be ratified, and this for two reasons. First, it was against public policy, as ratification might be used to exonerate the agent from criminal prosecution. And, next, it was claimed the agent had not acted in the name of his principal when he merely signed the principal's name, without more. Neither point is good. Ratification, of course, should not have any bearing on the criminal law and, plainly, the agent does disclose the purported principal's name in a forgery—only the pretended agency *relationship* is undisclosed. At all events, the Code now provides, with respect to negotiable paper, that "any unauthorized signature may be ratified," U.C.C. § 3–404(2). Moreover, the result is so reasonable, it may well become law generally.

Only a brief comment is needed regarding ratification by partners. Since partners are agents, § 7, supra, the law just discussed applies. The area in which ratification may be needed, however, requires that we observe the line between U.P.A. § 9(1) and 9(2). That is, any act "for apparently carrying on in the usual way" is within a partner's power, and thus needs no ratification. But any act "which is *not* apparently, etc.," must be "authorized by" *all* the partners. See, § 9(2), emphasis added. A bank in lending money to a firm, if either the amount or the purpose of the loan raises doubts as to the acting partner's authority, will request a prior consent signed by each partner. If it places the loan anyway, and relies on a subsequent ratification, U.P.A. § 9(2) requires unanimous action.

When ratification is not forthcoming, in the case just mentioned, the bank, as is true with respect to any third person, has additionally two main courses of action to recoup its losses. One, it may seek restitution from the purported principal. And, two, it may bring an action against the pretended agent. As to the first, see infra, § 56; the second, § 57.

§ 56. Restitution

Discussion of this topic will be brief, since the law relative to equitable remedies is not peculiar to Agency. It will be useful, however, to list some of the many *agency situations* in which such remedies are applied. See, § 22 supra. In a bank loan situation, when it develops that the "borrower's" agent lacked authority, and ratification has failed, the lending bank will look first to any funds credited to the third person's account. That is, the bank will charge back these credits to apply on the purported borrower's note. In essence this is restitution, by self help, since the third person has no standing "in good conscience" to retain the funds. For many years banks have sought to formalize the procedure by claiming a "banker's lien."

In the typical case, however, a good part of the unauthorized borrowing will have been drawn

out. Often the "agent" is at least quasi honest—
perhaps uncertain as to his authority—and will
have used the money to pay obligations which the
purported borrower owed to creditors. When
these are the facts, most courts require the borrower to repay the lender the amount of any benefit so received, and which in good conscience he
ought not keep. A case in point is Bannatyne v.
MacIver (1906) 1 K.B. 103, where Romer, L. J.,
said, "in equity . . . the lender is entitled to
stand in the same position as if the money had
originally been borrowed by the principal."

As a matter of procedure, the action is usually
at law for money had and received, although on
occasion a suit in equity for a constructive trust
may be the better remedy. When all the money
has been withdrawn almost at once, however,
a court may decide that the purported borrower
received no "benefit," and hence is not liable.
See, Credit Alliance Corp. v. Sheridan Theater
Co., Inc. (1925) 241 N.Y. 216, 149 N.E. 837. To
change the illustration, there has been much
litigation respecting sales of goods and property
by unauthorized agents, as in Cram v. Tippery,
supra. Again, as pointed out, the purported
buyer may not, "in good conscience," retain the
goods, and hence can be required to answer for
their fair value.

When the sales illustration is *reversed,* and it
is the *buyer's* agent who lacked authority, there

is an interesting ratification problem. That is, if the purported buyer retains the goods with knowledge of the facts, he cannot do so for long without being held to ratify. See, Seavey, Ratification by Silence (1954) 103 U.Pa.L.Rev. 30. Since it is at the seller's option at this point— either to treat it as ratification or not—it would seem the seller may, at his choice, either sue on the contract or for restitution, depending on which looks most advantageous to him. But, if the buyer moves first, he may either ratify or disaffirm, in which case the seller's option would seem to be gone. He surely would have no case for restitution, if the buyer, by ratification, has given him an action for the price on the affirmed contract.

§ 57. Unauthorized Agent

It is proposed now to examine into the responsibility, if any, of the agent who has acted *beyond* his express authority, or any apparent authority, assuming there has been no ratification. This is the third person's possible further recourse, in the situations discussed, supra, § 56. Of course, if the agent has been guilty of fraud, he may be required to answer to the third person upon tort principles. See, § 38, supra. However, the cases indicate that it may often be quite difficult to establish a *deceit*, since that requires showing: "Representation, falsity, scienter, deception and injury," as stated in Reno v. Bull (1919) 226 N.Y. 546, 124 N.E. 144.

Another course would be to require the agent to step into his purported principal's shoes, as a full-fledged *party* to the contract. Possibly because this would entail rewriting the contract, in effect, it has not often been done, except in special situations to be considered later. See, §§ 58 and 62. Last century, however, in Collen v. Wright (1857) 8 E. & B. 647, the court contrived an implied *warranty* of authority on the part of the agent. This had two virtues: it gave the third person an easily proven remedy; and, being a contract action, it survived the death of the agent before trial. Not only has this view been widely accepted, but the warranty has been held to be a continuing one. Thus the statute of limitations will ordinarily not defeat the third person. Moore v. Maddock (1929) 251 N.Y. 420, 167 N.E. 572, 64 A.L.R. 1189.

The content of the agent's warranty has become fairly well defined. It is not a warranty that the named principal will perform, or even that he has the capacity or financial ability to do so. See, Goldfinger v. Doherty (1934) 153 Misc. 826, 276 N.Y.S. 289 (infant principal). So also, it is not a warranty that the proposed action is not ultra vires of a corporate principal's powers. It *does* warrant that the agent has power to obligate the designated principal. Thus, where the principal had died prior to the transaction, or become mentally incompetent, the agent must answer for his consequent lack of authority. It is true that, as to the principal, the third person must at his peril ascertain the extent and existence of an agent's authority, § 46, supra, but as between agent and third person, that is the agent's responsibility.

The question of damages is troublesome. Since the agent's warranty is the basis of a contract action, it would seem to follow that breach of contract damages should be awarded. Thus, if an agent, without authority, sells a parcel of land for $5000, the hopeful buyer on showing that it was reasonably worth $10,000 on the market, should have the benefit of his bargain. And, a few English cases have so held. See, Godwin v. Francis (1870) L.R. 5 C.P. 295. But in this country the rule is otherwise. See Flora v. Hoeft (1922) 71 Colo. 273, 206 P. 381, where the court said: "The plaintiff lost no bargain, and no profits, because of the defendant's alleged deceit." The result, a tort recovery—damages naturally flowing from the wrong—in a contract action. See, Abel, Some Spadework on the Implied Warranty of Authority (1942) 48 W.Va.L.J. 96.

Ratification by the principal, meantime, introduces further complications. It is good law, however, that the effect is to *discharge* the agent on his warranty of authority. As stated in Sheffield

v. Ladue (1871) 16 Minn. 388, 10 Am.Rep. 145, "The plaintiffs [third persons] have got what they bargained for, and have no longer any cause of action for damages against the agent." The same has been said, although unnecessarily, in a case where the agent acted within his *apparent* authority. See, Dexter Sav. Bank v. Friend (C.C. Ohio 1898) 90 F. 703. Also, since Friend, the agent who had signed the note in suit, was not *wholly* without authority, "actual, implied or apparent," U.C.C. § 1–201(43), he could not well be held liable as a "party," even under the Code. See, U.C.C. § 3–404(1).

Further, upon ratification, the agent appears, also, to be relieved of responsibility to his principal. See, Triggs v. Jones (1891) 46 Minn. 277, 48 N.W. 1113, where Mitchell, J., said, "by a ratification of an unauthorized act, the principal absolves the agent from all responsibility for loss or damage growing out of the unauthorized transaction . . ." This upon the notion that the principal had a free choice, either to disavow the transaction and so incur no damages, or to ratify. Consistently, if the transaction is within the agent's apparent or ostensible authority— so that the principal would be liable anyway—so called "ratification" has been held not to release the agent. Pacific Vinegar & Pickle Works v. Smith (1907) 152 Cal. 507, 93 P. 85. These results seem oversimplified; the principal should be able to reserve his rights in either case.

This principle would seem also to apply to unauthorized *partners*, since they too are agents. However, when an unauthorized partner signs a contract for the firm, although he may not bind the firm, he surely will obligate himself, as a *party*. See, Bole v. Lyle (1955) 39 Tenn.App. 679, 287 S.W.2d 931. There is, accordingly, no need to use an implied warranty. Moreover, it would seem clear that ratification by the other partners would not release the active partner. Ratification in that case would simply make it clear that all partners—or the firm, if procedure permits, § 78, infra—could be held responsible.

Partnership law goes a step farther and gives the unauthorized partner an action for contribution, in a case where he acted after the partnership was dissolved without notice to him. U.P.A. § 34. The point is one the agency cases might well adopt. Thus an agent who has acted after the death of his principal, and without knowledge, should have indemnity against the estate for his warranty of authority losses.

§ 58. Contract Integration

The third person, in the situations we have been considering above, may have yet another string to his bow, if the contract was in writing and signed by the unauthorized agent; this depends on *how* the writing was signed. Agents, whether authorized or not, are often somewhat casual in the way they sign papers. Accordingly, they not infrequently run afoul of the parol evidence rule, that creation of the law courts which, like its counterpart the statute of frauds, is said to circumvent fraud and prevent injustice. See Corbin, The Parol Evidence Rule (1944) 53 Yale L.J. 603.

The parol evidence rule, simply stated, runs to the effect that, when a contract has been fully integrated and put in writing, it is the best evidence of the agreement. Or, as is often stated, parol evidence is not admissible to vary the terms of a written agreement. It might once have been argued that the rule applies only when *terms*, not *parties*, are in question, but it is too late for that now. Thus it is necessary, in any given case, to determine from what appears *within the four corners of the writing,* both what the text means, and who the parties to it are. There are two main exceptions: if ambiguous, parol evidence may be used to explain things; and, if there is fraud or mistake, parol evidence may be allowed to reform the agreement.

One point is fairly clear: If the agent—authorized or not—signs a note or other contract in his *own* name, he becomes a party, and parol evidence will not be heard to relieve him of responsibility. This was the holding in the much cited case of Higgins v. Senior (1841) 8 Mees. & W. 834, 151 Eng.Reprint 1278, in which the agent signed the sold note in suit in his own name, William Senior, for "one thousand tons of Varteg" iron. He evidently was authorized to sell for Varteg Iron Co., but the court held that he had obligated himself. In the court's view, the writing was not ambiguous. Accord, Nash v. Towne (1866) 72 U.S. (5 Wall.) 689, 18 L.Ed. 527.

It was recognized, at the same time, that the "sold note" in *Higgins* also could be enforced against Varteg Iron Works, if Senior were authorized. The statute of frauds would present no problem, even under the strict rule, since there was a writing binding on someone. See, U.C.C. § 8–319. Nor would the parol evidence rule apply, for the purpose would not be to *alter* the writing and exonerate the agent, but simply to *add* another party.

Plaintiff, thus, could sue Varteg Iron Company as if the contract had been properly signed: Varteg Iron Company, by William Senior, agent. There would be no need of a preliminary suit in equity to reform the contract. Indeed, such a suit, if brought, might well fail; aside from being unnecessary, there was no fraud, and the mistake, if any, may not have been mutual. See, Kegel v.

McCormack (1937) 225 Wis. 19, 272 N.W. 650, 111 A.L.R. 643. It is not unusual for agents to add their credit to that of the principal.

The common law rule, that words added to an agent's signature are mere *descriptio personae*, served to bring about much confusion. For example, in Casco Nat. Bank v. Clark (1893) 139 N.Y. 307, 34 N.E. 908, 36 Am.St.Rep. 705, the note in suit was signed "John Clark, Prest.," and the name "Ridgewood Ice Co.," appeared in the margin. Assuming that Clark had authority to borrow money for Ice Co., whose contract was it? The court held that Clark had made himself personally liable, that it was his contract. In the court's view the addition of "Prest.," to Clark's signature did nothing more than to identify *which* Clark was before the court. And, the addition of Ridgewood Ice Co., was only further identification.

Some courts approved. "It is better that a careless or ignorant agent should sometimes pay for his principal, than to subject the construction of valid written contracts to the manifold perversions, misapprehensions, and uncertainties of oral testimony." See, Sturdivant v. Hull (1871) 59 Me. 172, 8 Am.Rep. 409. But a construction so far out of line with commercial understanding could not endure. At all events, it was provided by N.I.L. § 20 that, if a person "adds to his signature words indicating that he signs for or on behalf of a principal, or in a representative capacity," he was not liable on the instrument "if he was duly authorized." Cf. U.C.C. § 3–403(2a). In the face of such a statute *Casco,* supra, would have gone the other way.

The case of the *unauthorized* signer finally reached the courts in New Georgia Nat. Bank v. J. & G. Lippmann (1928) 249 N.Y. 307, 164 N.E. 108, 60 A.L.R. 1344. The action was by a remote holder against either the company or its president, in the alternative, the note having been signed "J. & G. Lippmann, L. J. Lippmann, Pres." Plainly this was a proper signature to bind the company, not Lippmann personally. Nevertheless, Cardozo, J., for the court, stressed the words "duly authorized" in N.I.L. § 20, supra, and held, according to the negative implication, that Lippmann was individually responsible as a party, since he was *not* authorized.

Much can be said for such a holding on the facts of the case. That is, a remote holder expects and can fairly demand that *someone* be named as a "party." He might, of course, claim an action for breach of an implied warranty of authority, but, aside from being difficult to prove, it would ordinarily yield less than the face amount of the instrument. The Code fully approves the *New Georgia* rule, but then goes farther, and appears to give a payee or other immediate party an action against the *unauthorized agent* as a *party.*

See, U.C.C. § 3–404(1). This would seem to be a mistake of policy.

Code law, of course, applies only to negotiable paper, but the law in that area has often been persuasive as to writings generally. The rule stated in N.I.L. § 20, that an agent should not be personally liable, if he is authorized and signs in a representative capacity, is a good one. It pretty well does away with the old *descriptio personae* rule. On the other hand, there would seem little justification for adopting generally a rule that *any unauthorized* agent is liable as a *party*, especially when he has carefully signed to obligate his principal only. Of course, there may be exceptions. California by statute makes him a party, if he did not "in good faith" *believe* he had authority. West's Ann.Cal.Civil Code § 2343. Otherwise, it would seem, the third person has adequate redress in suing on the agent's warranty or—if the circumstances are appropriate—in having the instrument reformed to make the agent a party.

§ 59. Promoters' Contracts

The promoter is not an "agent," it is said, because for every agent there must be at least one principal. See § 4, supra. And, for the same reason, the promoter has no "authority." Hence, fortunately, contracts made by a promoter are not binding on the new corporation when it is duly organized and ready for business. The point, in fact, is more than a mere matter of legal semantics for, as said in Clifton v. Tomb (C.C.A. W.Va.1927) 21 F.2d 893, "if corporations could be held bound by all the secret undisclosed contracts of their promoters, few men would care to risk subscribing to their capital stock." See, Kessler, Promoters' Contracts (1961) 15 Rutgers L.Rev. 566.

It is *not* proposed to deal generally with the law of promoters—that is done elsewhere—but there are many points where a comparison with agency rules is useful. The benefit of some contracts, and some property acquired by the promoters, will definitely be wanted by the new organization. Conversely, the promoter will want to be released as promptly as may be from liability, if any, to third persons. An examination of these, and similar points, will throw light on their counterparts in the agency field. See, Ehrich & Bunzl, Promoters' Contracts (1929) 38 Yale L.J. 1011.

The theory upon which a newly formed corporation may take over a promoter's contracts on its behalf has been a troubled one. In the case of Kelner v. Baxter (1866) L.R. 2 C.P. 174, it was decided that it could not be done at all. The holding was based partly on statute and partly on an unbending notion of "contract." A few states in this country followed the *Kelner* lead, but today it is generally held that the new corporation may "adopt" the promoter's contracts on its behalf. This is not "ratification," as in agency, since there is no relation back. McArthur v. Times Printing Co. (1892) 48 Minn. 319, 51 N.W. 216, 31 Am.St.Rep. 653. The theory is of a new contract, the contract with the promoter being treated as an offer by the third person. Acceptance of this offer requires no more ritual than in the case of any contract. See, Morgan v. Bon Bon Co., Inc. (1917) 222 N.Y. 22, 118 N.E. 205.

Liability of the *promoter* to third persons depends on several variables. It is sometimes said, too generally, that promoters, though they "may assume to act on behalf of the projected corporation" and not for themselves, are nonetheless "personally liable." See, King Features Syndicate v. Courrier (1950) 241 Iowa 870, 43 N.W.2d 718. This statement is much too broad. If the promoter signed a contract in his own name, or purchases and uses goods intended for the new corporation, the promoter of course must answer. But when he signs in the name of the prospective corporation—"Ruth Realty Corp., by Charles Baum"—and the third person *knows* that the company has *not* yet been formed, there is no promoter liability. See, Weiss v. Baum (1926) 218 App.Div. 83, 217 N.Y.S. 820.

To be contrasted is the case where the third person *does not know* that the purported principal does not exist.   For example, a lease may be signed—"Food Shops, Inc., by H. T. Hagan, Pres."—before the company, Food Shops, Inc., has been formed.   See, Hagan v. Asa G. Candler, Inc. (1939) 189 Ga. 250, 5 S.E.2d 739, 126 A.L.R. 108.   The agency rule is clear enough: If one contracts as agent, when in fact he has no principal, he will be personally liable.   See, § 57, supra. That is, he becomes liable as a party to the contract.   And the promoter rule is the same, the promoter in *Food Shops, Inc.,* supra, was held to be liable for unpaid rent.

In *Food Shops, Inc.,* supra, the agency rule would also give the third person, at his election, an action for breach of *warranty of authority.* No cases are at hand, however, giving a similar remedy against a promoter; evidently, since promoters are not "agents," it has been too difficult to imply a warranty.   Another variation would occur, as well, if the projected corporation, Food Shops, Inc., when fully incorporated, were to "adopt" the lease contract.   Following the agency precedent, § 57, supra, the promoter would be discharged, as upon a ratification, since the third person would then have gotten what he bargained for.   But, here too, there appear to be no comparable holdings as to promoters.

The result is that the well advised "promoter" should shape his contract carefully.   There are several available patterns.   See O'Rorke v. Geary

(1903) 207 Pa. 240, 56 A. 541. For example, he could simply take an offer to be transmitted later to the new corporation, when organized and ready for business. But, if the third person should insist on personal liability pending incorporation—as is usual—the promoter should also insist that, upon incorporation and "adoption," he will be released. A few states have legislation on the point, both to regulate the "adoption" procedure, and to relieve the promoter from further responsibility. See, Johnson & Carlson v. Montreuil's Estate (1939) 291 Mich. 582, 289 N. W. 262.

A distant analogy in the partnership field is the situation presented when one partner assigns his interest and withdraws from the firm. Although the new firm becomes liable to existing firm creditors, the withdrawing partner *also* continues liable. U.P.A. § 41. The means by which he may extricate himself are discussed in § 82, infra.

§ 60. Undisclosed Principal; Liabilities

The new factor here, is that the agent has acted *without* disclosing his agency. Or, more realistically, the principal has chosen to carry on his affairs through agents, but without disclosure to third persons. Of course the principal, on discovery, can be held liable for his agent's torts; this, under the usual respondeat superior doctrine. See, § 30 supra. Indeed, rarely if ever is it possible for the third person to know of the employment relation at the moment of injury.

Likewise, the undisclosed principal may be liable upon his agent's *contracts* with third persons. Even though the agent purported to act only for himself, if he had authority and acted on behalf of the undisclosed principal, the principal can be held liable as a party to the contract. From the viewpoint of two-party contract law this has been condemned as "wholly anomalous." See, Ames, Undisclosed Principal—His Rights and Liabilities (1909) 18 Yale L.J. 443. And, plainly, there would be no "meeting of the minds," so to speak, since, by hypothesis, neither third person nor undisclosed principal knew of the other's existence. But, this aside, the result squares fairly well with notions of enterprise liability; if the undisclosed principal must answer for his agent's torts, why not also for his agreements; contract law can bend that much, and has.

The parol evidence rule, of course, would be no bar to the third person's action. The undisclosed principal's name may simply be *added* to the agent's contract with the third person. Cf. § 57 supra. However, when the agent has acted contrary to instructions, there has been difficulty. In the leading case, Watteau v. Fenwick [1893] 1 Q.B. 346, one Humble was manager for Fenwick in charge of a "beerhouse called the Victoria Hotel," but Humble appeared to third persons as the *owner*—his name only appeared above the door. On these facts the court held that Fenwick must answer for the price of certain cigars purchased by Humble from Watteau, even though contrary to instructions.

The Restatement fully approves the *Watteau* result, but on uncertain grounds. A few American courts have made use of apparent authority to reach the same end: "those clothing an agent with *apparent authority*" are bound, as "to parties dealing on the faith of such authority." See, Hubbard v. Tenbrook (1889) 124 Pa. 291, 16 A. 817, 2 L.R.A. 823, 10 Am.St.Rep. 585. The Restatement, however, holds that apparent authority is not applicable. For example, in *Watteau,* since the transaction was conducted throughout as though Humble were the *owner*, the Restatement would say it is not possible to speak of *agency*, much less of *apparent authority.* Accordingly, resort is had to a *new term,* "inherent agency power," which the agent is declared to have. Restatement, Second, Agency § 195 and Comment (b).

Which prompts the question, what are the antecedents of "inherent agency power?" What are its limits? It sounds contrived, much like the "imputed negligence" device used by torts writers when seeking to explain why an employer

—not at *fault* in any way—should be held liable under respondeat superior for his servants' misdeeds. See, § 30 supra. Judge Wills in *Watteau,* though, rested his case on the rule in partnership with respect to *dormant,* i. e., undisclosed partners. That is, any partner, dormant or otherwise, has always been liable in *contract* or *tort* for the actions of his active co-partner in carrying on ordinary firm business. For today, see U.P.A. §§ 9 and 13.

Whether "inherent agency power" is meant to derive from this law is not clear. However, in the few cases since § 195 was written, there has been no disposition to give the term a wide meaning. Thus, in Senor v. Bangor Mills (C.A.Pa. 1954) 211 F.2d 685, which was a suit upon a contract for nylon yarn negotiated, in his own name, by a special agent, the court held the undisclosed principal was *not* liable. Without discussing "inherent agency power," Judge Hastie insisted that, the agent being without authority to buy on credit, there must be some showing that the undisclosed principal placed the agent in a position which might induce third persons to rely upon him "as a responsible proprietor." Essentially, an apparent authority approach.

For the sake of analysis, however, concede that the Restatement is right when it says that *apparent authority* cannot apply. Perhaps *Watteau* may be supported on other grounds. What, in fact, was Humble's *actual* authority? Plainly it was to do what any *manager* might do, hire and fire, purchase supplies, pay bills, and so on. That Humble was asked to do this in the guise of an apparent "owner," surely can make no difference; if anything, his actual authority was enhanced thereby. In this context, then, the instruction *not to buy* cigars, was merely an attempt to *limit* Humble's fairly broad actual authority. And, of course, the courts have uniformly refused to sanction secret limitations in these circumstances. See, § 50 supra.

As a matter of fact, this appears to have been the basis on which Wills, J., decided the case; "it is clear law," he said, "that no limitation of authority as between the dormant and active partner will avail the dormant partner as to things within the ordinary authority of a partner." It will be noted that no mention was made of "apparent authority."

§ 61. Undisclosed Principal; Rights

While an undisclosed principal may be held *liable*, as just noted, upon contracts negotiated for him by his agent, he also has the affirmative *rights* of a party. Restatement, Second, Agency § 302. Indeed, to be a useful device, the law could not well be otherwise, but there are limitations.

A typical question arises, however, when a large corporation has need to buy considerable property for corporate purposes, and, to be sure of "fair" prices, proposes to remain wholly undisclosed, while a broker carries on the negotiations. When there has been no "fraud"—as by denying that the corporation is in any way involved—most courts have sanctioned the practice. See, Standard Steel Car Co. v. Stamm (1904) 207 Pa. 419, 56 A. 954, where the court said there is "nothing dishonest in law or in morals" in such a practice. As a party, the corporation has the usual action for damages, or even for specific performance, in case of breach. At the other extreme, most courts would say that if the third party has once *refused* to deal with a person, that person may not later circumvent the refusal by assuming the role of an undisclosed principal. The right of a person to select those with whom he will contract still has that much vitality.

A closer case came before Cardozo, J., in Kelly Asphalt Block Co. v. Barber Asphalt Paving Co. (1914) 211 N.Y. 68, 105 N.E. 88, L.R.A.1915C, 256, which was a suit by undisclosed principal against third person for breach of warranty on a contract for the purchase of paving blocks. It appeared that plaintiff buyer *suspected* that defendant would not sell to him directly, since he was a competitor, but there had been no prior refusal. In holding for the undisclosed principal buyer, Judge Cardozo said: "We are asked to hold that a contract complete in form becomes a nullity in fact because of a secret belief in the mind of the undisclosed principal . . . We cannot go so far."

It would be a mistake to conclude, however, that the undisclosed principal must be guilty of something in the nature of fraud to be denied recovery. For example, in Birmingham Matinee Club v. McCarty (1907) 152 Ala. 571, 44 So. 642, 13 L.R.A.,N.S., 156, 15 Ann.Cas. 237, suit was brought by the seller, an undisclosed principal, to have specific performance of a land contract. But the court denied recovery; the third person had contracted for the *agent's warranty,* not that of an unknown principal. If this were not so, "the elements of the contract reasonably attributable to personal confidence and trust, including the financial responsibility of the agent, with whom he alone deals as principal, would be stricken of force . . ."

Another illustration is found in the set-off cases. A third person having purchased goods which had been put into the possession of an agent, may have expected that he could set off a debt owed to him by the agent, in case of need. And, if the owner of the goods were in fact wholly undisclosed, most courts would allow the set off. In Hogan v. Shorb (1840) 24 Wend. (N.Y.) 458, for example, the court said in support of its holding that: "In a commercial community no rule short of this will afford sufficient protection to purchasers." And see: Restatement, Second, Agency § 306(1); Foreign Trade Banking Corp. v. Gerseta Corporation (1923) 237 N.Y. 265, 142 N.E. 607, 31 A.L.R. 932.

Consider the opposite situation, that is, the undisclosed principal may wish to settle accounts with his agent before the third person has demanded payment. Or, a not infrequent case, the principal may have advanced money or credit to his agent, even before the deal is made with the third person. If none of this money reaches the third person, what are the undisclosed principal's rights? When the principal was in fact wholly undisclosed, most courts have given the principal a defense to the extent of his payments to the agent. See, Laing v. Butler (1885) 37 Hun (N. Y.) 144, affirmed 108 N.Y. 637, 15 N.E. 442. Thus, a rough sort of justice, if the third person is to have his set-off against the agent, as just noted, so too the undisclosed principal is protected in his dealings with the agent, prior to disclosure. Accord, Cal.Civ.Code § 2335.

The Restatement departs from this law, however, and insists that there be something in the nature of an estoppel. It is only when the undisclosed principal has "settled accounts with an agent reasonably relying upon conduct of the other party" indicating that the agent has already paid the third person, that the principal is to be protected. Restatement, Agency § 208. The Restatement, plainly, takes an essentially non-commercial position. Compare, Senor v. Bangor Mills (C.A.Pa.1954) 211 F.2d 685.

§ 62. Partially Disclosed Principal

The customary term, "partially disclosed," is a clumsy way of describing a situation in which the third person knows that he is dealing with an agent, but does not know the identity of the principal. What is written above concerning the *liabilities* of a wholly undisclosed principal, § 60, applies equally to a partially disclosed principal. Most of what is said as to *rights*, § 61, above, also will apply; certainly the partially disclosed principal, as a party, has the rights of any principal to enforce *authorized* contracts made on his behalf by the agent. Moreover, while a *wholly undisclosed* principal may not ratify an unauthorized contract, for the somewhat artificial reason, that, by hypothesis, it could not have been made in his name, it would seem that the *partially* disclosed principal may ratify. See, Restatement, Second, Agency § 85.

A variance occurs, also, in the set-off cases; since the third person is assumed to have known of the agency, he cannot in fairness be allowed to set off his claims against the agent individually, when sued by the principal. Nor may the partially disclosed principal safely settle accounts with his agent. Of course, if the partially disclosed principal could show that he had done so because he had been misled by the third person, he might claim an estoppel. But that would not depend on agency principles.

The matter most litigated in the *partially disclosed* situation concerns the liability of the agent to third persons. In the wholly undisclosed case, as in *Watteau*, supra, § 60, the agent, Humble, was the only person known to the plaintiff and would be fully responsible as a party to the contract. He could not well have been liable on an implied warranty of authority, since he did not purport to act as an agent.

Indeed, the early criticism of the case appears to have centered on the point. How could the undisclosed principal be liable as a contracting party, when his agent, Humble, also was answerable as a party? Ames saw no way to reach the principal, except through the agent's right of indemnity, which would be non-existent in *Watteau*, since Humble acted contrary to instructions. The law, however, has solved the problem by saying there are *two* contracts, subject to third party election. See, § 63 infra.

When the principal is *fully disclosed*, it is ordinarily assumed that any authorized contract

made with third persons will be binding *only* on
the principal. Of course, the agent may expressly make himself personally liable as well, or the
parol evidence rule may operate to that end. See,
§ 58, supra. But the "partially disclosed" case
has been treated differently, and the third person
may hold the agent liable as a party. The reason is simply one of fairness: "to permit an agent
to turn over to his customer an undisclosed, and,
to the latter, unknown principal, might have the
effect to deny to the customer the benefit of any
available or responsible means of remedy or relief founded upon the contract." See, Argersing-
er v. MacNaughton (1889) 114 N.Y. 535, 21 N.E.
1022, 11 Am.St.Rep. 687.

Many cases have had to do with whether the
agent has made an *adequate* disclosure. Thus, in
Ell Dee Clothing Co., Inc. v. Marsh (1928) 247
N.Y. 392, 160 N.E. 651, the agent, representing
"London Lloyds," wrote a temporary binder or
contract of insurance. In practice, the risk would
be submitted to Lloyds and one or more members
of that association, at their election, would sign
as underwriters, and only later would a definitive
policy be issued. The court held that the agent
was individually liable on the binder, a loss having been suffered meanwhile: "Not only were
his supposed principals unknown .   .   .   in
fact there were none." The case is an extreme

example, since probably no one expected the agent to act as an insurance company.

A more usual illustration is Saco Dairy Co. v. Norton (1944) 140 Me. 204, 35 A.2d 857, 150 A.L.R. 1299. The defendant there, one Norton, was manager of a summer hotel called Breakwater Court, and had purchased a season's dairy supplies from plaintiff for the hotel, the supplies being billed to Breakwater Court as they were delivered. Actually, the hotel was owned by and operated for Mrs. Norton, the defendant's mother, and this fact was urged as a defense. The court, however, held that Norton was individually liable; there had not been a sufficient, or any, disclosure of his principal.

Two collateral questions are raised. The first has to do with possible torts, the second with the Fictitious Name statutes. One would assume that if a guest were to have been injured negligently by some employee of the hotel that Mrs. Norton, as owner and proprietor, and not Norton, the manager, would be liable. See, § 30 supra. Of course, Mrs. Norton must answer for, after all, she received the gains, if any, from the enterprise. However, a few cases would hold the manager liable in this situation, upon a showing that the employee at fault supposed he was working for the manager. See, Cockran v. Rice (1910) 26 S.D. 393, 128 N.W. 583, Ann.Cas.1913 B, 570.

[*194*]

Mrs. Norton, it appeared, was not at any time registered as owner of Breakwater Court, as required by statute in Maine. These statutes, however, were designed as an aid to creditors in finding ultimate debtors; there has been no disposition to say that registration gives *constructive* notice. See, Hunter v. Croysdill (1959) 169 Cal. App.2d 307, 337 P.2d 174. Thus, even if Breakwater Court had been duly registered, that would probably not have been a sufficient disclosure to relieve Norton of liability.

§ 63. The Election Doctrine

It will contribute to an understanding of the subject if it is looked at first from the third person's viewpoint. As discussed above, the third person certainly has rights on the contract he negotiated with the agent. Moreover, it is clear that—upon discovery—he may also hold the undisclosed, or partially disclosed, principal as a party to the contract. See, §§ 60, 62 supra. The election doctrine, developed by the courts, is based on the simple fact that—to use a common illustration—the third person sold but one bill of goods; that he *bargained* for but *one* buyer; and that, in simple fairness, he should have but one action, either that against the agent or the action against the principal—which comes to him more or less as a "windfall"—*but not both*. Hence the courts have done the logical thing and required an election. See, Georgi v. Texas Co. (1919) 225 N.Y. 410, 122 N.E. 238, so holding.

The result, of course, is truly an anomaly, *contract* rights against either of *two* promissors, not jointly, but *in the alternative*. Being an anomaly is not fatal. It will be recalled that Holmes regarded respondeat superior itself as an anomaly—a person not at fault should not be required to answer for another's wrongdoing— and yet it has survived rather nicely. See, § 30, supra. The real question is whether "election" in the agency field is at once fair, and serves a useful purpose. Much of the criticism of the doctrine—and there has been much—appears to stem from dislike of the common law rules concerning election of *remedies*, and, in the joint obligation area, of *parties*. But neither comparison is in point; the choice is plainly not between *remedies* and, since agent and principal are usually *not* co-partners, the rules concerning joint *parties* do not apply. See, U.P.A. § 13.

As a matter of perspective, there is virtually no law in the respondeat superior field requiring election. The injured third person may sue either the truck driver, for example, or his employer, or both together. See, Bradley v. Rosenthal (1908) 154 Cal. 420, 97 P. 875. That is, the action is "joint and several," and may be pursued until full *satisfaction* is received. Pennsylvania is in a small minority, and applies the same rule in the undisclosed principal *contract* area. See, Beymer v. Bonsall (1875) 79 Pa. 298. The prevailing view, however, as just noted, is to require an *election*; certainly there is no social urgency, as in the tort case, to require *satisfaction* in order to protect an innocent victim.

It does not follow, of course, that either agent or principal can *require* an election at any time. That might be useful, since it would allow the parties to settle their accounts earlier—in order to go about their other business—but there is no support for the practice. When the third person takes *judgment*, however, against either agent or principal, nearly everyone agrees that he has made a binding election. See, Restatement, Second, Agency §§ 210 and 337. In fact, it is well established that if both principal and agent are sued at one time, either may *require* election *before* judgment. Indeed, if they fail to do so, the point may be waived. See, Klinger v. Modesto Fruit Co., Inc. (1930) 107 Cal.App. 97, 290 P. 127.

There, of course, can be no "election" in any case until the essential facts are known. The situation before the court in North Carolina Lumber Co. v. Spear Motor Co. (1926) 192 N.C. 377, 135 S.E. 115, will illustrate. That was an action for the price of lumber sold by plaintiff to a contractor for use in remodeling a building owned by

Spear Motor, the contractor's agency being disputed. Owner and contractor were both sued in one action, and, when the contractor defaulted, early in the proceedings, plaintiff took judgment. Spear thereupon contended that this was an election, but the court held to the contrary, there could be no true choice so long as the agency was in dispute.

It may happen that the third person will have taken judgment against the wrong party, that is, against one unable to pay. As a matter of fairness, this can be seen as an ordinary business risk; the third person was not hurried in making his election. If, perchance, his unpaid judgment was against the agent, however, he also may claim rights by way of exoneration against the principal. See, Evans, Coleman & Evans, Ltd. v. Pistorino (1923) 245 Mass. 94, 139 N.E. 848. The court, there, was clear that Evans' judgment against the broker-buyer was an "election," but held that if the broker were to pay the judgment he would be entitled to indemnity from the defendants, his principals. That being true, it was an easy step, in equity, to order the defendants to pay plaintiff-seller the amount directly, in exoneration.

Opinions differ as to the fairness and utility of election in the agency field. See, Merrill, Election Between Agent and Undisclosed Principal (1933)

12 Neb.L.Bul. 100. In the writer's opinion, election is not only fairly well understood, but serves a useful commercial purpose. In fact, a case can be made to require election *prior* to judgment, as when, with full knowledge, burdensome legal proceedings are *started* against either party. See: Barrell v. Newby (1904) 62 C.C.A. 382, 127 F. 656; Comment (1929) 39 Yale L.J. 265.

§ 64. Sundry Statutes

The law of agency, for the most part, has been developed by the courts, case by case. The same may be said of partnership, except that in 1914 the Commissioners on Uniform State Laws proposed a Uniform Partnership Act (Appendix A hereto) and, later, a Uniform Limited Partnership Act (Appendix B hereto). Both statutes, designed in the main to codify prior case law, have been widely adopted. Aside from this, there are a number of short statutes bearing on Agency-Partnership, particularly in the undisclosed principal area, which it will be convenient to discuss now, with cross references to the sections in the text to which they are of most significance.

(a) *Fictitious Name Statutes.* Most states have statutes requiring persons doing business in the state under a trade or fictitious name to file the names and addresses of the persons so doing. These statutes have wide application; it is necessary, for example, to file the names of any partner, when the firm name does not disclose their membership and, of course, the names of dormant or silent partners.

The statutes differ mainly in the sanction to be imposed. A few states levy a fine for non-compliance, but most simply provide that no action may be maintained in any state court on any contract made in the fictitious name, "until the certificate has been filed": Cal.Civ.Code § 2468. However, it is a comparatively simple matter to file at any time, and thus comply with the statute. There are similar statutes requiring foreign corporations to register before doing business in the state.

The fictitious name statutes were rather plainly designed as an *aid to creditors*. A third person who may have negotiated with an agent representing persons unknown, using a trade name—Ajax Trading Co., for example—has only to consult the record. There is no question that a contract for the sale of goods, signed only in the trade name by an authorized agent, would be binding on the persons registered.

So, likewise, in the case of a partnership. At common law, under the aggregate theory, suit would be brought against all partners, "trading under the firm name and style of Ajax Trading Co." Since contract claims are joint, U.P.A. § 13, it was necessary to name each partner. Often it was uncertain who the partners were, which caused procedural delays. The fictitious name statutes are an aid; a better solution is to allow suit against the firm as an entity. See, § 78 infra.

Whether filing will relieve an agent from personal liability, however, is a question. To illustrate, consider the situation in Saco Dairy Co. v. Norton (1944) 140 Me. 204, 35 A.2d 857, 150 A.L.R. 1299. The action was for dairy products sold to Breakwater Court, a summer hotel, through Norton, who acted as manager for the owner, Mrs. Norton, his mother. Norton was held personally liable; there had been no sufficient disclosure the court said. See, § 62, supra.

As it happened, Mrs. Norton had not registered under the Maine statute, but, even if she had filed as owner, the decision should have been the same. That is, the fictitious name statutes were not designed to give *constructive* notice. See, Hunter v. Croysdill (1959) 169 Cal.App.2d 307, 337 P.2d 174. Hence, Norton would still not have made an adequate disclosure of his principal.

(b) *Statute of Frauds.* A long-standing problem has been the sufficiency of the memorandum either in the case of a sale of goods or of securities. It was Williston's view that the memorandum must constitute a contract, binding on someone, to satisfy the statute. For illustration, see Higgins v. Senior, discussed supra, § 58. The opposing view is that it is enough if the memorandum shows that a contract has been made *by someone* for the sale of specified goods or securities, at a stated price. The reasoning seems to be that since parol evidence is needed to show *delivery* of a contract—which is true—it follows that the memorandum itself need not contain the whole agreement, an obvious *non sequitur*.

In the case of Dodge v. Blood (1941) 299 Mich. 364, 300 N.W. 121, which was an action for specific performance, First of Michigan Corporation, a securities dealer, had sold certain shares of stock to plaintiff at a stated price. The confirmation slip, signed by First of Michigan, recited, however, that the sale had been made "as agents for an undisclosed principal." With the issue so presented, the court engaged in a long discussion to say that the confirmation slip was an adequate memorandum, even if no one was bound by it. However, at the end of the opinion, it added that First of Michigan "probably is bound" anyway. See, § 62, supra.

It is beyond the scope of this writing to discuss the Statute of Frauds as such. However, it may be noted that the Code has taken the less strict view; it is enough if there is "some writing" signed by or on behalf of the party "to indicate that a contract has been made for sale of a stated quantity of described securities at a defined or stated price . . . " U.C.C. § 8–319 (a). As in Dodge v. Blood, supra, this would seem to leave the agency question untouched.

(c) *Election.* The New York legislature recently added two clauses to its statutes specifying when a judgment, or the maintenance of an action, "shall *not* be deemed an election." (Emphasis added.) The first applies to joint actions, when "causes of action exist against several persons." Civ.Pr.Law and Rules, § 3002(a). This reads plainly on the respondeat superior situation and makes it clear for New York that the tort claimant is not to be defeated by taking judgment against either the negligent agent or his employer. As such the statute merely confirms the general law that the action is joint and several.

It was evidently intended, however, to apply also to the joint *contract* action. And, in particular, to the partnership situation, as presented in Crehan v. Megargel (1922) 234 N.Y. 67, 136 N.E. 296. Plaintiffs there had first brought suit in Massachusetts for breach of contract and taken judgment against several partners. This was urged as an "election," barring suit against the defendant partners in New York. However, the court pointed out that defendants could not have been served in the Massachusetts action, under the circumstances, and held that, there could be no true election. See, § 27 supra.

The new statute makes the point abundantly clear. It also effectively abrogates the common law rule of election of *parties* as it applied to joint obligations generally. Like the common law rule concerning the election of *remedies,* it is hard to find a modern reason to support election in either area. The view that a plaintiff may not be allowed "to trifle with the courts" is not very substantial. See remarks of Clark, J., in Ore Steamship Corp. v. Hassel (C.C.A.1943) 137 F.2d 326.

The second clause, § 3002(b), reads upon a situation where a person has "causes of action .   .   . against an agent and his undisclosed principal." In such case, contrary to New York and general case law, it is stated that judgment, if unsatisfied, shall *not* be "deemed an election of remedies." Plainly, the draftsman was confused; third persons do not have two causes of action, against the agent *and* the undisclosed principal. As most, he has but *one* action, against one party or the other, in the alternative. See, Georgi v. Texas Co., noted supra § 63. Secondly, the issue obviously does not concern an election of "remedies," as the statute has it, but of *parties,* a very different matter. Nonetheless, the clause is on the books, and, however muddle headed, must be reckoned with.

(d) *Written Authority.* As discussed above, § 52, several states have short statutes requiring that an agent's authority be in writing when the contract to be negotiated must itself be in writing to be effective. The California provision is Cal. Civ.Code § 2309. This is the modern counterpart of the equal dignity rule at common law, which required that the agent's authority be in writing and under seal. The present question is whether such statutes apply without qualification in the undisclosed principal situation.

In Marr v. Postal Union Life Ins. Co. (1940) 40 Cal.App.2d 673, 105 P.2d 649, the court refused to apply § 2309: "Respondents believed, as they had a right to believe . . . that they were dealing with the Underwriters as principal. Consequently respondents could not be expected to inquire as to the existence of written authority to the agent when they had no knowledge that the Underwriters [were] anything but the principal." Cf. Wloczewski v. Kozlowski (1947) 395 Ill. 402, 70 N.E.2d 560.

PART III

FORMS OF ENTERPRISE

§ 65. Scope

The circumstance that two or more persons may join forces to conduct an enterprise, whether by themselves or through agents, is not new. A great many forms and terms of association have been developed. Moreover, the purposes for which associations may be formed are many, covering as they do almost the whole range of profit and non-profit activities in a free society. It is proposed in the next several sections to examine some of these forms, with particular regard to the liabilities of associates. The concluding sections have mainly to do with claims to assets, claims of creditors and associates, upon dissolution of the enterprise.

§ 66. Partnership

One of the oldest forms of business organization, certainly the one in widest use today—the corporation excepted—is the partnership. Indeed, until the middle of last century incorporation was hard to come by, since special legislation was required. In spite of its long use, however, there has always been litigation as to when a partnership, in one of its forms, may be said to exist.

This must be decided, of course, as a necessary first step in determining the liability of the associates.

Prior to the adoption of U.P.A. § 6, many cases were consumed by a search for the "intent" of the parties. Some cases even now are bothered by the question. Under the Act, however, it is clear that no specific intent to form a partnership, as such, is needed; what is required is a showing that the parties *voluntarily* associated together, as the statute reads, "to carry on as co-owners a business for profit." See, § 7 above. That the association be voluntary is, of course, a necessary safeguard to the members, since their relationship is a personal one. See, § 19, supra.

The present test, thus, is largely objective in nature. Even so, each word and phrase of the definition has caused some question. The phrase "carry on" is evidently intended to say that the Act applies to the ordinary business or commercial enterprise as a going concern. It does not include the "joint venture," which often is for but a single transaction. See, § 68 infra. Whether the parties are associated to "carry on" a business, may also be determined by objective evidence.

The next phrase, "as co-owners," has caused some trouble. A few courts have failed to make allowance for the practice by which one associate gives the firm the *use* of property, but not the *ownership*, and have found no partnership to exist. It was well established last century, however, that it is only necessary to show a community of interest in, or a co-ownership of, the *business* and a right to share in its profits. See, Champion v. Bostwick (1837) 18 Wend. 175, 31 Am.Dec. 376, and infra § 79. It would seem that U.P.A. § 6 was intended to codify this law.

To reverse the facts, there have been cases in which the parties are *co-owners* of a given property and yet have been held *not* to be partners. An example is where property, say, a business publication, has been willed to several persons as joint tenants. Or, a more typical example, the co-ownership of a car. On these facts alone there would be no partnership, nor even a joint venture. This for the reason that there would be no *association* in either a business or a venture for profit. Co-ownership alone is not enough. See, U.P.A. § 7(2).

The last phrase, that the association be one "for profit," is the essence of the thing. See, § 33 supra. Profit, also, may be determined by objective proof. Usually the parties stipulate for an agreed share of any profits, but if they should not do so, the Act provides that they shall share *equally* "in the profits and surplus remaining after all liabilities" have been "satisfied." See, U.P.A. § 18 (a). The question whether profits are really "profits," or a disguised payment of rent, interest, wages and so on, will be explored in § 72, infra.

§ 67. Background

The present definition of partnership, U.P.A. § 6, conceals a long course of prior litigation. Late in the 18th century two ship agents in different cities were held to be liable as partners, since they had agreed to share profits at fixed times. Waugh v. Carver (1793) 2 H.Bl. 235. This upon the principle that "he who takes a moiety of all the profits indefinitely shall, by operation of law, be made liable to losses . . . ." Whether the two ship agents were actually partners later became immaterial; it was held that in any case persons so situated should be partners as to third persons.

In England the case of Cox v. Hickman (1860) 8 H.L.Cas. 268, 11 Eng.Rept. 431, was the turning point. It broke away dramatically from the generality that profit sharing, alone, is a *conclusive* test of partnership. See, Eastman v. Clark (1872) 53 N.H. 276, 16 Am.Rep. 192, for a good account. For at least a century courts in this country have reiterated the point, over and over again. Nevertheless, as discussed above, though not *conclusive*, an agreement to share profits continues to be *essential*. Indeed, this factor in the partnership cases offers strong support for the point that respondeat superior itself ordinarily rests on the profit-taking factor, rather than on "control", or the hypothetical "right to control." See, § 33 supra.

The notion that persons who are not partners as to each other may be partners as to third persons is met head-on by the Uniform Act. It provides that, except for estoppel situations, "persons who are not partners as to each other are not partners as to third persons." See, U.P.A. § 7(1). The many situations where a person has been held out to be a partner, creating a so-called partnership by estoppel, are provided for in U.P.A. § 16. And, see infra, § 81.

Finally, there remains a trace, at least, of Waugh v. Carver, supra, in U.P.A. § 7(4). There it is provided that "receipt by a person of a share of the profits of a business is prima facie evidence that he is a partner in the business." Of course, prima facie evidence is really a far cry from *conclusive* proof. The sharing of *gross returns*, as distinguished from *profits,* is of little probative value to establish partnership, U.P.A. § 7(3).

§ 68. Joint Venture

A joint venture (or *ad*venture) is said to be mainly distinguishable from partnership by the fact that, ordinarily, it is for but a single transaction. See generally, State, etc. v. Bland (1946) 355 Mo. 706, 197 S.W.2d 669, 168 A.L.R. 929. Often it may be for several related transactions, which is much the same thing. In any case, the distinction is that the associates do not engage to "carry on" a business, as partnership is defined by the Uniform Act. Cf. § 66, supra. Thus, the joint venture, a type of partnership, may be defined as an association of two or more persons to carry *out* one or a few transactions for profit, or for commercial gain or benefit.

The additional purpose, "for commercial gain or benefit," also represents a departure from the strict definition of partnership. See, U.P.A. § 6. In effect, it defines a partnership category intermediate to that of the Uniform Act, which must be for "profit," and joint *enterprise,* where the association is often one for purely social purposes. See, § 69, infra. It should be noted, however, that this line between joint venture and joint enterprise has not always been drawn in the decisions; at times, in fact, the two terms appear to be used interchangeably.

An example of a joint venture "for commercial gain or benefit," is Judge v. Wallen (1915) 98 Neb. 154, 152 N.W. 318. It appeared there that two salesmen, representing different employers, had agreed to use one car when covering their territories, and to share expenses. The relationship plainly was not for "profit," in the usual sense, nor was it for a social lark. The Nebraska court (though it called the relationship a "joint enterprise"), quite properly held that *each* salesman was liable to a third person injured by the negligence of the salesman who was driving at the time and in the scope of the venture. That result, of course, could be reached easily on partnership principles. See, § 33, supra.

Another typical illustration of "joint venture" occurs when one person, having land and money, associates with a contractor, having construction skills, to build one or more houses for sale, the "profit" or "gains," if any, to be divided equally. The cases are quite uniform, in this situation, that *either* associate may be held liable to third persons in case of injury caused by the negligence of one associate or his employees. See, Keiswetter v. Rubenstein (1926) 235 Mich. 36, 209 N.W. 154, 48 A.L.R. 1049, so holding.

Likewise, each associate could be held liable upon a contract negotiated by one in the scope of the venture. In fact, the *Keiswetter* court went on to say: "While under the present state of the law courts do not treat a joint venture as in all respects identical with a partnership, the contractual relations of the parties and nature of their association are so similar and closely akin to a partnership that it is commonly held that their rights and liabilities are to be tested by the same rules that govern partnerships."

It is true, moreover, that much partnership law will apply equally to the joint venture; it also is a fiduciary relationship, each associate is in some sense an agent of the others, and so on. Indeed, there is some opinion that the joint venture, as a type of partnership, need not be classified separately. See, Mechem, The Law of Joint Adventures (1931) 15 Minn.L.Rev. 644. However, the cautious view is that there are, or may come to be, several variances, between the joint venture partnership, and the partnership governed by the Uniform Act (Appendix A hereto).

In recent years there has been wide use of "joint venture" between corporations. An oil company, say, may form a venture with an exploration company; a chemical company may set up a venture with a construction company to test a new process; and so on. There has been little litigation; and the early question whether a corporation may be a member of such a venture is now fairly well settled in the affirmative. In fact, the associates now often form a new corporation to handle the venture, each associate taking its proportionate number of the shares, thus avoiding many partnership questions.

§ 69. Joint Enterprise

Unlike joint venture, the term "joint enterprise" is of fairly recent origin. Joint adventure, in fact, was in use in early sailing ship days, when the venture may have consisted of a joint interest in a ship's cargo—wine, flour or other goods—which, hopefully, would be sold at the end of the voyage for a gain or profit. See, Hourquebie v. Girard (C.C.Pa.1808) 12 Fed.Cas. 593, No. 6,732. In 1815, Lord Eldon said that "a joint adventure . . . [is] as proper a partnership as any other," and held that one adventurer would be liable upon instruments signed by the other within the scope of the venture. See, Davison v. Robertson (1815) 3 Dow 218, 229.

"Joint enterprise," on the other hand, seems to have come in with the motor vehicle: "While it is by no means impossible that the principle may be applied to other activities, the very great majority of the decisions applying it have involved the use of motor vehicles." Restatement, Second, Torts § 491, comment (b). This has meant, for example, that if one member, while driving on a *joint enterprise*, should negligently injure a third person, each member of the enterprise must answer. And, conversely, if suit is brought *against* the third person for *his* negligence, plaintiff member may be charged with any contributory negligence of the member driver, insofar as that is still a defense. See: Restatement, Second, Torts § 491(1).

The critical question, therefore, concerns how "joint enterprise," is to be defined. In a leading case, the court said there were four elements: (1) a contract, (2) a common purpose, (3) a community of interest, and (4) an equal right to a voice, accompanied by an equal right of control. See Carboneau v. Peterson (1939) 1 Wash.2d 347, 374, 95 P.2d 1043, 1054. The Restatement agrees, but quietly inserts the word "pecuniary" before the word "interest" in paragraph (3). See, Restatement, Second, Torts § 491, comment (c). The word *pecuniary* did not appear in the first edition, nor has it been a *requirement* in a great many cases.

Nevertheless, there has been a steady tendency in recent years to require a pecuniary purpose. Thus, when one of four Hooten brothers, returning from a deer hunting trip, negligently collided with a car in which plaintiff was riding, the court refused recovery against any but the driver: "[T]he concept of joint adventure or enterprise should be confined to business enterprises . . . ." Edlebeck v. Hooten (1963) 20 Wis.2d 83, 121 N.W.2d 240. And see, Clemens v. O'Brien (1964) 85 N.J.Super. 404, 204 A.2d 895.

Quite evidently the Wisconsin court does not distinguish between joint enterprise and joint venture. See, § 68, supra. This raises a basic question, will "joint enterprise" as above defined, survive at all. Perhaps it should simply be merged with "joint venture," where the object has always been one of "profit" or "commercial gain." The ultimate test is one of social policy, to be determined as cases arise over the years. See, Decline & Fall of Joint Enterprise (1965) 19 Rutgers L. Rev. 532.

It may well be there is a place for a *non-pecuniary* "joint enterprise," as a separate concept. By stressing point (4) in the *Carboneau* definition, supra, a good theoretical basis can be provided. That is, if it can be shown clearly that the associates not only have a common purpose, but that each member has an "equal right of control" over the enterprise, it is not too difficult to find each member liable for losses. It will be recalled that one rationalization for respondeat superior—a closely related liability equation—is that the master has "control" over the actions of his servant. See, § 30, supra. That doctrine has long applied in both pecuniary and non-pecuniary settings.

One difficulty seems to have been that, in many cases, the *control* factor has not been fully developed in evidence. If in fact it existed! When the association is for "profit," as in a partnership, mutual control of the business follows as an incident of the relationship. See, U.P.A. § 18(e).

The same may be said of the "joint venture" for commercial gain or benefit. But in the "joint enterprise," as defined in *Carboneau,* supra, mutual control must be proven. It is the gist of the concept. See, Poutre v. Saunders (1943) 19 Wash.2d 561, 143 P.2d 554; Murphy v. Keating (1939) 204 Minn. 269, 283 N.W. 389.

§ 70. Rights Between Associates

The rights of a partner to bring an action for an accounting to redress losses, that is, to have contribution, was discussed, supra, § 24. By analogy this law would seem also to apply to the *joint venture,* since it too is a form of partnership. But the point is not clear and this may be another difference between partnership and joint venture. As for the non-pecuniary *joint enterprise,* the Restatement has a simple provision allowing an injured associate to recover directly, and in full, from the associate at fault. See, Restatement, Second, Torts § 491(2).

For the sake of concreteness, consider the facts before the court in Eagle Star Ins. Co. v. Bean (C.C.A.Wash.1943) 134 F.2d 755. That was an action by one associate, O'Leary, or his insurance carrier, against the other associate, Olympia Supply Company, a partnership, for the loss of a mill, caused by the negligence of one Abe Bean, an employee of Olympia. The agreement was that the mill would be purchased by O'Leary, which was done, that Olympia would dismantle the mill, and that the gain or profit, if any, to be derived from the sale of salvaged materials was to be divided between the two associates.

Plainly this was a joint venture, as the lower court held. See, § 68, supra. The point to the contrary, that O'Leary did not have *equal* control, was easily answered by saying that the parties had delegated the dismantling operation to Olympia Supply at the outset. Nor was it material that the associates did not share *equally* in profits. Whether plaintiff should have been required to ask for an *accounting,* however, does not appear to have been considered. On these facts, the lower court denied all recovery, except against the said Abe Bean, and its holding was affirmed on appeal.

The crux of the case, as it was argued, centered on who should be responsible for Abe Bean's negligence. It was urged that his negligence should be *imputed* to Olympia Supply, his employer, and that under the torts rule, when suit is between associates, the negligence of one associate will not be *imputed* to the other. Thus, judgment should be for O'Leary. The trial court, however, held for Olympia, and its holding was affirmed, the court on appeal saying that Abe Bean's negligence should be "imputed to neither" O'Leary nor Olympia.

It is submitted that the decision in this case was right; the court saw clearly enough that it was dealing with a *joint venture,* and that the *whole* loss should not be put on one member. Had Abe Bean injured a third person, however, both associates could have been held liable. See, *Keiswetter,* supra, § 68. Whether Abe's negligence was to be charged to each associate, or to neither, as the court found, would make little difference. In either case, the most that O'Leary should ultimately recover for the loss of his mill would be *contribution,* not indemnity. See, § 24, supra. Associates in a joint venture, like co-partners generally, *share* losses.

As noted above, the torts rule in the case of the *joint enterprise* is to the contrary; that is, an associate may have full recovery. See, Restatement, Second, Torts § 491(2). Two points may be made. First, the measure of care owed by one associate to another is surely less than that to third persons. They do not, ordinarily, engage that each will be infallible. This is clearly the rule as between co-partners (and probably coventurers) as to business or pecuniary risks: "There is no general principle of partnership which renders one partner liable to his copartners for his honest mistakes." Per Rugg, C. J., in Hurter v. Larrabee (1916) 224 Mass. 218, 112 N.E. 613.

Secondly, the rule of § 491(2) ignores the *joint enterprise* entirely, and sees only the tort. This, it is submitted, is a mistake. Moreover, that rule has not always been followed in the courts. See, Johnson v. Fischer (1940) 292 Mich. 78, 290 N.W. 334.

§ 71. Problems of Proof

The third person encounters some interesting points when he seeks to show that the defendant he has named is liable as a member of a partnership. Or, of a joint venture. Of course, if plaintiff can show that the defendant *shared* in the profits of the business, he has a prima facie case, a good start. See, § 67 supra. Presumably, the partnership rule, that receipt of a share of the profits will be prima facie evidence, applies equally to the joint venture.

If, perchance, the parties-defendant have put the terms of their association in writing, the plaintiff's task is greatly simplified. Even so, as pointed out supra, § 46, the *contract* is not the *partnership*. Indeed, the partnership may have changed course several times over the years. As a practical matter this means that evidence may be needed to establish the scope of the business at the time when plaintiff's cause of action arose; the parol evidence rule does not apply here.

With a written contract of association in evidence, the court's task is primarily to see whether the terms of the writing satisfy U.P.A. § 6, as discussed above. Not infrequently, however, the parties will have specified that "this agreement is not intended to constitute a partnership." Or, occasionally, a reverse statement! See: Fenwick v. Commission (1945) 133 N.J.L. 295, 44 A.2d 172. In either case, most courts pay little attention to such declarations; the controlling question is whether, in fact, the parties associated together to carry on a business as co-owners for profit. Or, to carry out a venture.

When there is no contract, and partnership is disputed, the third person has a more difficult time. He may have to make out his case largely by circumstantial evidence. However, if he can establish as a framework that the named defendants were in fact associated together for some purposes, this may permit the introduction of letters or memoranda as original evidence binding on each associate to show that in fact the purpose was to carry on a business for profit. This, on simple agency principles.

The conspiracy cases afford a carefully worked out precedent. For example, in *Gypsum,* it was established that the defendants had met together to sign common patent license agreements, with provisions for price fixing, a seemingly innocent activity. See, United States v. U. S. Gypsum Co. (1947) 333 U.S. 364, 68 S.Ct. 1525. The Government, however, was then able to introduce various writings, binding on the writer as an admission, and on the associates as original evidence, to show that there was a plan or scheme "to fix prices and stabilize the industry." This was held to show a violation of the Sherman Act.

From time to time, when an effort at incorporation falls short, it has been sought to hold the promoters individually liable as partners. Supposedly, their natural state! If the corporation has achieved de facto status—a matter not to be treated here—most courts hold that the promoters incur no personal liability to third persons. See, Tisch Auto Supply Co. v. Nelson (1923) 222 Mich. 196, 192 N.W. 600. If de facto status has *not* been achieved, however, it by no means follows that the organizers are liable as partners. Again that depends on a showing that they have associated together as stated in U.P.A. § 6. See Baker v. Bates-Street Shirt Co. (C.A.A.Me.1925) 6 F.2d 854.

§ 72. Profits as Profits

Last century a prolific source of partnership litigation concerned the question, as it was put, whether profits were really shared as "profits." Lenders, for example, contended that they had only contracted for a share to gain a flexible interest return. Landlords urged that any share in profits they may have received was merely as rental. Necessarily, there was a wide variety of holdings, for the courts saw little alternative but to seek out an illusory "intent of the parties" as a basis of decision.

The Uniform Act did not take a position either pro or con in the various situations. Rather, it got at the matter indirectly by providing that no "inference" of partnership "shall be drawn" from the receipt of profits, when they are received in any of five listed situations. See, § 7(4)(a)(b) (c)(d) and (e). Actually, of course, the Act is thus weighted heavily in favor of the non-entrepreneur. No-inference, is scarcely a presumption, but it has had something of the same effect.

The celebrated case of Cox v. Hickman, noted supra § 67, will illustrate. In that case a debtor, B. Smith & Son, being in financial difficulty, entered into a deal of arrangement with creditors, some 101 in number, including the defendant Cox, by which the Stanton Iron Works was assigned to trustees, to be operated by them, the net income to be paid to the creditors until their claims were satisfied. As noted above, the court held that the defendant creditors were not partners, even though they not only received *profits* but had been given very large powers of *control*.

The court's opinion is not very helpful, since it said "the real ground" on which to put partnership liability is mutual agency. As pointed out in Meehan v. Valentine (1892) 145 U.S. 611, 12 S.Ct. 972, 36 L.Ed. 835, however, agency is an *incident* of partnership, not a *test*. In retrospect, however, what the court appears to have been reaching for was a means by which to differentiate the entrepreneur (or enterpriser), on the one hand, from mere creditors, on the other. Such a result is in keeping with our law, which has selected out the enterpriser as the one most able to carry risks of doing business.

In general, the American courts reached the *Hickman* result, but there were holdings to the contrary. See, Purvis v. Butler (1891) 87 Mich. 248, 49 N.W. 564. The Uniform Act resolved the conflict by saying that when *profits* are received as "a debt by installments or otherwise," there is no prima facie "inference" of partnership. After all, a random group of creditors is not likely to be the best economic risk bearer. If they assert some control, it is at most transitory and secondary.

The lender who took a portion of the profits, as *interest,* was also generally successful. Such was the case of Meehan v. Valentine, noted above. Likewise the landlord, in most cases, was allowed to take rent, as a percentage of profits, without becoming liable as a partner. So with the agent whose salary consisted of a share in profits, or the seller of a business and its good will, when the price was determined by a share of future profits. These results, too, are favored by the Uniform Act, § 7(4)(a)(b) & (c).

In a leading case under the Act, the New York court also decided for the lender. See, Martin v. Peyton (1927) 246 N.Y. 213, 158 N.E. 77. There the defendants had loaned some $2,500,000 worth of liquid securities to the firm of K. N. & K., with very large powers of control reserved, mainly by way of veto, and were to receive 40 percent of any profits until the securities were returned. Action was by creditors of K. N. & K. The court found, easily enough, that a loan of securities is a "loan" within U.P.A. § 7(4)(d). Its holding that the lenders were not partners was at least consistent with the *no-inference* aspect of the section, but that was not discussed.

The result, of course, is to put lenders in much the same situation as limited partners. See, § 74, infra, where the point is discussed. The issue centers on the matter of control. In *Martin* there was no evidence of what actual control was exercised by the lenders, the court deciding the case on the papers in evidence, which were carefully drawn to disavow partnership. Plainly, however, a point may be reached when the lender's control transcends what is necessary as *security* and becomes a part of *operations*.

The widespread and often informal practice of operating a farm "on shares" affords a comparison. It resulted in considerable litigation, at common law, both by contract and tort creditors of the farmer. Most courts, however, ultimately found for the landowner; he and the share cropper were not partners. This result, moreover, is greatly supported by U.P.A. § 7(3), which says that a "sharing of gross returns does not of itself establish a partnership . . ." After all a share in crops, i. e., in gross returns, is very different from a share of "profits"; they may not even be ascertained until an account is taken of the "losses" involved.

§ 73. Associations Not for Profit

There seem always to have been a very large number of voluntary, non-profit, unincorporated associations in social and business life. They include clubs, exchanges, pools, committees, circles, lodges, parties, syndicates, unions, churches, foundations, leagues, societies and so on. Some are formed to attain special advantages for their members; others to advance the welfare of mankind. Not being organized to carry on a business for profit, they must depend on law apart from that of partnership. In any case, before going on to special forms of partnership, it will be useful to consider here what makes for membership liability in a non-partnership association.

The law in this area is distinguished by its uncertainties. A typical association is the Oregon Telephone Federation. The association was established by vote at a mass meeting of telephone users with a purpose to engage a rate expert to appear before the Public Service Commission to gain a reduction in rates. See, Cousin v. Taylor (1925) 115 Ore. 472, 239 P. 96, 41 A.L.R. 750. Whether rates were actually reduced or not, the rate expert was not paid for his efforts, and brought suit against the agents with whom he had dealt and also against some fourteen members of the Federation at large.

Most courts would agree with the holding that the defendant agents *were* liable. Since the Federation, at common law, was not a legal entity, and could not be held liable as such, the court said that the agent's liability followed from the agency rule that when an agent acts for a non-existent principal, the agent himself becomes liable. Another ground would be that the agents had not disclosed who their principals were. See, § 62, supra. Somewhat inconsistently, however, the court held also that it was error to dismiss as to the fourteen defendant members. That is, the court said the contract with plaintiff would be binding "upon them as principals."

The basis of the member's liability presents a problem. Presumably, each defendant member in

Cousin voted *for* the action taken, but was that essential? It would seem so. There are cases, however, involving better established associations, with a charter and by-laws, for example, in which a non-assenting member has been held liable. It may be possible there, as in the case of a lodge, to show that the action taken was within the stated purposes of the association. See, Security-First Nat. Bank v. Cooper (1944) 62 Cal. App.2d 653, 145 P.2d 722. In *Cousin*, however, only those who voted "yes" might be held as joint principals.

It should make little difference whether the question is raised directly or in an agent's action for indemnity. However, in a leading case involving a club, the Cercle Francais, the court refused recovery to an agent trustee who asked for indemnity. See, Wise v. Perpetual Trustee Co., (1903) A.C. 139, 149, 150, in which Lord Lindley said, "Clubs are associations of a peculiar nature. They are not partnerships . . . " Continuing, "the feature which distinguishes them from other societies is that no member as such becomes liable" to any charge, except to pay his dues. And, the "trustees of a club are the last persons" to assert a contrary view.

Thus, it would seem, clubs are a separate category, but the point is not clear. In a recent case involving the Lancashire Utility Poultry Society, a dues paying association, the court had to decide who should be held liable for losses caused by the society's "testers," employed to examine poultry for disease. See, Bradley Egg Farm, Ltd. v. Clifford (1943) 2 All E.R. 378. Although such testing was well within the purposes of the society, the court put liability, not on the members, but on the council set up to manage its affairs. The third person's contract for testing was said to have been made with them, not the Society, or the members, as joint principals. See, (1943) 21 Can.Bar Rev. 852.

These, at best, are representative holdings in the field. The only clear consensus is that in one way or another liability will be put on management, that is, on the agents who conduct affairs. In many states now there are procedural statutes saying that any unincorporated association *may* sue or be sued *in its common name*, thus giving it at least a measure of identity. See, Cal.Civ.Proc. § 388, and § 78 infra. What bearing these statutes may have is largely for the future.

Some things may be conjectured. For example, in a case such as *Cousin*, supra, the defendant agents could be said to have had a principal and have disclosed its name, i. e., Telephone Federation. Hence, some new argument must be devised to hold the agents liable. If judgment is taken against the association, however, it will, at best, reach the common assets. Any recovery against the members, individually, must rest on due service, and an additional showing, similar to that in *Cooper*, supra.

§ 74.　Limited Partnerships

The limited partnership is strictly a matter of statute. Its purpose is obvious, to provide limited liability—as in the case of the corporation shareholder for investment funds. Following the Waugh v. Carver decision, supra § 72, it had become hazardous even to *loan* funds to enterprise, except on a fixed interest basis. The available alternatives, the dormant and sub-partner contracts, had obvious limitations. See, infra, § 75. At all events, in 1822, New York adopted the first limited partnership act in this country and it became a model for similar statutes in other states. Now, these statutes have been superseded by the Uniform Limited Partnership Act, which has been adopted in all but a few states (Appendix B hereto). See Lewis, The Uniform Limited Partnership Act (1917) 65 U.Pa.L.Rev. 715. Recently, the National Conference of Commissioners on Uniform State Laws approved a revised Uniform Limited Partnership Act (1976). See, Vol. 6 Uniform Laws Annotated (West Publishing Co., 1977 pocket supp.). This new statute, to the extent approved by the individual states, will supersede the existing Act.

It is a relatively simple matter to form a limited partnership. Any number of persons may do so, but, of course, not fewer than two, one general partner and one special or limited partner. All that is needed is to fill out and swear to a certificate giving names, type of business, capital and so on, in compliance with U.L.P.A., § 2, thus to advise the commercial world. Last century the penalty for an inaccurate statement was to convert special partners into general partners, which might entail serious losses. Moreover, the requirement was strictly, even zealously, enforced.

The turning point came in a case where the certificate recited that $10,000 "had been actually and in good faith paid in cash" by the special partner when, in fact, a certified check had been given for the amount. See, White v. Eiseman (1892) 134 N.Y. 101, 31 N.E. 276. A rather picayune claim, since the check had been paid in due course, but of the kind being recognized.

In holding for the limited partner, Vann, J., said: "The primary object of the act authorizing limited partnerships was to encourage those having capital to become partners with those having skill, by limiting the liability of the former to the amount actually contributed to the firm." Continuing, he recognized the need for accurate public notice of the arrangement, but said the provision to that effect "was not designed as a trap to catch the innocent and unwary . . ." The Uni-

form Act abandons the penalty altogether, but
gives an injured third person a damage action.
See, U.L.P.A. § 6.

A related question concerns the *defectively organized* limited partnership.   The Uniform Act
provides that a person who has contributed capital
"erroneously believing that he has become a limited partner," is not "by reason of his exercise
of the rights of a limited partner," a "general
partner   .   .   .   ., provided that on ascertaining the mistake he promptly renounces his interest in the profits of the business   .   .   ." U.L.
P.A. § 11.   A similar question arises in the case
of the corporation, where the courts have used
the concept of a "de facto corporation" to shield
innocent shareholders.   See, § 71, supra.

In the leading limited partnership case the parties did not file in time to come within the Illinois statute.   See, Giles v. Vette (1924) 263 U.S.
553, 44 S.Ct. 157, 68 L.Ed. 441.   They never attempted to organize under the Uniform Act, since
the Illinois version did not authorize limited partnership to do a brokerage business.   However, the
supposed limited partners returned all profits previously received and, presumably, renounced any
claim to future profits.

On these facts the Supreme Court, after declar-
ing that § 11 was "broad and highly remedial,"
held that the *erroneous believers* were not liable

to creditors of the business. It is an open question whether it would have sufficed, if defendants had merely *renounced* any interest in profits. See, Gilman Paint & Varnish Co. v. Legum (1951) 197 Md. 665, 80 A.2d 906, 29 A.L.R.2d 286.

With these questions to one side, the limited partner would seem to have reached fairly safe ground, for the Act states: "The limited partners as such shall not be bound by the obligations of the partnership." U.L.P.A., § 1. But a possible pitfall lurks in the phrase, "as such." That is, to state the thing positively, a limited partner *may* become "liable as a general partner" if "in addition to the exercise of his rights and powers as a limited partner, he takes part in the control of the business." U.L.P.A., § 7. The rights of a limited partner, as stated in the Act, are mainly those of supervision and, of course, "to the return of his contribution," if the firm is still solvent. See, U.L.P.A. § 10.

The courts are now in the process of deciding, case by case, what may constitute impermissible *control*. When the limited partners, in a farming venture, for example, take it upon themselves to decide what crops are to be planted, and even to require the general partner to resign as manager, they plainly have crossed the line. See, Holzman v. De Escamilla (1948) 86 Cal.App.2d 858, 195 P.2d 833. There is some question whether it must be shown that third persons were misled, but estoppel surely is not a part of the equation. The statute need only be complied with as written.

The "control" question may arise anywhere, as, for example, in a real estate development setting, where the limited partnership is a convenient and much used device. That is, the promoters may form a syndicate to acquire property, say, to build a motel or an apartment house. Later a limited partnership is formed, with the promoters as general partners and those who are to finance the transaction taking stock as limited partners. If the charter so provides, this stock may be transferable. See, U.L.P.A. § 19. Indeed, the certificate is probably negotiable. See, U.C.C. §§ 8–102, 8–105. The relationship between limited partners is not a fiduciary one; it compares more closely with that of a lender-debtor relationship. Cf. §§ 19 and 22, supra.

A case in this setting came up recently in New York. See, Riviera Congress Associates v. Yassky (1966) 18 N.Y.2d 540, 277 N.Y.S.2d 386, 223 N.E.2d 876. There it was alleged that the general partners had leased firm property to another concern in which they were interested, and then cancelled the rental contract. The big question was whether the 350 or so limited partners had any remedy at all. Finally, borrowing from the corporation precedent (See, § 23, supra), five of the limited partners brought a derivative action, on behalf of the partnership, against the general partners for the amount of the unpaid rent, alleging fraud and breach of fiduciary duty. The court, by Fuld, J., decided for the plaintiffs, thereby establishing a useful precedent.

It is a nice question, necessarily not passed on by Judge Fuld, whether by bringing their action the five limited partners did not assert such "control of the business" as to become general partners. However, "control" as used in the statute would seem to refer to a positive influence on future action in an on-going business. At most, the five were engaged in a salvage operation. If this view is taken, however, it accords very well with the loan cases, where control is permissible when it is basically a veto power given as security. See, Martin v. Peyton, § 72, supra.

All of which poses the question, whether the limited partnership has real advantages over the loan transaction. The control point may be a standoff, but the greater detail of the Uniform Act and possible tax advantages in individual cases are on the side of the partnership. See generally, Crane, Are Limited Partnerships Necessary? (1933) 17 Minn.L.Rev. 351. Crane gives a qualified vote in the affirmative to his question.

§ 75. Dormant, Dummy and Sub-Partners

The oldest device, no doubt, by which to limit— or even eliminate—personal liability as a partner, is that of the dormant or silent partner. That is, by remaining unknown, a partner could share in the profits, even have some control, and yet escape liability to creditors—at least, for a time. On discovery, however, the point was clear, as it is under the Act, that he would be fully liable to creditors, either in tort or contract. See, U. P.A. § 15.

The question most litigated today is whether a dormant partner must give the usual notice to creditors, on withdrawal, to avoid liability. See, § 50, supra. In a leading common law case, the court put the burden on the defendant to establish that, in fact, he had been a dormant partner prior to withdrawal, that is, that he had been both *inactive* and *unknown*. See, Rowland v. Estes (1899) 190 Pa. 111, 42 A. 528, where he was unable to establish the second negative, and so was personally liable.

The Uniform Act does not define dormant partner, a point on which the common law courts were not in agreement. It is clear, though, that —however defined—the dormant partner, like any other partner, *must* give the usual notice to prior dealers, and a notice by advertisement to all others, upon retirement. See, U.P.A. § 35(1b). A failure to do so would operate—at the very least —to charge his share of the firm *assets* with liability to creditors.

Whether he would also be personally liable is a different question.   Here the Act gives recognition to the fact that he was in some sense dormant.   That is, he may escape *personal* liability if he can show that he was: "So far *unknown* and *inactive* in partnership affairs that the business reputation of the partnership could not [reasonably] be said to have been in any degree due to his connection with it."   See, U.P.A. § 35(2b).   Thus, he must still prove a negative, but it has been shifted to the "reputation of the partnership," the real issue, and an easier matter to prove.   See, Warner v. Modano (1960) 340 Mass. 439, 164 N.E.2d 904, where the court added the word "reasonably" to the section.

All in all, it would seem the would-be dormant partner might better insist on becoming a limited partner, if the situation would permit.   The sub-partner's contract is very different.   In fact, he is not a partner at all in the principal firm.   To illustrate, if A, B, and C are associated together as a partnership, The Ajax Trading Co., D and C may form a separate partnership as to C's interest only.   Perhaps C needed additional money to complete his contribution to Ajax.

In this situation D would share in such profits and losses as might come to C, in the Ajax partnership.   He would have no control of Ajax affairs.   The common law courts have been quite uniform in holding that D, as a sub-partner,

[*237*]

would not be liable to the Ajax creditors.   See, Burnett v. Snyder (1880) 81 N.Y. 550, 37 Am. Rep. 527.   The Uniform Act would seem to have no provision to the contrary.   But this may overstate the matter, for surely C would have recourse against his co-partner, D, for contribution, in event of loss in the Ajax business.   And, this right at least could be reached by the creditors. See generally, Rowley, Risk Evasion Through Sub-Partnership (1930) 30 Col.L.Rev. 674.

The sub-partner may easily be distinguished from a dummy partner.   Indeed, the latter is essentially an agent for an undisclosed principal. See, § 60 supra.   In a leading case, one Karste, a banker, refused to become a partner with Johnson in the firm of Peter Johnson & Co., but suggested that Mrs. Healy should go in with Johnson as a general partner, and an agreement was drawn up on this basis.   Thus the paper record showed Mrs. Healy to be a partner, and she would no doubt be liable to third persons as such.

As a matter of fact, however, Karste furnished Mrs. Healy with the $8500 she put in as her share of the capital in Johnson & Co., and it was further understood that Karste should be entitled to *all* of any profits obtained.   At the trial it was urged that Karste was merely a sub-partner, but the court said: "Where the so-called 'sub-partner' owns the entire interest, including profits and property, he must be considered as the real partner . . . ." See, Webb v. Johnson (1893) 95 Mich. 325, 54 N.W. 947.

§ 76. Joint Stock Associations

The joint stock association came into wide use late in the 18th and early in the 19th centuries in response to the needs of an expanding economy. Corporations were a matter of special legislation, with charters often difficult to obtain. However, it was plain that any group of persons could form a *partnership*, and *by contract* gain at least some of the advantages of incorporation. In particular, there was need to be able to sell shares to the public, thereby greatly to increase the capital available to enterprise. See Maitland, The Unincorporate Body, Collected Papers (1911) vol. II pp. 271–284.

It was a relatively easy matter, moreover, to provide for transferable shares. While partnership is a personal relationship, a partner's rights in this respect may be waived at the outset in the partnership agreement. At all events, the scheme succeeded. Although the so-called Bubble Act, an attempt at regulation, was passed late in he 18th century to discourage speculation, it was repealed in 1825. Of course, it was also necessary to provide against termination of the partnership upon death of any casual shareholder—or at his whim on sale of his shares—but this too was accomplished by contract. In fact, it has been held today that the dissolution provisions of the Uniform Act do not apply. State Street Trust Co. v. Hall (1942) 311 Mass. 299, 41 N.E.2d 30, 156 A.L.R. 13.

Some things could not be attained by contract. Since a partnership was not regarded as an entity at common law, the joint stock association could neither sue nor be sued. Likewise, and for the same reason, it could not hold title to real property. The last posed little difficulty, as the organizers had at hand the trust device, whereby title could be put in the name of one or more persons to hold as trustees for the association. See, § 77, infra. The first, however, required legislation. New York, last century, provided the necessary means whereby to sue and be sued. In fact, it stated a priority, by requiring suit against the association before suit might be had against the share-partners. See Westcott v. Fargo (1875) 61 N.Y. 542.

Two corporate advantages, however, were never fully attained. The first, a means to concentrate management in a board of directors, came to give little trouble, as the early courts declared quite positively that "All who have dealings with a joint stock company know that the authority to manage the business is conferred upon the directors . . . " See, Burnes v. Pennell (1849) 2 H.L.Cas. 497. Plainly, it would not do if any shareholder, as a partner, might act for the company.

However, the attempt to gain limited liability, comparable to that of a corporation, never succeeded. Something could be done by contract with the third person, that is, he could be asked to agree to look only to company assets. See generally, Hibbs v. Brown (1907) 190 N.Y. 167, 82 N.E. 1108. But, tort claims, of course, could not be so handled. In any case, with the "so-called vegetable oil scandal" of 1963, and the prospect of large losses, it is reported that a number of joint stock associations—including American Express Company—changed to the corporate form. See, In re Ira Haupt & Co. (D.C.N.Y. 1965) 240 F.Supp. 369.

Thus, the long and useful career of the joint stock association would seem to almost have come to an end. It is not reported that new associations are being formed, nor indeed is there any apparent need for them. This account, however, may prove useful, when we consider the Business Trust. See infra, § 77. For a general study, see Warren, Corporate Advantages Without Incorporation (1929) pp. 327–404.

§ 77. The Business Trust

The line between a business trust, often called a Massachusetts Trust, and a joint stock association, is easily drawn. While the stock association held only its real estate in trust, the organizer of the business trust put everything, the business and *all* assets, in the hands of trustees to manage. Perhaps they only sought at first to avoid a rule in some states that corporations could not deal in land. See, Owens, Business Organization and Combination (1934) pp. 67–80. That reason, however, is no longer valid in most states, and yet the business trust continues in use.

The entity problem gave no serious difficulty. The law has long regarded trustees, not the estate, as principals, with the capacity of any individual to sue and be sued. Thus, when the Hope Oil Trust, for example, engaged to buy goods, in an amount of $180, from plaintiff, it was clearly the obligation of the trustees. See, Betts v. Hackathorn (1923) 159 Ark. 621, 252 S.W. 602, 31 A.L.R. 847. Indeed, it was said long ago: "When a trustee contracts as such, unless he is bound no one is bound, as he has no principal. The trust estate cannot promise . . . ." Taylor v. Davis (1884) 110 U.S. 330, 4 S.Ct. 147.

It was also a relatively easy matter to reach the capital market. That is, the trustees will simply issue transferable certificates of interest in the trust, and these may then be sold to the public. A similar device is used in the sale of rail and air line equipment. The manufacturer will sell to a bank or trust company, which in turn will lease the equipment to the railroad or air line. Public participation is gained by the bank, which puts everything in trust and then issues and sells equipment trust certificates, a well regarded security.

A basic question, of course, is that of limited liability. Certificate holders, however, are not principals, but merely beneficiaries of the trust, or, *cestui que trustent*, in trust language. And, as such, it has long been established law that they are not to be held answerable for debts and obligations incurred by the trustees, who are not agents. It was so held, in fact, in Betts v. Hackathorn, cited supra. Only a few states have refused to recognize the business trust, relying on a rather strained construction of their constitutions to that end. But see, Goldwater v. Oltman (1930) 210 Cal. 408, 292 P. 624, 71 A.L.R. 871.

Most litigation in recent years has dealt with the problem of control. An assertion of control, as by the creditor-beneficiaries in Cox v. Hickman, supra § 72, would be fatal; an ostensible trust would be converted thereby into a simple agency. See, §§ 4 and 17, supra. True, the plaintiff lost in Cox v. Hickman, but the *holding* was merely that the trust beneficiaries were not partners. There are many cases which indicate that they *would* be liable as joint principals. In fact, if the certificate holders are given no more than the power to elect trustees annually, or to fill vacancies, that alone is usually held to be enough control to defeat the trust.

In view of these risks, it is customary, in third party dealings, to stipulate that recourse may not be had against the certificate holders. Or, for that matter, against the trustees, personally. So far as possible, the purpose is to put the trust assets only behind the obligations incurred by the trustees on behalf of the trust. It has been held that it is not enough that the third person has read the trust agreement and is aware of this purpose. To have any effect as to him, the limitations must actually appear in his contract with the trustees. See Larson v. Sylvester (1933) 282 Mass. 352, 185 N.E. 44.

The position of trustee, in a business trust, is thus a precarious one. His first recourse, in case of loss, is by way of indemnity from the estate. As a matter of procedure in some states the third person's action against the trustee is virtually an action against the estate. The serious question—should this remedy not suffice—is whether the trustee may also reach the certificate holder for indemnity. The trust agreement is usually drawn to negative such an attack. Notwithstanding, the possibility exists, but at least it may be said no cases are at hand testing the point.

Now for a brief evaluation of the business trust as a vehicle for business use. At one time it appears to have enjoyed a tax advantage, but Mr. Justice Hughes has made it clear that a trust is a corporation for purposes of the Internal Revenue Laws. See: Morrissey v. Commissioner (1935) 296 U.S. 344, 56 S.Ct. 289; and Smith, Associates Classified as Corporations (1946) 34 Cal.L.Rev. 461. Also, most states have ruled that an out-of-state trust must register as a foreign corporation to do business in their jurisdictions. Whether there may be tax advantages in individual cases is outside the scope of this text.

One significant business trust advantage may exist. This lies in the fact that the powers of the trustees to obligate the estate are usually more limited, and perhaps more definitely stated, than those of directors. Moreover, no doctrine of apparent authority has appeared, or is likely to appear in the decisions; it has been customary, in fact, to construe a trustee's powers quite strictly. See, Fulda and Pond, Tort Liability of Trust Estates (1941) 41 Col.L.Rev. 1332. Of course, the certificate holders sacrifice control, but they may participate in profits, with immunity from the claims of creditors, matters of no small concern. Moreover, a trust indenture, carefully specifying in advance the powers of the trustees, can make up to a degree for the loss of day-by-day control.

§ 78.   To Sue or Be Sued

A recent development, by which an unincorporated association is given the capacity to sue and be sued, may have more than procedural significance. Many states have long had so-called "common name" statutes, designed to give creditors the right to sue "associates" in order to reach the general assets of the partnership or other unincorporated association in which they are members. The next step has been to expand the "common name" idea and virtually give the "association" itself entity status, at least as a matter of procedure.

The operative part of the California statute, passed in 1967, reads as follows:

"(a) Any partnership or other unincorporated association, whether organized for profit or not, may sue and be sued in the name which it has assumed or by which it is known.

"(b) Any member of the partnership or other unincorporated association may be joined as a party in an action against the unincorporated association .   .   ." See, West's Ann.Cal.Code Civ.Proc. § 388.

It will be useful to examine § 388 in some detail to see what changes have been made in prior law. In the first place, the common name statutes provided expressly that "the joint property of the associates" could be reached by a judgment. This wording is gone, but probably a judgment today against an "association" would reach such assets, and no more. That is, in the case of a partnership, the property contributed to the firm by the partners, and any money or other property held in common, would be reachable. Nothing is stated as to priority, which presumably is to be controlled by general law. See infra, § 87.

This construction is bolstered by the point that, if a plaintiff would reach other assets, he is authorized to serve and join any "member" in his action as well. That is, it is further provided in § 388(b), that a judgment may also be had against a member "based on his personal liability," and this, "whether such liability be joint, joint and several, or several." Probably this last serves as an amendment to U.P.A. § 15(b), which provides, as at comon law, that partners are liable only "jointly" on all contract actions. If so, the change is welcome, as the common law rule was productive mainly of delay and annoyance. See, Crehan v. Megargel (1922) 234 N.Y. 67, 136 N.E. 296.

Whether the section will also permit a *partner* or other member to *bring* suit against his own firm or association is not wholly clear. At common law the partner's remedy, on partnership causes, was for an accounting. See, U.P.A. § 22.

When he sought to recover at law directly, on non-partnership causes, it was urged that he could not be both plaintiff and defendant. However, there have been a number of well-reasoned cases permitting a partner to recover from his firm, naming himself as one defendant. As a member, of course, he must contribute to the loss. See, Smith v. Hensley (Ky., 1962) 354 S.W.2d 744, 98 A.L.R.2d 340. (Suit by partner for damage to his truck.)

In the case of a partnership this conclusion would seem to mean that U.P.A. § 13 has been amended by striking out the limiting words, "not being a partner in the partnership." The section thus would say that "the partnership" *may* be held liable to anyone—partner or any other—for injury caused by the wrongful conduct of a partner "acting in the ordinary course of the business." It has long been recommended that § 13 should be so amended anyway. See, Crane, Liability of Unincorporated Association (1963) 16 Vand.L.Rev. 319.

Some support for this view is gained from the holding in Marshall v. Int. Longshoremen (1962) 57 Cal.2d 781, 371 P.2d 987, 22 Cal.Rptr. 211, the case which paved the way for § 388 in California. In *Marshall*, a member of a labor union had been injured by a fall over a concrete obstruction in the Union's parking lot, and he brought suit against the Union and also against certain officers and members of the Union. The court was troubled by the point discussed above, that a member has no standing to sue his own association, but refused to accept it. Then, after a skillful review of the many situations in which a union has been treated virtually as an entity, it took the next step, and gave recovery against the Union itself.

However, the lower court's dismissal of the action against the *members* was sustained. The court said that "members of labor unions are not to be held vicariously liable," but liability, if at all, must rest "upon their personal participation in, or authorization, of such acts." Thus, it would seem that members at large are given much the same position as corporate shareholders or limited partners now enjoy. They are not to be held liable, nor presumably do they have any authority to act, except as they may have crossed the line and taken "part in the control of the business." See: U.L.P.A. § 7, discussed supra § 74; Thomas v. Dunne (1955) 131 Colo. 20, 279 P.2d 427.

More or less concealed in all this is the point that even the "association" is not *liable*, except as plaintiff can show that his action grew out of *authorized* conduct of association agents, members or any other. Subtly the association has been given entity status, not only in the respect that it may be sued, but also in the respect that *it* may appoint agents. This is a necessary first step, for example, to bring the respondeat superior doctrine into play. When taken, it also would reverse such a case as Cousin v. Taylor, discussed supra § 73, since the "Oregon Telephone Federation" of that case would have the capacity to engage an agent to enter contracts binding on *it*. See generally, Security-First National Bank v. Cooper et al. (1944) 62 Cal.App. 2d 653, 145 P.2d 722.

These results were obtained, in each case, by dressing the association involved "in garb of the entity concept," which, we are told, is not too important, "provided the fictional personification is . . . not used as a premise for syllogistic thrusts elsewhere." Per Weintraub, C. J., in Mazzuchelli v. Silberberg (1959) 29 N.J. 15, 148 A.2d 8. The question in *Mazzuchelli* was whether defendant partner was entitled to the usual employer's immunity from common law suit, plaintiff employee having already received compensation from the firm for his injuries. See generally, § 27, above. The court found for the defendant. Although the statute recognized the partnership as an "entity" for purposes of compensation, the partners still were employers, entitled to the statutory immunity. In other words, there are limits to the entity idea.

§ 79. Capital Contributions

In one respect, at least, the Uniform Partnership Act embraced the entity theory. That is, the statute was drafted to say that *it*—the partnership—could acquire, hold and dispose of real property. Of course, businessmen and accountants had long proceeded on that assumption, at least as to cash and goods. Only land caused a problem, for the common law said a partnership, not being a legal entity, could not conceivably take title. See generally, Woodward v. McAdam (1894) 101 Cal. 438, 35 P. 1016. Fortunately, this now has been changed. See, U.P.A. § 8.

Thus the way is clear for a partner to "contribute" land *directly* to the partnership as his share of capital, much as he always could contribute goods or cash. The point may not be too significant, since a partner could make his conveyance of land to a partner or other person in trust for the partnership. It helps, however, to make a related point clear that, upon contribution, the cash, goods, or real estate becomes the property of the partnership. The contributor's only remaining interest is "his share of the profits and surplus, and the same is personal property." See, U.P.A. § 26.

Probably the element most essential to a going concern, of whatever form, is the capital with which it does business. It is capital that makes the world go round. In the case of a corporation, equity capital, so-called, is raised by the sale of shares of stock. Again, the shareholder's interest is personal property; he has no interest in any tangible property. This means that, on dissolution, the shareholder, like the partner, received his distributive portion of any assets and surplus remaining after the debts are paid.

There are important differences, however. Upon dissolution, the partner is entitled to have his "contribution" *returned.* As a matter of priority, the liabilities to creditors are paid first, next any to partners, and thirdly those "owing to partners in respect of capital." See, U.P.A. § 40(b) III. Moreover, after his contribution has been repaid, the partner may also "share equally in the profits and surplus remaining" after all liabilities are satisfied. See, U.P.A. § 18(a). The limited partner, however, after the return of his contribution, is given no similar right to share in the residual partnership assets. See, U.L.P.A. § 23.

A contribution, thus, is a partnership liability to be repaid, but it is not a loan. As further evidence, the partner does not receive interest in respect of his contribution, in the absence of a contrary agreement. That is, he may have interest "*only* from the date when repayment should be made." (Emphasis added.) See, U.P.A.

§ 18(d). Likewise, a partner has no claim to salary. See, U.P.A. § 18(f). The reasoning seems to be, in each of these situations, that, since the partner has contracted to share in partnership gains, no other recompense is to be implied in the usual case.

A principal source of litigation has been to determine the question of fact, whether cash, goods or given properties have indeed been *contributed*. In many cases, the partner may merely have given the *use* of his property to the firm. For example, in *Keiswetter*, § 68 supra, Hammel carefully retained title to the land which figured in the joint venture. Only the *use* was contributed. Thus, had plaintiff obtained judgment against the *venture only*, he would not have been able to reach the Hammel lots. Of course, as a procedural matter, he could not have recovered against the venture, since it had no "common name." See generally, § 78 supra.

By way of further illustration, a contest may develop between a firm creditor, on the one hand, and an individual creditor of a partner, on the other. In Clements v. Jessup (1883) 36 N.J.Eq. 569, where that was the situation, the question turned on whether the debtor partner had in fact *contributed* certain goods and chattels used in the business. Holding that they had been contributed, it followed that the individual creditor, who claimed by right of purchase at an attachment sale, took nothing. Otherwise, had the partner merely given the "use" of his goods and chattels, an opposite result would follow. See, In re Amy (C.C.A.N.Y.1927) 21 F.2d 301 (property was an Exchange seat).

Also, if plaintiff's claim were to rest on an attachment of the debtor partner's *interest in the partnership,* rather than on specific goods, the court indicated that again plaintiff would lose. At most, a sale under such an attachment would convey only the interest of the partner *after* the firm debts had been paid, which obviously was not the case before court. Moreover, the long established rule that firm creditors have priority over individual creditors of a partner might itself have defeated plaintiff's claim on the facts presented. See, § 85 infra.

The Uniform Act, in fact, now goes one step farther, and outlaws the attachment altogether, when it is sought to be used to reach a partner's personal interest in his firm. See, U.P.A. § 25 (2)(c). A judgment creditor, however, may initiate proceedings for a "charging order" to much the same end, where all claims may be heard. See: U.P.A. § 28; Gose, *The Charging Order* (1953) 28 Wash.L.Rev. 1.

§ 80. Contributions to Contributors

The point that each partner must contribute to the payment of the claims of the general creditors has been discussed. See, § 24 supra. The question here is whether partners, including those who engaged only to give services, must likewise contribute to make good a co-partner's initial contribution to capital. The point usually arises at dissolution, when it may be found that the money on hand, after the general creditors have been paid, is not sufficient to repay contributors. There is resistance, especially on the part of the service partners.

At common law it was fairly well established that *all* partners must contribute to pay contribution losses. In a leading case, Whitcomb v. Converse (1875) 119 Mass. 38, 20 Am.Rep. 311, four partners had agreed to engage in a dry goods commission business. Two of the partners contributed the whole of the capital in unequal proportions; they also were to give some services. The other two made no cash contribution, but agreed to give all of their time to the business. Profits were to be divided equally.

The business appears to have suffered a $25,000 loss, and Whitcomb accordingly brought a bill in equity against the other three partners to have his cash contribution repaid in full. The court pointed out that the four partners had agreed to share profits equally, and said that "by implication of law" they each "must share the losses in the same proportion." No exception was made in favor of the service partners. In fact, since one partner had become bankrupt, each solvent partner's share was increased from one fourth to one third, thereby to make up the difference.

The Uniform Act, it would seem, has codified this result, since it provides, without qualification, that "each partner . . . must contribute towards the losses, whether of capital or otherwise . . . " See, U.P.A. § 18(a). Nevertheless, there is a sense of unfairness, as may be illustrated by Moseley v. Taylor (1917) 173 N.C. 286, 91 S.E. 1035, L.R.A.1917E, 875. The money partner there had contributed $5000 to a "horse and mule business at Raleigh, N. C.," and Will Taylor, the service partner, agreed to manage the business for one year, profits to be divided equally. After six months, the money partner died, thus dissolving the partnership, and the court ordered the $3676.69 on hand, after the creditors had been satisfied, to be paid to the money partner, or his estate, in partial repayment of his contribution.

Thus, in *Moseley*, Will Taylor, who had claimed one half of the sum on hand, got nothing. The court said that the rule contended for by Taylor would be very unfair; it would mean that if Moseley had died "the next day" after the venture was

[*256*]

started, Taylor must be paid $2500, or half of the initial contribution, and for doing nothing. Of course, the court's rule is equally unfair, for if Taylor had worked the full year, when Moseley up and died, it would mean that he had *lost* everything. Plainly the situation is one which calls for a carefully drafted agreement, perhaps one crediting the capital account of the service partner with the agreed value of his services as the work progresses.

A few courts have implied an agreement. In their view the parties, by their profit sharing arrangement, must have given *equal* weight to services and cash. Such a solution, however, is not very realistic. The California court, for its part, has refused to apply the rule altogether, but its decision is suspect, since the supposed joint venture before it was probably a mere hiring, compensation to be determined by profits. See, Kovacik v. Reed (1957) 49 Cal.2d 166, 315 P.2d 314. The case may not have been well argued, for the court leaned heavily on non-contribution or use cases, where plainly the risk is not on the partnership anyway. See generally, § 79, supra.

§ 81. The Incoming Partner

At common law, any change in membership served to work a *dissolution* of the partnership. Typically, this would happen, either when a new partner was taken into the firm, or when an existing partner should die or seek to withdraw and dispose of his interest. The Uniform Act does not list the *addition* of a partner as a cause of dissolution, § 29, but neither does it deny the point. In any case, it is proposed to explore the situation in this section on the common law basis. The problems involved, when a partner withdraws voluntarily, or when he dies, will be discussed next, §§ 82 and 83. See generally, Bromberg, Partnership Dissolution (1965) 43 Tex.L.Rev. 631.

A partner may join an existing partnership in either of two principal ways: (1) he may acquire the interest of a retiring partner, paying him any agreed consideration; or (2) he may negotiate directly with the partnership, making such contribution to capital as may be required. Of course, a partner may sell his interest at any time—it being personal property, U.P.A. § 26— but the buyer does not become a partner until full consent is given. See, U.P.A. § 18(g). Also, it is agreed that—apart from special contract—the incoming partner is not liable personally upon the prior debts of the firm. That is, "he becomes one of the firm for the future, and not for the past." See, Wolff v. Madden (1893) 6 Wash. 514, 33 P. 975.

It sometimes happens that, in prior dealings, the incoming partner allowed his name to be used as if he were already a partner. As a result, he may be held to have become a partner by estoppel, at least as to creditors. See, U.P.A. § 16. And, even though there is no estoppel, the purchaser of a partner's interest may have been permitted to exercise such control of affairs—to make sure of a satisfactory liquidation—that a court may find him to have become a partner with full responsibility to creditors. See Freeman v. Huttig Sash & Door Co. (1913) 105 Tex. 560, 153 S.W. 122. Except for situations of this sort, however, the incoming partner is uniformly held not answerable for past transactions.

In view of this law, it comes as something of a surprise to read in the Uniform Act that an incoming partner "is liable" for all obligations arising *prior* to his admission. The explanation, however, lies in the proviso, "except that this liability shall be satisfied only out of partnership property." See, U.P.A. § 17. Probably there was no better way to state the matter, on the aggregate theory, to make sure that a retiring partner's interest in the firm assets would remain liable to existing creditors. In fact, such creditors are given an additional protection, for it seems clear that any new money brought in by the incoming partner will likewise be subject to their claims. See, U.P.A. § 41(1).

There has been a question whether the sale of a partner's interest, as above, might be vulnerable under the Bulk Sales laws. It may be argued, first, that the statute does not apply, since the partner does not sell "goods," but merely his interest in any surplus on liquidation. In the next place, the Commercial Code now provides that such transfers are not within the Act, if the transferee becomes bound to pay his transferor's debts and gives public notice of the fact. See, U.C.C. § 6–103(6). Since the incoming partner does just that, U.P.A. § 41, the question may now be considered at rest, that is, assuming the incomer does not fail to give notice.

§ 82.   The Outgoing Partner

It is now proposed to examine the problems of the outgoing partner. Typically, he will either have sold out his interest to an existing partner of the firm or disposed of it to an incoming partner. Problems arising when a partner dies or retires and it is desirable to continue the business without liquidation will be considered next, § 83. In general, outgoing partners have two classes of creditors to think about. Possible liability to one of these, that is, to *new* creditors of the ongoing business, is readily manageable. All that is required is that the notices stated in U.P.A. § 35 be given. See discussion, §§ 50 and 51, supra.

Existing creditors of the firm, and hence also of the outgoing partner, present more of a problem. Of course, it is routine for the buyer to engage to pay all such claims. That is part of the agreement when a partner sells his interest. Creditors at least become third party beneficiaries thereby. Indeed, the Uniform Act takes things a step farther, and expressly provides that "if the business is continued without liquidation of the partnership affairs, creditors of the first or dissolved partnership *are also creditors* of the partnership so continuing the business." See, U.P.A. § 41(1), emphasis supplied.

This would seem to make very sure that old firm creditors are not to lose their claims to the *assets* of the business. Likewise, it may be said, they do not lose their right to pursue individual partners, including the outgoing partner, on their *personal liability*. See, U.P.A. § 36(1). The outgoing partner usually gives prompt notice of the situation to existing creditors, and many courts have found that he is then to be put in the position of a surety, with the new firm as principal debtor.

The Uniform Act, in fact, has given some sanction to the surety theory. It does not mention the word surety, but provides that the outgoing partner shall be discharged from liability to any creditor who consents "to a material alteration in the nature or time of payment" of the creditor's claim. See, U.P.A. § 36(3). Thus, the Act has singled out one suretyship defense, probably the most common one, and made it available to the outgoing partner.

How much farther suretyship law may be used is a problem. A double problem in fact, because sometimes suretyship law itself is not clear. For example, there has been litigation on the question whether the outgoing partner may call upon firm creditors to take prompt action against their debtor, the on-going firm. Unless this is done, valuable assets may often be dissipated and lost and, if they are, the outgoing partner demands that he be discharged accordingly. See, Comment, The Doctrine of Paine v. Packard (1928) 37 Yale L.J. 971.

The courts that refuse this defense justify their position by saying: "It would not be *just* . . . to impose upon the creditor the duty of suing the continuing partner . . . " See, Faricy v. J. S. Brown Mercantile Co. (1930) 87 Colo. 427, 288 P. 639. Interestingly enough, the New York view to the contrary uses the same reasoning, the surety *is* discharged because it would be "unjust for the creditor, by delaying to sue, to expose the surety" to the increased hazard of loss. See, Colgrove v. Tallman (1876) 67 N.Y. 95, 23 Am. Rep. 90.

The upshot is that the outgoing partner has only one real safeguard, that is, to obtain a release from existing creditors. This could have been done readily at one time, by offering the new firm's undertaking as consideration. But, since the Act gives the creditor such an action anyway (see, U.P.A. § 41(1), discussed above), perhaps an additional consideration is needed. The Act itself suggests that an "agreement" to discharge the partner "may be inferred from the course of dealing." See, U.P.A. § 36(2). Since, presumably, such an agreement would be effective, an explicit written release surely would not be less so. This, without waiting for a "course of dealing" to ripen.

§ 83. Death of Partner

When a general partner dies, the partnership is perforce "dissolved." See, U.P.A. § 31(4). So also, when a partner becomes "incapable of performing his part of the partnership contract," a court, by decree, may order dissolution. See, U.P.A. § 32(1)(b). The next step might well be to liquidate the business. In many cases, however, the parties wish to continue on at the old stand, and to avoid the expense and disruption of a winding up. See, § 84, next infra. It is proposed now to examine some of the problems involved when this is the case.

The orderly way to handle the matter, of course, is by contract. That is, since the possibility of premature dissolution is easily foreseeable, it is only good sense to provide for the contingency. There are an infinite number of such contracts; even an agreement of joint tenancy—

survivor take all—has been enforced. It is more usual, however, to give the firm, or the surviving partner or partners, an option to purchase the share of the partner who dies. It is possible to name a set price, but in most cases provision is made for an evaluation.

Even when this is the case, there may be problems. For example, there may be uncertainty whether the deceased partner's estate is entitled to a share of the "good will." This is true particularly in the case of a professional partnership, as for example, a medical clinic. While some courts are of the view that there can be no element of good will in such case, the better position is to the contrary. After all, "good will" is not so much a personal matter as an expectancy arising from a name or place or way of doing business, which has found favor among customers. See generally, Kalez v. Miller (1944) 20 Wash.2d 362, 147 P.2d 506.

Another troublesome question is that of insurance. Increasingly, it has become practice to take out insurance on each partner to provide funds with which to pay a partner's estate, when his time has come. See generally, Fahr, The Business Purchase Agreement and Life Insurance (1950) 15 Law & Contemp.Prob. 316. There is no question that there is an insurable interest. If the policy happens to have been written to show the partner's individual estate as beneficiary, that has caused litigation. When partnership funds were used to pay premiums, however, there is at least a presumption that the policy belongs to the firm. See: U.P.A. § 8(2); Quinn v. Leidinger (1932) 110 N.J.Eq. 663, 160 A. 537.

The parties, however, may wish to take a different course entirely. That is, it may have been provided by agreement, or by the deceased partner's will, that his share in the assets should simply remain in the business, as part of the continuing firm's general assets. Moreover, depending on conditions, this may well be a prudent thing to do. No doubt the consent of the continuing partners would be needed, but they would seem to have little reason to object. At all events, by such an arrangement the estate would continue to enjoy its share of the profits.

Of course, if the business should *not* prosper the estate would stand to lose. But, loss would be limited to the assets left in the business; it should incur no individual liability to new creditors of the on-going business. This is true because it is very clear that, by so doing, neither the estate nor the estate representative would become a partner in the new firm. See, U.P.A. § 18(g). As for existing creditors at the time of dissolution, nothing is changed; the estate would remain liable or not, as discussed subsequently, § 84. Incidentally, the rights of such creditors against the on-going business are well protected. See, U.P.A. § 41.

The result is that the estate is given a position very similar to that of a limited partner. The Wisconsin court, in fact, has gone a step farther, and recognized that an administrator of a deceased partner's estate has power to effect such an arrangement, *without* prior authorization. See, Blumer Brewing Corp. v. Mayer (1936) 223 Wis. 540, 269 N.W. 693, 111 A.L.R. 1087. After all, the partner's interest in the firm is personal property and thus fully within the administrator's jurisdiction. The court was careful to point out, however, that if the administrator should act without court order, he might well run risk of personal liability, should the business not succeed.

Comparison is invited with the situation existing when a partner brings about dissolution *in violation* of the partnership contract. See, U.P.A. § 31(2). Here the shoe is on the other foot, and the on-going partners are given power to *require* the wrongdoer to leave his share of the assets in the business until the end of the agreed term. This, with the proviso, that the on-going partners "secure the payment" of the value of his interest, less damages for breach, "by bond approved by the court.' See, U.P.A. § 38(2)(b).

§ 84. Winding Up

After dissolution, all efforts to continue the business having failed, the next step is to "wind up" partnership affairs. See, U.P.A. § 37. Essentially the *action* is for an accounting, but the *job* entails many things, sale of the assets, collection of claims, paying creditors, returning capital contributions, distributing any surplus, and so on. If there is no surplus, the partner to wind up the business has the painful duty of calling on his erstwhile partners, or their estates, for contribution. See, § 80, supra. A final settlement, of course, may be reached without the aid of a court, but the books are full of cases where some partner, or his estate, has demanded a formal accounting. Moreover, that is his right. See, U.P.A. § 22.

It will be useful at this point to re-examine the concept of "dissolution." Actually, nothing much happens upon dissolution; it may be likened to a sign or signal that cause exists for a subsequent liquidation or winding up. See, U.P.A. § 29. Thus, as discussed above, dissolution may be waived. A good example is when transferable shares are issued, as in the case of a joint stock association, the fact of issuance carries with it an implied waiver (it may also be express) that a sale of shares, or even the death of a shareholder, will not cause dissolution. See generally,

Bromberg, Partnership Dissolution (1965) 43 Texas L.Rev. 631.

So the partner to wind up the business has a job of liquidation; the partnership, in theory, still subsists until "termination." U.P.A. § 30. Moreover, his authority is rather strictly limited to what is reasonably necessary to liquidation, but this would allow the liquidator to engage counsel, for example, to bring an action for the recovery of partnership assets. The fee and costs in such case would be properly chargeable to the partnership. In fact, contrary to the usual case, the liquidating partner himself is entitled to reasonable compensation for his work. See, U.P.A. § 18(f).

The Uniform Act does not state which partner has responsibility for a winding up. Where there are but two, and one dies, the job has usually fallen to the lot of the survivor. Indeed, the matter would seem to be one for arrangement between the interested parties; any partner may require winding up by a court in a proper case. U.P.A. § 37. So likewise, a *limited partner* may have the partnership dissolved and its affairs terminated, when that is necessary to obtain the return of his contribution. U.L.P.A. § 16(4). It has been held that the trustees of a business trust are the proper persons to do a winding up of the trust.

By way of guidelines, the liquidator must act fairly and with reasonable promptness. This does not mean that he must put the assets up in bulk at a forced sale. Depending on circumstances, a sale at retail may be the best course; the liquidator may even buy new goods, on behalf of the estate, to round out a line. The job is greatly aided by the fact that all co-partners, including the representative of a deceased partner, are under strict fiduciary duties. Affirmatively, this means they must render on demand true and full information of all things affecting the partnership. U.P.A. § 20. And, of course, they must account for any property of the partnership, or profits derived therefrom, which they may hold. See, U.P.A. § 21.

One of the problems confronting the liquidator is that of valuation. Even when contributions are to be returned in kind, it is necessary to put a value on the returned property before it is possible to determine shares in any cash surplus remaining. Also, there has been frequent litigation testing *when* valuation should be made. The estate of a deceased partner, for example, may demand payment according to the book value at the time of dissolution. However, this ignores the fact that liquidation is an involved process, and it may be much fairer to await a settlement of all accounts before putting a value on any partner's share.

By way of further illustration of the "valuation" problem, consider this situation: Partner A put in a mill, then valued at £24,000, as his contribution to capital; partner B contributed services and £2500 cash; profits were to be divided equally. After dissolution, the mill was sold for £57,000 and the good will and movable equipment for some £48,000. Partner A demanded both sums, since, after all, it was *his* mill that had been sold. But, plainly, A was only entitled to £24,000, the value placed on his contribution when made. See, § 79 supra. It was the *partnership* mill which was sold, and B was entitled to share equally with A in any *gain* only. See generally, Robinson v. Ashton (1875) L.R. 20 Eq. 25.

In a leading New York case, the liquidator acted promptly, perhaps too promptly, when he returned some $80,000 to a limited partner, the amount of his contribution. At the time, however, it was thought there were sufficient assets in hand to pay creditors. When this proved not to be the case, the question was whether the limited partner could be required to return the $80,000 he had received. The court held, in effect, that the assets of the firm in liquidation were in the nature of a trust fund, and that any partner could be required to repay, with interest, any funds received before the creditors were fully paid. See generally, Kittredge v. Langley (1930) 252 N.Y. 405, 169 N.E. 626, 67 A.L.R. 1087.

The rule is much the same in the case of a corporation in liquidation. The *Kittredge* case, however, illustrates another point, that the job of winding up is not without risk. In the event the limited partner in *Kittredge* should not be able to repay any part of the $80,000, the other partners would seem to have an action against the liquidator for the loss.

§ 85. Distribution

Assuming that business is not to continue and the winding up process has gone so far as to reduce the property to cash, the next step is distribution. When the business has been profitable, the *order* of distribution would seem to make little difference. Nonetheless, since this fact cannot well be known in advance, it is usual to follow the order developed through the years and carefully laid out in the statute. U.P.A. § 40(a)(b). In fact, that procedure is useful, probably necessary, in order to arrive at the exact amount of any *profit* to be distributed.

First off, liabilities owing to creditors, other than partners, are to be paid, and then those to partners. The subordination of the claims of partners—as for money loaned—is due to the thought that it would not be seemly for a partner to "compete" with his own creditors. Next in order, liabilities "owing to partners in respect of capital" are to be paid. See, § 79 supra. Finally, the sum remaining, in the happy event that the business was successful, is to be divided equally, or according to any agreed ratio, and paid to the partners as profits. See, U.P.A. § 18(a).

The foregoing order seems logical enough, but it conceals a controversy involving the claims of *personal,* non-partnership, creditors of a partner. According to the aggregate theory, all partners are individually and directly liable to firm creditors—as joint debtors on contract claims—and thus, when *firm* creditors hold unpaid judgments against one or more partners, it is essential to each that, in liquidating the estate, firm assets be used so far as possible in payment. The concealed point is that by this order of distribution a partner's *personal* creditors are effectively foreclosed from any right to participate in such assets.

Consistently, as noted above, they have no power to *attach* a partner's interest. See, § 79 supra.

In the early cases, it was sometimes said that a partner has a "lien" on partnership assets. Probably though, this was but an inept way of describing a partner's right to this order of distribution as just discussed. A partner who has sold goods to his firm, for example, certainly has no lien on them enforceable on liquidation.

What are *partnership claims,* of course, is a question of law and fact. A non-partner, held liable to creditors by estoppel as an *ostensible* partner, U.P.A. § 16, is said to have no *equity* to insist that *partnership* assets be used as above to pay his creditors. The point, however, is in some dispute. See generally, Broadway Nat. Bank v. Wood (1896) 165 Mass. 312, 43 N.E. 100.

In the case of a *limited* partnership the order of distribution is much the same. See, U.L.P.A. § 23. That is, partnership assets are to be used first to pay partnership creditors. As might be expected, limited partners are then given priority over general partners, both in the payment of any income due them, and also in the repayment of their capital contributions. Following that, the remaining estate is distributed to the general partners, first in repayment of claims for money advanced, next for "profits," and then "in respect to capital."

§ 86. Dual Priorities

It is equally well settled, perhaps as a result, that the *individual* creditors of a partner are first to be paid out of his *personal* assets. Only then do partnership creditors have any standing; they are then admitted to share equally, or *pari passu,* with unpaid personal creditors in any assets remaining. Thus a balanced remedy, sometimes called the "jingle" rule, established by the equity courts two or more centuries ago. See, *MacLachlan*, Bankruptcy (1956) p. 424.

The reasons for the first branch of the rule, that partnership creditors look first to partnership assets, are as uncertain as the rule itself is certain. The second branch of the rule was reached only after much debate. In a leading case, affirming the second branch, Bartley, C. J., put it this way: "[P]erfect equality between the joint and individual creditors, is, perhaps, rarely attainable. That it is, however, more equal and just, as a general rule, than any other which can be devised, *consistently with the preference to the partnership creditors in the joint estate,* cannot be successfully controverted." See, Rodgers v. Meranda (1857) 7 Ohio St. 179 (Emphasis added.)

It has been urged that the priority rule as respects the partnership is confirmation of the entity theory. That is, the firm is treated as an entity when it is said that *its* creditors have priority of payment from *its* assets. While this is true enough, there is little evidence that the early courts reasoned in that way. Rather, since the action was in equity, they started from the premise that "equality is equity," and while they clearly viewed the partnership as an entity, that was not the basis for their holding.

However that may be, for purposes of bankruptcy today, the partnership definitely is to be regarded as an entity. That is, the partnership, as such, may be declared bankrupt. See, Fed. Bankruptcy Act, 11 U.S.C.A. § 23. There has been resistance when the trustee has demanded, as part of the process of marshalling its assets, that each partner turn in his personal assets for administration, but the trustee has prevailed. See, In re Ira Haupt & Co. (D.C.N.Y.1965) 240 F.Supp. 369. Indeed, as the courts have said, it is hard to conceive of a bankrupt *partnership,* when one or more of its partners is solvent.

Moreover, the Act adopts explicitly the dual priorities rule as above discussed: "(g) The net proceeds of the partnership property shall be appropriated to the payment of the partnership debts and the net proceeds of the individual estate of each general partner to the payment of his individual debts." See, § 5(g), 11 U.S.C.A. § 23. The section goes on to say that should any surplus remain in any general partner's estate, after paying his individual debts, that surplus shall be added to the partnership property, if needed, to pay its debts. Thus, whatever its rational basis, the dual priorities rule is law.

§ 87. Priorities at Law

It is essential to keep the foregoing discussion of distribution priorities in context. They are a creation of equity and have no application at law. In other words, it is still true that a partnership creditor may hold any partner liable for firm debts "to the last farthing and the last acre" as of old. Indeed, as noted above, the way has been made easier by recent legislation in effect removing the requirement of joint action. See, § 78 supra. It follows that if such a creditor were to recover a judgment for, say $50,000, the defendant then would have the arduous task of seeking out his co-partners for contribution.

It would seem, however, that things seldom come to such a pass. At some point it may be found that either the partner, or the firm, is bankrupt, and then the trustee will liquidate assets as above discussed. Or, the personal creditors of the partner—rather than lose access to $50,000 in assets—may succeed in having a receiver appointed, who will distribute the full estate to personal creditors first. Or, more likely, there may be cause for dissolution, U.P.A. § 31, in which case the partner then in charge of winding up will apply firm assets first, as above discussed. See, §§ 85 and 86.

These possibilities aside, there has been a growing trend, at law, to insist that a partnership creditor bring his action first against the firm. Only after he has exhausted the assets held in common has he any standing to sue a partner individually.

See generally, Horn's Crane Service v. Prior (1967) 182 Neb. 94, 152 N.W.2d 421, so holding. Looking at the question through the eyes of the creditor, however, whom did he *expect* to hold? The question has been much debated and has received a variety of answers through the years. See Lewis, The Uniform Partnership Act (1915) 24 Yale L.J. 617.

Today, it would seem, the well advised creditor must increasingly expect to look first to the credit of the partnership. Not that we have gone as far with the entity theory as to say he may now hold the firm *only*. The individual credit of a partner is still of major importance, but the trend is definitely to require creditors to look first to the firm. Of course as a legal matter, in a given case, it will depend on the law of the particular state. But enough has been said to suggest that the question does not turn on the expectations of a hypothetical creditor.

Last century, in the case of the joint stock association, it was expressly provided that a creditor must exhaust his remedy against the association before suit might be brought against a shareholder-partner. See, Westcott v. Fargo (1875) 61 N.Y. 542. But that was a special situation, an attempt to give the firm attributes of a corporation. So also, the effort of trustees of a business trust by use of contract to the same end has its own reasons. See, §§ 76 and 77, supra. However, though the reasons differ, these two illustrations also point in the direction of centralized primary liability.

§ 88. Finally

It is well to stand aside a moment and view the Agency-Partnership institution as an anthropologist might look at it. One has the impression that, under the watchful guidance of the judiciary, the institution has served the English speaking tribes fairly and rather well, in their search for economic security and the good life. See, very generally, *Ardrey,* The Social Contract (1970).

APPENDIX A

UNIFORM PARTNERSHIP ACT

---

§ 1. Name of act. This act may be cited as Uniform Partnership Act.[1]

§ 2. Definition of terms. In this act, "Court" includes every court and judge having jurisdiction in the case.

"Business" includes every trade, occupation, or profession.

"Person" includes individuals, partnerships, corporations, and other associations.

"Bankrupt" includes bankrupt under the Federal Bankruptcy Act or insolvent under any state insolvent act.

"Conveyance" includes every assignment, lease, mortgage, or encumbrance.

"Real property" includes land and any interest or estate in land.

§ 3. Interpretation of knowledge and notice. (1) A person has "knowledge" of a fact within the meaning of this act not only when he has actual knowledge thereof, but also when he has

[1] For a list of adoptions and references to pertinent case law, see Vol. 6 Uniform Laws Annotated (West Publishing Co. 1969).

[*279*]

knowledge of such other facts as in the circumstances shows bad faith.

(2) A person has "notice" of a fact within the meaning of this act when the person who claims the benefit of the notice:

(a) States the fact to such person, or

(b) Delivers through the mail, or by other means of communication, a written statement of the fact to such person or to a proper person at his place of business or residence.

§ 4. Rules of construction. (1) The rule that statutes in derogation of the common law are to be strictly construed shall have no application to this act.

(2) The law of estoppel shall apply under this act.

(3) The law of agency shall apply under this act.

(4) This act shall be so interpreted and construed as to effect its general purpose to make uniform the law of those states which enact it.

(5) This act shall not be construed so as to impair the obligations of any contract existing when the act goes into effect, nor to affect any action or proceedings begun or right accrued before this act takes effect.

§ 5. Rules for cases not provided for in this act. In any case not provided for in this act the rules of law and equity, including the law merchant, shall govern.

§ 6. Partnership defined. (1) A partnership is an association of two or more persons to carry on as co-owners a business for profit.

(2) But any association formed under any other statute of this state, or any statute adopted by authority, other than the authority of this state, is not a partnership under this act, unless such association would have been a partnership in this state prior to the adoption of this act; but this act shall apply to limited partnerships except in so far as the statutes relating to such partnerships are inconsistent herewith.

§ 7. Rules for determining the existence of a partnership. In determining whether a partnership exists, these rules shall apply:

(1) Except as provided by section 16 persons who are not partners as to each other are not partners as to third persons.

(2) Joint tenancy, tenancy in common, tenancy by the entireties, joint property, common property, or part ownership does not of itself establish a partnership, whether such co-owners do or do not share any profits made by the use of the property.

(3) The sharing of gross returns does not of itself establish a partnership, whether or not the persons sharing them have a joint or common

right or interest in any property from which the returns are derived.

(4) The receipt by a person of a share of the profits of a business is prima facie evidence that he is a partner in the business, but no such inference shall be drawn if such profits were received in payment:

(a) As a debt by installments or otherwise,

(b) As wages of an employee or rent to a landlord,

(c) As an annuity to a widow or representative of a deceased partner,

(d) As interest on a loan, though the amount of payment vary with the profits of the business,

(e) As the consideration for the sale of a goodwill of a business or other property by installments or otherwise.

§ 8. Partnership property. (1) All property originally brought into the partnership stock or subsequently acquired by purchase or otherwise, on account of the partnership, is partnership property.

(2) Unless the contrary intention appears, property acquired with partnership funds is partnership property.

(3) Any estate in real property may be acquired in the partnership name. Title so acquired can be conveyed only in the partnership name.

(4) A conveyance to a partnership in the partnership name, though without words of inheritance, passes the entire estate of the grantor unless a contrary intent appears.

§ 9. **Partner agent of partnership as to partnership business.** (1) Every partner is an agent of the partnership for the purpose of its business, and the act of every partner, including the execution in the partnership name of any instrument, for apparently carrying on in the usual way the business of the partnership of which he is a member binds the partnership, unless the partner so acting has in fact no authority to act for the partnership in the particular matter, and the person with whom he is dealing has knowledge of the fact that he has no such authority.

(2) An act of a partner which is not apparently for the carrying on of the business of the partnership in the usual way does not bind the partnership unless authorized by the other partners.

(3) Unless authorized by the other partners or unless they have abandoned the business, one or more but less than all the partners have no authority to:

(a) Assign the partnership property in trust for creditors or on the assignee's promise to pay the debts of the partnership,

(b) Dispose of the good-will of the business,

(c) Do any other act which would make it impossible to carry on the ordinary business of a partnership,

(d) Confess a judgment,

(e) Submit a partnership claim or liability to arbitration or reference.

(4) No act of a partner in contravention of a restriction on authority shall bind the partnership to persons having knowledge of the restriction.

§ 10. **Conveyance of real property of the partnership.** (1) Where title to real property is in the partnership name, any partner may convey title to such property by a conveyance executed in the partnership name; but the partnership may recover such property unless the partner's act binds the partnership under the provisions of paragraph (1) of section 9, or unless such property has been conveyed by the grantee or a person claiming through such grantee to a holder for value without knowledge that the partner, in making the conveyance, has exceeded his authority.

(2) Where title to real property is in the name of the partnership, a conveyance executed by a partner, in his own name, passes the equitable interest of the partnership, provided the act is one within the authority of the partner under the provisions of paragraph (1) of section 9.

(3) Where title to real property is in the name of one or more but not all the partners, and the record does not disclose the right of the partnership, the partners in whose name the title stands may convey title to such property, but the partnership may recover such property if the partners' act does not bind the partnership under the provisions of paragraph (1) of section 9, unless the purchaser or his assignee, is a holder for value, without knowledge.

(4) Where the title to real property is in the name of one or more or all the partners, or in a third person in trust for the partnership, a conveyance executed by a partner in the partnership name, or in his own name, passes the equitable interest of the partnership, provided the act is one within the authority of the partner under the provisions of paragraph (1) of section 9.

(5) Where the title to real property is in the names of all the partners a conveyance executed by all the partners passes all their rights in such property.

§ 11. Partnership bound by admission of partner. An admission or presentation made by any partner concerning partnership affairs within the scope of his authority as conferred by this act is evidence against the partnership.

§ 12. Partnership charged with knowledge of or notice to partner. Notice to any partner of any matter relating to partnership affairs, and the knowledge of the partner acting in the particular matter, acquired while a partner or then present to his mind, and the knowledge of any other partner who reasonably could and should have communicated it to the acting partner, operate as notice to or knowledge of the partnership, except in the case of a fraud on the partnership committed by or with the consent of that partner.

§ 13. Partnership bound by partner's wrongful act. Where, by any wrongful act or omission of any partner acting in the ordinary course of the business of the partnership or with the authority of his co-partners, loss or injury is caused to any person, not being a partner in the partnership, or any penalty is incurred, the partnership is liable therefor to the same extent as the partner so acting or omitting to act.

§ 14. Partnership bound by partner's breach of trust. The partnership is bound to make good the loss:

(a) Where one partner acting within the scope of his apparent authority receives money or property of a third person and misapplies it; and

(b) Where the partnership in the course of its business receives money or property of a third person and the money or property so received is misapplied by any partner while it is in the custody of the partnership.

§ 15. Nature of partner's liability. All partners are liable

(a) Jointly and severally for everything chargeable to the partnership under sections 13 and 14.

(b) Jointly for all other debts and obligations of the partnership; but any partner may enter into a separate obligation to perform a partnership contract.

§ 16. Partner by estoppel. (1) When a person, by words spoken or written or by conduct, represents himself, or consents to another representing him to any one, as a partner in an existing partnership or with one or more persons not actual partners, he is liable to any such person to whom such representation has been made, who has, on the faith of such representation, given credit to the actual or apparent partnership, and if he has made such representation or consented to its being made in a public manner he is liable to such person, whether the representation has or has not been made or communicated to such person so giving credit by or with the knowledge of the apparent partner making the representation or consenting to its being made.

(a) When a partnership liability results, he is liable as though he were an actual member of the partnership.

(b) When no partnership liability results, he is liable jointly with the other persons, if any, so consenting to the contract or representation as to incur liability, otherwise separately.

(2) When a person has been thus represented to be a partner in an existing partnership, or with one or more persons not actual partners, he is an agent of the persons consenting to such representation to bind them to the same extent and in the same manner as though he were a partner in fact, with respect to persons who rely upon the representation. Where all the members of the existing partnership consent to the representation, a partnership act or obligation results; but in all other cases it is the joint act or obligation of the person acting and the persons consenting to the representation.

§ 17. Liability of incoming partner. A person admitted as a partner into an existing partnership is liable for all the obligations of the partnership arising before his admission as though he had been a partner when such obligations were incurred, except that this liability shall be satisfied only out of partnership property.

Part IV—Relations of Partners to One Another

§ 18. Rules determining rights and duties of partners. The rights and duties of the partners in relation to the partnership shall be determined, subject to any agreement between them, by the following rules:

(a) Each partner shall be repaid his contributions, whether by way of capital or advances to the partnership property and share equally in the profits and surplus remaining after all liabilities, including those to partners, are satisfied; and must contribute towards the losses, whether of capital or otherwise, sustained by the partnership according to his share in the profits.

(b) The partnership must indemnify every partner in respect of payments made and personal liabilities reasonably incurred by him in the ordinary and proper conduct of its business, or for the preservation of its business or property.

(c) A partner, who in aid of the partnership makes any payment or advance beyond the amount of capital which he agreed to contribute shall be paid interest from the date of the payment or advance.

(d) A partner shall receive interest on the capital contributed by him only from the date when repayment should be made.

(e) All partners have equal rights in the management and conduct of the partnership business.

(f) No partner is entitled to remuneration for acting in the partnership business, except that a surviving partner is entitled to reasonable compensation for his services in winding up the partnership affairs.

(g) No person can become a member of a partnership without the consent of all the partners.

(h) Any difference arising as to ordinary matters connected with the partnership business may be decided by a majority of the partners; but no act in contravention of any agreement between the partners may be done rightfully without the consent of all the partners.

§ 19. **Partnership books.** The partnership books shall be kept, subject to any agreement between the partners, at the principal place of business of the partnership, and every partner shall at all times have access to and may inspect and copy any of them.

§ 20. **Duty of partners to render information.** Partners shall render on demand true and full information of all things affecting the partnership to any partner or the legal representative of any deceased partner or partner under legal disability.

§ 21. **Partner accountable as a fiduciary.** (1) Every partner must account to the partnership for any benefit, and hold as trustee for it any profits derived by him without the consent of the other partners from any transaction connected with the formation, conduct, or liquidation of the partnership or from any use by him of its property.

(2) This section applies also to the representatives of a deceased partner engaged in the liquidation of the affairs of the partnership as the personal representatives of the last surviving partner.

§ 22. **Right to an account.** Any partner shall have the right to a formal account as to partnership affairs:

(a) If he is wrongfully excluded from the partnership business or possession of its property by his co-partners,

(b) If the right exists under the terms of any agreement,

(c) As provided by section 21,

(d) Whenever other circumstances render it just and reasonable.

§ 23. **Continuation of partnership beyond fixed term.** (1) When a partnership for a fixed term or particular undertaking is continued after the termination of such term or particular undertaking without any express agreement, the rights and duties of the partners remain the same as they were at such termination, so far as is consistent with a partnership at will.

(2) A continuation of the business by the partners or such of them as habitually acted therein

during the term, without any settlement or liquidation of the partnership affairs, is prima facie evidence of a continuation of the partnership.

Part V—Property Rights of a Partner

§ 24. Extent of property rights of a partner. The property rights of a partner are (1) his rights in specific partnership property, (2) his interest in the partnership, and (3) his right to participate in the management.

§ 25. Nature of a partner's right in specific partnership property. (1) A partner is co-owner with his partners of specific partnership property holding as a tenant in partnership.

(2) The incidents of this tenancy are such that:

(a) A partner, subject to the provisions of this act and to any agreement between the partners, has an equal right with his partners to possess specific partnership property for partnership purposes; but he has no right to possess such property for any other purpose without the consent of his partners.

(b) A partner's right in specific partnership property is not assignable except in connection with the assignment of rights of all the partners in the same property.

(c) A partner's right in specific partnership property is not subject to attachment or execution, except on a claim against the partnership. When partnership property is attached for a partnership debt the partners, or any of them, or the representatives of a deceased partner, cannot claim any right under the homestead or exemption laws.

(d) On the death of a partner his right in specific partnership property vests in the surviving partner or partners, except where the deceased was the last surviving partner, when his right in such property vests in his legal representative. Such surviving partner or partners, or the legal representative of the last surviving partner, has no right to possess the partnership property for any but a partnership purpose.

(e) A partner's right in specific partnership property is not subject to dower, curtesy, or allowances to widows, heirs, or next of kin.

§ 26. Nature of partner's interest in the partnership. A partner's interest in the partnership is his share of the profits and surplus, and the same is personal property.

§ 27. Assignment of partner's interest. (1) A conveyance by a partner of his interest in the partnership does not of itself dissolve the partnership, nor, as against the other partners in the absence of agreement, entitled the assignee, during the continuance of the partnership to interfere in the management or administration of the partnership business or affairs, or to require any information or account of partnership transactions, or to inspect the partnership books; but it merely entitles the assignee to receive in accordance with his contract the profits to which the assigning partner would otherwise be entitled.

(2) In case of a dissolution of the partnership, the assignee is entitled to receive his assignor's interest and may require an account from the date only of the last account agreed to by all the partners.

§ 28. **Partner's interest subject to charging order.** (1) On due application to a competent court by any judgment creditor of a partner, the court which entered the judgment, order, or decree, or any other court, may charge the interest of the debtor partner with payment of the unsatisfied amount of such judgment debt with interest thereon; and may then or later appoint a receiver of his share of the profits, and of any other money due or to fall due to him in respect of the partnership, and make all other orders, directions, accounts and inquiries which the debtor partner might have made, or which the circumstances of the case may require.

(2) The interest charged may be redeemed at any time before foreclosure, or in case of a sale

being directed by the court may be purchased without thereby causing a dissolution:

(a) With separate property, by any one or more of the partners, or

(b) With partnership property, by any one or more of the partners with the consent of all the partners whose interests are not so charged or sold.

(3) Nothing in this act shall be held to deprive a partner of his right, if any, under the exemption laws, as regards his interest in the partnership.

Part VI—Dissolution and Winding Up

§ 29. Dissolution defined. The dissolution of a partnership is the change in the relation of the partners caused by any partner ceasing to be associated in the carrying on as distinguished from the winding up of the business.

§ 30. Partnership not terminated by dissolution. On dissolution the partnership is not terminated, but continues until the winding up of partnership affairs is completed.

§ 31. Causes of dissolution. Dissolution is caused: (1) Without violation of the agreement between the partners,

(a) By the termination of the definite term or particular undertaking specified in the agreement,

(b) By the express will of any partner when no definite term or particular undertaking is specified,

(c) By the express will of all the partners who have not assigned their interests or suffered them to be charged for their separate debts, either before or after the termination of any specified term or particular undertaking,

(d) By the expulsion of any partner from the business bona fide in accordance with such a power conferred by the agreement between the partners;

(2) In contravention of the agreement between the partners, where the circumstances do not permit a dissolution under any other provision of this section, by the express will of any partner at any time;

(3) By any event which makes it unlawful for the business of the partnership to be carried on or for the members to carry it on in partnership;

(4) By the death of any partner;

(5) By the bankruptcy of any partner or the partnership;

(6) By decree of court under section 32.

§ 32. Dissolution by decree of court. (1) On application by or for a partner the court shall decree a dissolution whenever:

(a) A partner has been declared a lunatic in any judicial proceeding or is shown to be of unsound mind,

(b) A partner becomes in any other way incapable of performing his part of the partnership contract,

(c) A partner has been guilty of such conduct as tends to affect prejudicially the carrying on of the business,

(d) A partner wilfully or persistently commits a breach of the partnership agreement, or otherwise so conducts himself in matters relating to the partnership business that it is not reasonably practicable to carry on the business in partnership with him,

(e) The business of the partnership can only be carried on at a loss,

(f) Other circumstances render a dissolution equitable.

(2) On the application of the purchaser of a partner's interest under sections 27 or 28:

(a) After the termination of the specified term or particular undertaking,

(b) At any time if the partnership was a partnership at will when the interest was assigned or when the charging order was issued.

§ 33. General effect of dissolution on authority of partner. Except so far as may be necessary to wind up partnership affairs or to complete transactions begun but not then finished, dissolution terminates all authority of any partner to act for the partnership,

(1) With respect to the partners,

(a) When the dissolution is not by the act, bankruptcy or death of a partner; or

(b) When the dissolution is by such act, bankruptcy or death of a partner, in cases where section 34 so requires.

(2) With respect to persons not partners, as declared in section 35.

§ 34. Right of partner to contribution from co-partners after dissolution. Where the dissolution is caused by the act, death or bankruptcy of a partner, each partner is liable to his co-partners for his share of any liability created by any partner acting for the partnership as if the partnership had not been dissolved unless

(a) The dissolution being by act of any partner, the partner acting for the partnership had knowledge of the dissolution, or

(b) The dissolution being by the death or bankruptcy of a partner, the partner acting for the partnership had knowledge or notice of the death or bankruptcy.

§ 35. Power of partner to bind partnership to third persons after dissolution. (1) After dissolution a partner can bind the partnership except as provided in Paragraph (3).

(a) By any act appropriate for winding up partnership affairs or completing transactions unfinished at dissolution;

(b) By any transaction which would bind the partnership if dissolution had not taken place, provided the other party to the transaction

(I) Had extended credit to the partnership prior to dissolution and had no knowledge or notice of the dissolution; or

(II) Though he had not so extended credit, had nevertheless known of the partnership prior to dissolution, and, having no knowledge or notice of dissolution, the fact of dissolution had not been advertised in a newspaper of general circulation in the place (or in each place if more than one) at which the partnership business was regularly carried on.

(2) The liability of a partner under Paragraph (1b) shall be satisfied out of partnership assets alone when such partner had been prior to dissolution

(a) Unknown as a partner to the person with whom the contract is made; and

(b) So far unknown and inactive in partnership affairs that the business reputation of the partnership could not be said to have been in any degree due to his connection with it.

(3) The partnership is in no case bound by any act of a partner after dissolution

(a) Where the partnership is dissolved because it is unlawful to carry on the business, unless the act is appropriate for winding up partnership affairs; or

(b) Where the partner has become bankrupt; or

(c) Where the partner has no authority to wind up partnership affairs; except by a transaction with one who

(I) Had extended credit to the partnership prior to dissolution and had no knowledge or notice of his want of authority; or

(II) Had not extended credit to the partnership prior to dissolution, and, having no knowledge or notice of his want of authority, the fact of his want of authority has not been advertised in the manner provided for advertising the fact of dissolution in Paragraph (1bII).

(4) Nothing in this section shall affect the liability under Section 16 of any person who after

dissolution represents himself or consents to another representing him as a partner in a partnership engaged in carrying on business.

§ 36. Effect of dissolution on partner's existing liability. (1) The dissolution of the partnership does not of itself discharge the existing liability of any partner.

(2) A partner is discharged from any existing liability upon dissolution of the partnership by an agreement to that effect between himself, the partnership creditor and the person or partnership continuing the business; and such agreement may be inferred from the course of dealing between the creditor having knowledge of the dissolution and the person or partnership continuing the business.

(3) Where a person agrees to assume the existing obligations of a dissolved partnership, the partners whose obligations have been assumed shall be discharged from any liability to any creditor of the partnership who, knowing of the agreement, consents to a material alteration in the nature or time of payment of such obligations.

(4) The individual property of a deceased partner shall be liable for all obligations of the partnership incurred while he was a partner but subject to the prior payment of his separate debts.

§ 37. Right to wind up. Unless otherwise agreed the partners who have not wrongfully dissolved the partnership or the legal representative of the last surviving partner, not bankrupt, has the right to wind up the partnership affairs; provided, however, that any partner, his legal representative or his assignee, upon cause shown, may obtain winding up by the court.

§ 38. **Rights of partners to application of partnership property.** (1) When dissolution is caused in any way, except in contravention of the partnership agreement, each partner as against his co-partners and all persons claiming through them in respect of their interests in the partnership, unless otherwise agreed, may have the partnership property applied to discharge its liabilities, and the surplus applied to pay in cash the net amount owing to the respective partners. But if dissolution is caused by expulsion of a partner, bona fide under the partnership agreement and if the expelled partner is discharged from all partnership liabilities, either by payment or agreement under section 36(2), he shall receive in cash only the net amount due him from the partnership.

(2) When dissolution is caused in contravention of the partnership agreement the rights of the partners shall be as follows:

(a) Each partner who has not caused dissolution wrongfully shall have,

[*302*]

(I) All the rights specified in paragraph (1) of this section, and

(II) The right, as against each partner who has caused the dissolution wrongfully, to damages for breach of the agreement.

(b) The partners who have not caused the dissolution wrongfully, if they all desire to continue the business in the same name, either by themselves or jointly with others, may do so, during the agreed term for the partnership and for that purpose may possess the partnership property, provided they secure the payment by bond approved by the court, or pay to any partner who has caused the dissolution wrongfully, the value of his interest in the partnership at the dissolution, less any damages recoverable under clause (2aII) of the section, and in like manner indemnify him against all present or future partnership liabilities.

(c) A partner who has caused the dissolution wrongfully shall have:

(I) If the business is not continued under the provisions of paragraph (2b) all the rights of a partner under paragraph (1), subject to clause (2aII), of this section,

(II) If the business is continued under paragraph (2b) of this section the right as against his co-partners and all claiming through them in respect of their interests in the partnership, to have the value of his interest in the partnership, less any damages caused to his co-partners by the dissolution, ascertained and paid to him in cash, or the payment secured by bond approved by the court, and to be released from all existing liabilities of the partnership; but in ascertaining the value of the partner's interest the value of the good-will of the business shall not be considered.

§ 39. Rights where partnership is dissolved for fraud or misrepresentation. Where a partnership contract is rescinded on the ground of the fraud or misrepresentation of one of the parties thereto, the party entitled to rescind is, without prejudice to any other right, entitled,

(a) To a lien on, or right of retention of, the surplus of the partnership property after satisfying the partnership liabilities to third persons for any sum of money paid by him for the purchase of an interest in the partnership and for any capital or advances contributed by him; and

(b) To stand, after all liabilities to third persons have been satisfied, in the place of the creditors of the partnership for any payments made by him in respect of the partnership liabilities; and

(c) To be indemnified by the person guilty of the fraud or making the representation against all debts and liabilities of the partnership.

§ 40. Rules for distribution. In settling accounts between the partners after dissolution, the following rules shall be observed, subject to any agreement to the contrary:

(a) The assets of the partnership are:

(I) The partnership property,

(II) The contributions of the partners necessary for the payment of all the liabilities specified in clause (b) of this paragraph.

(b) The liabilities of the partnership shall rank in order of payment, as follows:

(I) Those owing to creditors other than partners,

(II) Those owing to partners other than for capital and profits,

(III) Those owing to partners in respect of capital,

(IV) Those owing to partners in respect of profits.

(c) The assets shall be applied in the order of their declaration in clause (a) of this paragraph to the satisfaction of the liabilities.

(d) The partners shall contribute, as provided by section 18(a) the amount necessary to satisfy the liabilities; but if any, but not all, of the partners are insolvent, or, not being subject to process, refuse to contribute, the other parties shall contribute their share of the liabilities, and, in the relative proportions in which they share the profits, the additional amount necessary to pay the liabilities.

(e) An assignee for the benefit of creditors or any person appointed by the court shall have the right to enforce the contributions specified in clause (d) of this paragraph.

(f) Any partner or his legal representative shall have the right to enforce the contributions specified in clause (d) of this paragraph, to the extent of the amount which he has paid in excess of his share of the liability.

(g) The individual property of a deceased partner shall be liable for the contributions specified in clause (d) of this paragraph.

(h) When partnership property and the individual properties of the partners are in possession of a court for distribution, partnership creditors shall have priority on partnership property and separate creditors on individual property, saving the rights of lien or secured creditors as heretofore.

(i) Where a partner has become bankrupt or his estate is insolvent the claims against his separate property shall rank in the following order:

(I) Those owing to separate creditors,

(II) Those owing to partnership creditors,

(III) Those owing to partners by way of contribution.

§ 41. Liability of persons continuing the business in certain cases. (1) When any new partner is admitted into an existing partnership, or when any partner retires and assigns (or the representative of the deceased partner assigns) his rights in partnership property to two or more of the partners, or to one or more of the partners and one or more third persons, if the business is continued without liquidation of the partnership affairs, creditors of the first or dissolved partnership are also creditors of the partnership so continuing the business.

(2) When all but one partner retire and assign (or the representative of a deceased partner assigns) their rights in partnership property to the remaining partner, who continues the business without liquidation of partnership affairs, either alone or with others, creditors of the dissolved partnership are also creditors of the person or partnership so continuing the business.

(3) When any partner retires or dies and the business of the dissolved partnership is continued as set forth in paragraphs (1) and (2) of this section, with the consent of the retired partners or the representative of the deceased partner, but without any assignment of his right in partnership property, rights of creditors of the dissolved partnership and of the creditors of the person or partnership continuing the business shall be as if such assignment had been made.

[*307*]

(4) When all the partners or their representatives assign their rights in partnership property to one or more third persons who promise to pay the debts and who continue the business of the dissolved partnership, creditors of the dissolved partnership are also creditors of the person or partnership continuing the business.

(5) When any partner wrongfully causes a dissolution and the remaining partners continue the business under the provisions of section 38 (2b), either alone or with others, and without liquidation of the partnership affairs, creditors of the dissolved partnership are also creditors of the person or partnership continuing the business.

(6) When a partner is expelled and the remaining partners continue the business either alone or with others, without liquidation of the partnership affairs, creditors of the dissolved partnership are also creditors of the person or partnership continuing the business.

(7) The liability of a third person becoming a partner in the partnership continuing the business, under this section, to the creditors of the dissolved partnership shall be satisfied out of partnership property only.

(8) When the business of a partnership after dissolution is continued under any conditions set forth in this section the creditors of the dissolved partnership, as against the separate creditors of

the retiring or deceased partner or the representative of the deceased partner, have a prior right to any claim of the retired partner or the representative of the deceased partner against the person or partnership continuing the business, on account of the retired or deceased partner's interest in the dissolved partnership or on account of any consideration promised for such interest or for his right in partnership property.

(9) Nothing in this section shall be held to modify any right of creditors to set aside any assignment on the ground of fraud.

(10) The use by the person or partnership continuing the business of the partnership name, or the name of a deceased partner as part thereof, shall not of itself make the individual property of the deceased partner liable for any debts contracted by such person or partnership.

§ 42. Rights of retiring or estate of deceased partner when the business is continued. When any partner retires or dies, and the business is continued under any of the conditions set forth in section 41(1, 2, 3, 5, 6), or section 38(2b), without any settlement of accounts as between him or his estate and the person or partnership continuing the business, unless otherwise agreed, he or his legal representative as against such persons or partnership may have the value of his interest at the date of dissolution ascertained, and shall receive as an ordinary creditor an amount equal to the value of his interest in the dissolved partnership with interest, or, at his option or at the option of his legal representative, in lieu of interest, the profits attributable to the use of his right in the property of the dissolved partnership; provided that the creditors of the dissolved partnership as against the separate creditors, or the representative of the retired or deceased partner, shall have priority on any claim arising under this section, as provided by section 41(8) of this act.

§ 43. Accrual of actions. The right to an account of his interest shall accrue to any partner, or his legal representative, as against the winding up partners or the surviving partners or the person or partnership continuing the business, at the date of dissolution, in the absence of any agreement to the contrary.

Part VII—Miscellaneous Provisions

§ 44. When act takes effect. This act shall take effect on the _____ day of _____ one thousand nine hundred and _____.

§ 45. Legislation repealed. All acts or parts of acts inconsistent with this act are hereby repealed.

APPENDIX B

UNIFORM LIMITED PARTNER-SHIP ACT

(Omitted: §§ 29, 30, 31)

§ 1. Limited partnership defined.[1] A limited partnership is a partnership formed by two or more persons under the provisions of Section 2, having as members one or more general partners and one or more limited partners. The limited partners as such shall not be bound by the obligations of the partnership.

§ 2. Formation. (1) Two or more persons desiring to form a limited partnership shall

(a) Sign and swear to a certificate, which shall state

I. The name of the partnership,

II. The character of the business,

III. The location of the principal place of business,

IV. The name and place of residence of each member; general and limited partners being respectively designated,

V. The term for which the partnership is to exist,

[1] For a list of adoptions and references to pertinent case law, see Vol. 6 Uniform Laws Annotated (West Publishing Co. 1969).

VI. The amount of cash and a description of and the agreed value of the other property contributed by each limited partner,

VII. The additional contributions, if any, agreed to be made by each limited partner and the times at which or events on the happening of which they shall be made,

VIII. The time, if agreed upon, when the contribution of each limited partner is to be returned,

IX. The share of the profits or the other compensation by way of income which each limited partner shall receive by reason of his contribution,

X. The right, if given, of a limited partner to substitute an assignee as contributor in his place, and the terms and conditions of the substitution,

XI. The right, if given, of the partners to admit additional limited partners,

XII. The right, if given, of one or more of the limited partners to priority over other limited partners, as to contributions or as to compensation by way of income, and the nature of such priority,

XIII. The right, given, of the remaining general partner or partners to continue the business on the death, retirement or insanity of a general partner, and

XIV. The right, if given, of a limited partner to demand and receive property other than cash in return for his contribution.

(b) File for record the certificate in the office of [here designate the proper office].

(2) A limited partnership is formed if there has been substantial compliance in good faith with the requirements of paragraph (1).

§ 3. Business which may be carried on. A limited partnership may carry on any business which a partnership without limited partners may carry on, except [here designate the business to be prohibited].

§ 4. Character of limited partner's contribution. The contributions of a limited partner may be cash or other property, but not services.

§ 5. A name not to contain surname of limited partner; exceptions. (1) The surname of a limited partner shall not appear in the partnership name, unless

(a) It is also the surname of a general partner, or

(b) Prior to the time when the limited partner became such the business had been carried on under a name in which his surname appeared.

(2) A limited partner whose name appears in a partnership name contrary to the provisions of paragraph (1) is liable as a general partner

to partnership creditors who extend credit to the partnership without actual knowledge that he is not a general partner.

§ 6. Liability for false statements in certificate. If the certificate contains a false statement, one who suffers loss by reliance on such statement may hold liable any party to the certificate who knew the statement to be false.

(a) At the time he signed the certificate, or

(b) Subsequently, but within a sufficient time before the statement was relied upon to enable him to cancel or amend the certificate, or to file a petition for its cancellation or amendment as provided in Section 25(3).

§ 7. Limited partner not liable to creditors. A limited partner shall not become liable as a general partner unless, in addition to the exercise of his rights and powers as a limited partner, he takes part in the control of the business.

§ 8. Admission of additional limited partners. After the formation of a limited partnership, additional limited partners may be admitted upon filing an amendment to the original certificate in accordance with the requirements of Section 25.

§ 9. Rights, powers and liabilities of a general partner. (1) A general partner shall have all the rights and powers and be subject to all the restrictions and liabilities of a partner in a partnership without limited partners, except that without the written consent or ratification of the specific act by all the limited partners, a general partner or all of the general partners have no authority to

(a) Do any act in contravention of the certificate,

(b) Do any act which would make it impossible to carry on the ordinary business of the partnership,

(c) Confess a judgment against the partnership,

(d) Possess partnership property, or assign their rights in specific partnership property, for other than a partnership purpose,

(e) Admit a person as a general partner,

(f) Admit a person as a limited partner, unless the right so to do is given in the certificate,

(g) Continue the business with partnership property on the death, retirement or insanity of a general partner, unless the right so to do is given in the certificate.

§ 10. Rights of a limited partner. (1) A limited partner shall have the same rights as a general partner to

(a) Have the partnership books kept at the principal place of business of the partnership, and at all times to inspect and copy any of them,

(b) Have on demand true and full information of all things affecting the partnership, and a formal account of partnership affairs whenever circumstances render it just and reasonable, and

(c) Have dissolution and winding up by decree of court.

(2) A limited partner shall have the right to receive a share of the profits or other compensation by way of income, and to the return of his contribution as provided in Sections 15 and 16.

§ 11. **Status of person erroneously believing himself a limited partner.** A person who has contributed to the capital of a business conducted by a person or partnership erroneously believing that he has become a limited partner in a limited partnership, is not, by reason of his exercise of the rights of a limited partner, a general partner with the person or in the partnership carrying on the business, or bound by the obligations of such person or partnership; provided that on ascertaining the mistake he promptly renounces his interest in the profits of the business, or other compensation by way of income.

§ 12. **One person both general and limited partner.** (1) A person may be a general partner and a limited partner in the same partnership at the same time.

(2) A person who is a general, and also at the same time a limited partner, shall have all the

rights and powers and be subject to all the restrictions of a general partner; except that, in respect to his contribution, he shall have the rights against the other members which he would have had if he were not also a general partner.

§ 13. Loans and other business transactions with limited partner. (1) A limited partner also may loan money to and transact other business with the partnership, and, unless he is also a general partner, receive on account of resulting claims against the partnership, with general creditors, a pro rata share of the assets. No limited partner shall in respect to any such claim

(a) Receive or hold as collateral security any partnership property, or

(b) Receive from a general partner or the partnership any payment, conveyance, or release from liability, if at the time the assets of the partnership are not sufficient to discharge partnership liabilities to persons not claiming as general or limited partners,

(2) The receiving of collateral security, or a payment, conveyance, or release in violation of the provisions of paragraph (1) is a fraud on the creditors of the partnership.

§ 14. Relation of limited partners inter se. Where there are several limited partners the members may agree that one or more of the limited partners shall have a priority over other limited partners as to the return of their contributions, as to their compensation by way of income, or as to any other matter. If such an agreement is made it shall be stated in the certificate, and in the absence of such a statement all the limited partners shall stand upon equal footing.

§ 15. Compensation of limited partner. A limited partner may receive from the partnership the share of the profits or the compensation by way of income stipulated for in the certificate; provided, that after such payment is made, whether from the property of the partnership or that of a general partner, the partnership assets are in excess of all liabilities of the partnership except liabilities to limited partners on account of their contributions and to general partners.

§ 16. Withdrawal or reduction of limited partner's contribution. (1) A limited partner shall not receive from a general partner or out of partnership property any part of his contribution until

(a) All liabilities of the partnership, except liabilities to general partners and to limited partners on account of their contributions, have been paid or there remains property of the partnership sufficient to pay them,

(b) The consent of all members is had, unless the return of the contribution may be rightfully demanded under the provisions of paragraph (2), and

(c) The certificate is cancelled or so amended as to set forth the withdrawal or reduction.

(2) Subject to the provisions of paragraph (1) a limited partner may rightfully demand the return of his contribution

(a) On the dissolution of a partnership, or

(b) When the date specified in the certificate for its return has arrived, or

(c) After he has given six months' notice in writing to all other members, if no time is specified in the certificate either for the return of the contribution or for the dissolution of the partnership.

(3) In the absence of any statement in the certificate to the contrary or the consent of all members, a limited partner, irrespective of the nature of his contribution, has only the right to demand and receive cash in return for his contribution.

(4) A limited partner may have the partnership dissolved and its affairs wound up when

(a) He rightfully but unsuccessfully demands the return of his contribution, or

(b) The other liabilities of the partnership have not been paid, or the partnership property is insufficient for their payment as required by paragraph (1a) and the limited partner would otherwise be entitled to the return of his contribution.

§ 17. Liability of limited partner to partnership. (1) A limited partner is liable to the partnership

(a) For the difference between his contribution as actually made and that stated in the certificate as having been made, and

(b) For any unpaid contribution which he agreed in the certificate to make in the future at the time and on the conditions stated in the certificate.

(2) A limited partner holds as trustee for the partnership

(a) Specific property stated in the certificate as contributed by him, but which was not contributed or which has been wrongfully returned, and

(b) Money or other property wrongfully paid or conveyed to him on account of his contribution.

(3) The liabilities of a limited partner as set forth in this section can be waived or compromised only by the consent of all members; but a waiver or compromise shall not affect the right of a creditor of a partnership who extended credit or whose claim arose after the filing and be-

fore a cancellation or amendment of the certificate, to enforce such liabilities.

(4) When a contributor has rightfully received the return in whole or in part of the capital of his contribution, he is nevertheless liable to the partnership for any sum, not in excess of such return with interest, necessary to discharge its liabilities to all creditors who extended credit or whose claims arose before such return.

§ 18. Nature of limited partner's interest in partnership. A limited partner's interest in the partnership is personal property.

§ 19. Assignment of limited partner's interest. (1) A limited partner's interest is assignable.

(2) A substituted limited partner is a person admitted to all the rights of a limited partner who has died or has assigned his interest in a partnership.

(3) An assignee, who does not become a substituted limited partner, has no right to require any information or account of the partnership transactions or to inspect the partnership books; he is only entitled to receive the share of the profits or other compensation by way of income, or the return of his contribution, to which his assignor would otherwise be entitled.

(4) An assignee shall have the right to become a substituted limited partner if all the mem-

bers (except the assignor) consent thereto or if the assignor, being thereunto empowered by the certificate, gives the assignee that right.

(5) An assignee becomes a substituted limited partner when the certificate is appropriately amended in accordance with Section 25.

(6) The substituted limited partner has all the rights and powers, and is subject to all the restrictions and liabilities of his assignor, except those liabilities of which he was ignorant at the time he became a limited partner and which could not be ascertained from the certificate.

(7) The substitution of the assignee as a limited partner does not release the assignor from liability to the partnership under Sections 6 and 17.

§ 20. **Effect of retirement, death or insanity of a general partner.** The retirement, death or insanity of a general partner dissolves the partnership, unless the business is continued by the remaining general partners

(a) Under a right so to do stated in the certificate, or

(b) With the consent of all members.

§ 21. **Death of limited partner.** (1) On the death of a limited partner his executor or administrator shall have all the rights of a limited partner for the purpose of settling his estate, and such power as the deceased had to constitute his assignee a substituted limited partner.

(2) The estate of a deceased limited partner shall be liable for all his liabilities as a limited partner.

§ 22. **Rights of creditors of limited partner.** (1) On due application to a court of competent jurisdiction by any judgment creditor of a limited partner, the court may charge the interest of the indebted limited partner with payment of the unsatisfied amount of the judgment debt; and may appoint a receiver, and make all other orders, directions, and inquiries which the circumstances of the case may require.

(2) The interest may be redeemed with the separate property of any general partner, but may not be redeemed with partnership property.

(3) The remedies conferred by paragraph (1) shall not be deemed exclusive of others which may exist.

(4) Nothing in this act shall be held to deprive a limited partner of his statutory exemption.

§ 23. **Distribution of assets.** (1) In settling accounts after dissolution the liabilities of the partnership shall be entitled to payment in the following order:

(a) Those to creditors, in the order of priority as provided by law, except those to limited partners on account of their contributions, and to general partners,

(b) Those to limited partners in respect to their share of the profits and other compensation by way of income on their contributions,

(c) Those to limited partners in respect to the capital of their contributions,

(d) Those to general partners other than for capital and profits,

(e) Those to general partners in respect to profits,

(f) Those to general partners in respect to capital.

(2) Subject to any statement in the certificate or to subsequent agreement, limited partners share in the partnership assets in respect to their claims for capital, and in respect to their claims for profits or for compensation by way of income on their contributions respectively, in proportion to the respective amounts of such claims.

§ 24. When certificate shall be cancelled or amended. (1) The certificate shall be cancelled when the partnership is dissolved or all limited partners cease to be such.

(2) A certificate shall be amended when

(a) There is a change in the name of the partnership or in the amount or character of the contribution of any limited partner,

(b) A person is substituted as a limited partner,

(c) An additional limited partner is admitted,

(d) A person is admitted as a general partner,

(e) A general partner retires, dies or becomes insane, and the business is continued under section 20,

(f) There is a change in the character of the business of the partnership,

(g) There is a false or erroneous statement in the certificate,

(h) There is a change in the time as stated in the certificate for the dissolution of the partnership or for the return of a contribution,

(i) A time is fixed for the dissolution of the partnership, or the return of a contribution, no time having been specified in the certificate, or

(j) The members desire to make a change in any other statement in the certificate in order that it shall accurately represent the agreement between them.

§ 25. Requirements for amendment and for cancellation of certificate.

(1) The writing to amend a certificate shall

(a) Conform to the requirements of Section 2(1a) as far as necessary to set forth clearly the change in the certificate which it is desired to make, and

(b) Be signed and sworn to by all members, and an amendment substituting a limited partner or adding a limited or general partner shall be signed also by the member to be substituted or added, and when a limited partner is to be substituted, the amendment shall also be signed by the assigning limited partner.

(2) The writing to cancel a certificate shall be signed by all members.

(3) A person desiring the cancellation or amendment of a certificate, if any person designated in paragraphs (1) and (2) as a person who must execute the writing refuses to do so, may petition the [here designate the proper court] to direct a cancellation or amendment thereof.

(4) If the court finds that the petitioner has a right to have the writing executed by a person who refuses to do so, it shall order the [here designate the responsible official in the office designated in Section 2] in the office where the

certificate is recorded to record the cancellation or amendment of the certificate; and where the certificate is to be amended, the court shall also cause to be filed for record in said office a certified copy of its decree setting forth the amendment.

(5) A certificate is amended or cancelled when there is filed for record in the office [here designate the office designated in Section 2] where the certificate is recorded

(a) A writing in accordance with the provisions of paragraph (1), or (2) or

(b) A certified copy of the order of court in accordance with the provisions of paragraph (4).

(6) After the certificate is duly amended in accordance with this section, the amended certificate shall thereafter be for all purposes the certificate provided for by this act.

§ 26. **Parties to actions.** A contributor, unless he is a general partner, is not a proper party to proceedings by or against a partnership, except where the object is to enforce a limited partner's right against or liability to the partnership.

§ 27. **Name of act.** This act may be cited as The Uniform Limited Partnership Act.

§ 28. **Rules of construction.** (1) The rule that statutes in derogation of the common law are to be strictly construed shall have no application to this act.

(2) This act shall be so interpreted and construed as to effect its general purpose to make uniform the law of those states which enact it.

(3) This act shall not be so construed as to impair the obligations of any contract existing when the act goes into effect, nor to affect any action or proceedings begun or right accrued before this act takes effect.

APPENDIX C

REFERENCES TO PARTNERSHIP LAWS

UNIFORM LIMITED PARTNERSHIP ACT

UNIFORM PARTNERSHIP ACT

APPENDIX C

UNIFORM PARTNERSHIP ACT—Continued

UNIFORM PARTNERSHIP ACT—Continued

APPENDIX D

REFERENCES TO RESTATEMENT

RESTATEMENT, SECOND, AGENCY (1958)

APPENDIX D

RESTATEMENT, SECOND, AGENCY (1958)—Continued

* Restatement, Agency (1933)

*

INDEX

References are to Pages

INDEX

[*347*]

INDEX

[*349*]

PARTNER BY ESTOPPEL

See Partnership Dissolution

PARTNERSHIP

See also Business Trust; Joint Enterprise; Joint
Venture; Limited Partnership; Partnership Dissolution; Partnership Property

Generally, 12 et seq., 206 et seq.

Agency, relation to, 13

At will, 30

Basic concept,

Aggregate theory, 13, 200, 201, 259, 272

Entity theory, 13, 250, 251, 274, 275

Consent,

Assignment of rights without, 29

Contract by parties, 30

Implied, 29

Control,

Negative covenants compared, 40, 41

Right to control, 32

Defined, 12, 26

Earmarks,

Gross returns, 210

Intention, 207, 223

Mutual agency, 224

Profit sharing, 209, 210

Fiduciary obligations, 48

Gains, entitled to, 26 et seq.

Personal relationship,

Generally, 36 et seq.

Forced dissolution, 37 et seq.

Profits as "profits",

Generally, 222 et seq.

Agent's salary, 224, 225

Farm on shares, 226

Interest to lender, 224

Loan of securities, 225

Payments to creditors, 223, 224

Rent, 224

Share gross returns, 226

INDEX

References are to Pages

[*355*]

INDEX

References are to Pages

[*359*]

INDEX

[*363*]

INDEX